DATE REMOVED
1 6 JUL 2021
STOCK

A-level Study Guide

Business Studies

...sed and updated

Barry Brindley

Martin Buckley

Series Consultants: Geoff Black and Stuart Wall

Project Manager: Stuart Wall

Pearson Education Limited

Edinburgh Gate, Harlow

Essex CM20 2JE, England

and Associated Companies throughout the world

© Pearson Education Limited 2000, 2004

British Library Cataloguing in Publication Data

A catalogue entry for this title is available from the British Library.

ISBN 0-582-78414-X

First published 2000

Reprinted 2001

Updated 2004

Set by 35 in Univers, Cheltenham

Printed by Ashford Colour Press, Gosport, Hants

The business environment

This chapter looks at the ways in which the business environment impacts upon the organization. You will find that most specialist departments within the organization will be surveying their environments. In doing so they will be looking for trends in business activity or in attitudes and asking the question 'what are the likely impacts upon the organization?' Because each firm is individual you will find that each has a unique environment and will be affected differently to other firms in the same industry. You may also find that a large firm working in several different markets faces several very different environments.

Exam themes

→ The nature and purpose of business activity.

→ The role of price and profits in resource allocation.

→ Business classification and its impact upon business activity and decision-making.

→ The pressures on business to change.

→ The effects of political, economic, social and technological change upon the structure and activities of business.

→ The effects of competition on business behaviour.

→ The impact of size upon business operations.

→ The role of the state and the EU.

Topic checklist

○ AS ● A2	AQA	EDEXCEL	OCR	WJEC
The market	○	○	○	○
Markets and competition	○	○	○	○●
Macro-economic factors	○	○	○	○●
Controlling the economy	○●	●	○●	○●
Social and demographic influences	○	○●	○●	○●
Technological influences	○	●	○●	○
Business and the law	○	○●	○●	○●
Business and society	●	●	○●	○
Business and the natural environment	●	●	○●	○
The European Union (EU)	●	●	●	○●

The market

In a capitalist or free enterprise economy 'the market' is at the heart of the economic system. It is in the market that buyers and sellers interact and thus determine the prices and quantities of the goods and services exchanged.

Demand

Demand refers to the quantity of a product (good or service) that consumers are willing and able to purchase at a given price. The majority of demand curves are downward sloping from left to right, such as D_1D_1 in diagram (a) below showing that as price falls, demand for the product *expands*. This is because the product is now cheaper, becoming relatively more attractive to the consumer. Conversely, when the price rises, demand *contracts* as the product becomes relatively less attractive to purchase when compared with others the consumer can buy.

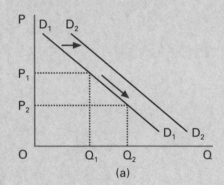
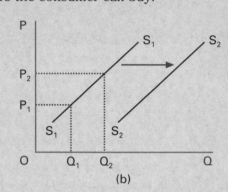

(a)   (b)

The demand curve may also *shift* so that more or less is demanded at any given price. Diagram (a) also shows a separate demand curve D_2D_2 that has *shifted to the right* of the original demand curve. This is because factors other than the price of the product have changed. These factors are known as the **conditions** (or **determinants**) **of demand**, and include

→ changes in income of consumers
→ changes in tastes of consumers
→ changes in price of substitutes or complements in consumption
→ demographic changes

Supply

Supply refers to the quantity of a product that producers are willing and able to supply at a given price. The majority of supply curves are upward sloping from left to right, such as S_1S_1 in diagram (b), showing that as price rises, supply of the product *expands*. This is because the price rise induces existing producers to produce more and may also attract less efficient producers to the industry. Conversely as the price falls, existing producers will produce less (supply *contracts*) and marginal producers will leave the market. These *movements along* the supply curve are due solely to a change in the price of the product.

Like the demand curve, the supply curve may also *shift* so that more or less is supplied at a given price. In diagram (b), the supply curve S_2S_2 has shifted to the right, indicating that more of the product is supplied at any particular price. Behind this shift in the supply curve are changes in the **conditions** (or **determinants**) **of supply**, which include

→ changes in the price of production inputs
→ changes in technology
→ changes in the price of other goods
→ changes in taxes or subsidies

Price determination ●●●

In a free market prices are determined by the intersection of demand and supply. As diagram (c) shows, the **equilibrium price** is where the quantity demanded is the same as the quantity supplied; at price P_1 the quantity Q_1 is both demanded and supplied. Of course, price may be set at levels other than the equilibrium price. In diagram (c) at price P_2 there is **excess supply** and the unsold product brings pressure to reduce prices. However at price P_3 there is **excess demand** with pressure to raise prices. In each case the pressure to reduce or raise prices is only stopped at the equilibrium price P_1.

You should be aware that the equilibrium price may change if any of the conditions of demand or supply change. Diagram (d) shows the impact on equilibrium price of a *decrease in supply* (price rises from P_1 to P_2).

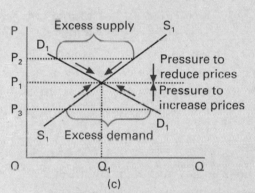

(c)

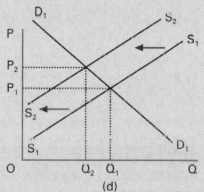

(d)

The role of profit ●●●

Profit is revenue minus cost. Profit will often guide firms as to how to use scarce resources, e.g. deciding how much of alternative products to produce. Profit also has a number of other functions.

→ *It is a reward for risk taking.* Entrepreneurs can never be sure their ideas are going to be successful as people have freedom of choice.
→ *It is a spur to efficiency.* To achieve maximum profits the firm seeks to use its resources as efficiently as possible in order to keep costs to the minimum (e.g. improve methods of production).
→ *It provides the resources for expansion.* Roughly 60% of all profits are 'ploughed back' into the business.

Exam questions
answers: pages 24–5

1   Assess the impact of a sharp rise in petrol prices on the sales of cars. (15 min)

2   At different times governments have imposed:
    (a) maximum price legislation or
    (b) minimum wage legislation.
    Discuss the impacts of *one* of these types of legislation on firms, individuals and the government. (30 min)

Checkpoint 3

Can you show the impact on an initial equilibrium price/quantity for apples of
(a) tastes changing towards apples
(b) a fall in costs of apple production?

Links

Price sensitivity is measured by calculating the price elasticity of demand. See page 71.

Action point

Think about the impact on price P_1 of an increase in supply, decrease in demand, increase in demand.

Checkpoint 4

Profit is an important business objective but there are others. What are they?

Check the net

Look at how the following companies use their profits.
www.marks.and.spencer.co.uk
www.sainsburys.co.uk

Examiner's secrets

Using diagrams can help make your answer clearer. It may also help you to think of short-term and long-term time periods.

Markets and competition

Competition is admired because it prevents a firm from raising prices or reducing quality in order to increase profits. The more competitive the market, the less likely it is that the consumer will be exploited.

The spectrum of competition

Not all markets are equally competitive. At one extreme is the 'ideal' of a **perfectly competitive market**, where market forces ensure the consumer obtains the products they want at the lowest possible price.

At the other extreme is **pure monopoly**, where one seller controls the market and can manipulate quantity (or quality) so as to raise prices and profits. Between these two extremes we have the more usual market situations of **monopolistic competition** and **oligopoly**. The characteristics of each form of competition are shown below.

Perfect competition	Monopolistic competition	Oligopoly	Monopoly (pure)
→ undifferentiated product	→ differentiated product	→ differentiated product	→ no subsitutes
→ free entry	→ free entry	→ barriers to entry	→ barriers to entry
→ many sellers	→ many sellers	→ few sellers	→ single seller
→ price takers	→ price takers	→ price makers	→ price maker
→ low profits	→ low profits	→ high profits	→ high profits
		→ interdependent	

Competition and profits

In highly competitive situations the firm may find the price it can charge is determined by the actions of consumers and other firms in the industry. That firm is said to be a **price taker**. In such situations the firms will be keen to lower costs, perhaps through adopting new production methods, in the hope of obtaining a *competitive advantage* over their rivals.

In many markets though the firm is a **price maker**, exercising some degree of control over price and profits. The key lies in the ability of the firm to produce a **differentiated product** and so insulate itself from competition. The more unique the product is perceived to be, the fewer will be the number of satisfactory substitutes, thereby strengthening the firm's market position and its control over price.

Any higher profits that arise from this situation though may act as a magnet to other firms. To prevent these firms entering the industry and competing away profits there must be **barriers to entry**. The amount of capital required to set up is often a major barrier to new firm entry.

Many large firms in this country could be described as oligopolies. The extent of oligopoly is often measured through the **concentration ratio**. For UK industry as a whole the five firm concentration ratio stands at around 50% and in many cases is far higher. In such situations firms are less likely to compete on price (e.g. fear of 'price warfare') but non-price competition may become very important.

Fixing the market ●●●

There have been many attempts by firms to manipulate the market to their own advantage. It is for this reason that most national governments (and the EU) have introduced legislation to control unfair competition.

In the UK the government has power to investigate

→ monopoly situations, including local monopolies
→ proposed mergers and takeover bids
→ anti-competitive practices

Where an activity is thought to be against the public interest the government may refuse to allow a merger to go ahead, seek assurances from firms that they will not act in certain ways in the future, or fine them if they have acted illegally.

Market failure ●●●

The role of a market is to ensure that resources are allocated efficiently. At times though the market 'fails'. For example, an *oligopolistic industry* often results in higher prices and profits and unusually high expenditures on advertising and promotion.

Market failure may also occur because of **externalities**. The situation arises when only *private costs* are included in the price of the product. Thus if a firm making chemicals is allowed to pump its waste material into the river or sea rather than treat it, then the price of chemicals will be lower and more will be purchased than if all the costs, including *social costs*, had been taken into account.

Governments may also intervene in markets for reasons of *equity* (fairness), e.g. taxing high earners to support pensioners.

Exam questions
answers: page 25

1   A. Loonat has just taken over control of his father's engineering business. The firm operates in a very competitive environment with very low profit margins. Can you suggest potential strategies that he might adopt to improve competitiveness? (15 min)

2   According to various newspaper reports British motorists may pay up to 30% more for a new car than if they bought the same model on the continent. Equally the price of a train journey from Wakefield to London can cost over £100 or as little as £30. What factors enable firms to charge these different prices? Why would firms want to do this? (30 min)

3   A recent article on a pensioner stated that she had difficulty in affording even basic items of clothing. Presents for her grandchildren were out of the question. Council house rent had climbed to a level where many pensioners had to claim housing benefit whilst heating bills in winter were far too high.
    (a) Where prices are set by the market, why can't some people afford them? (10 min)
    (b) If everything was provided through the market, what sort of needs would 'poor' people have to go without? (10 min)
    (c) How does the government try to overcome this problem? (10 min)

Watch out!

Be familiar with the work of the *Competition Commission* and the *Office of Fair Trading* in the UK (see pages 16–17). Also check out aspects of EU competition policy.

Jargon

A cartel exists when a group of firms agree production or sales quotas for each member. These arrangements allow firms to make greater profits than when trading independently.

Checkpoint 2

Can you give some other examples of *externalities*?

Action point

Can you list some of the *social costs* in this example?

Check the net

For more on markets and competition visit www.bized.ac.uk

Examiner's secrets

The concept of externalities and its implications for business and society will appear in most examinations. Be aware of the benefits of the market system in allocating resources as well as its 'failures'.

Macro-economic factors

All organizations operate in a macro-economic environment over which they have no control. Nevertheless it is important that firms understand the impact that macro-economic factors may have on their operations.

Inflation

Inflation may be caused by **cost push** or **demand pull** influences. It may also be *imported*.

→ *Business may benefit from mild inflation.* Rising prices are often associated with high levels of demand, and may encourage firms to expand production. Unemployment will tend to fall, further increasing the demand for goods generally. Rising prices may also raise the profit margin, increasing the total level of profits and resulting in share prices rising on the stock exchange.

→ *Businesses may also suffer as a result of inflation.* If inflation is higher than in neighbouring countries, domestic products become uncompetitive and may lose market share. Input prices will also tend to rise, putting pressure on current prices and profits. Inflation may also cause interest rates to rise.

Employment and unemployment

The *structure* of employment has changed dramatically over time. In 1800 most employees worked in the **primary sector**, but by 1900 a majority worked in the **secondary sector** and by 2000 the majority of employees worked in the **tertiary sector**. Employment and unemployment also vary between *regions*. Much of South-East England has very high levels of employment, while North-East England has relatively high levels of unemployment.

Levels of unemployment vary throughout the **business cycle**. For example levels of unemployment may be significantly higher during a *recession*, resulting in a much lower level of demand for goods and services. On the other hand unemployment will be lower in periods of *recovery*, though even with the UK experiencing a high level of demand for goods and services, around 5% of the population remain unemployed.

Unemployment may be either frictional or structural. **Frictional unemployment** may be temporary, e.g. people in between jobs, in seasonal jobs, etc. **Structural unemployment** occurs where the skills of the employee are not those that are required in the labour market. It is often associated with declining industries but may also arise as a result of a firm changing its processes so that it is now looking for employees with a different range of skills.

In situations where the firm does find difficulty in recruiting labour, firms have four major remedies. They may limit (or not expand) their business activities, pay for the retraining of employees, try to poach skilled labour from another firm by paying higher wages, or look at different technologies which avoid the use of labour. All of these remedies impose costs and burdens on the firm.

Checkpoint 1

Can you briefly explain each of these causes of inflation?

Watch out!

Whereas mild inflation may bring benefits which outweigh costs there is always the risk of *hyper-inflation*, i.e. very rapid rises in price.

Check the net

For information on inflation www.bankofengland.co.uk and on unemployment www.oecd.org www.tuc.org

Checkpoint 2

Define each of these sectors. (See also page 32.)

Example

In 1999, unemployment in Merseyside was over 9% compared with 2.6% in the South-East.

Watch out!

Even with unemployment around 4% or 5%, employers are finding it difficult to recruit new staff.

Don't forget

You should be aware of the major argument about whether 'work should be taken to the workers' or 'workers should move to the work'.

International trade and exchange rates

International trade provides us with those products we cannot produce ourselves and also those products which can be more efficiently produced abroad. For the businessman, free international trade provides both benefits and costs.

→ On the *benefit* side, the firm has a much larger market for its product, e.g. the Single European Market contains almost 400 million people. A larger market gives opportunities for scale economies and more efficient production.

→ On the *cost* side the firm may find that competition is fiercer and that to survive it must reduce prices and profit margins. To compete internationally the firm may be forced to look for ways to produce more efficiently, to modify its product so that it is more attractive to the customer, and to look for new products to replace existing ones. Additionally if the firm does enter foreign markets it is likely to incur additional costs, including those from using foreign currency.

The **exchange rate** is the value of one currency measured in terms of another. So, in early 2000, £1 would buy you 250 Spanish pesetas. Yet only a few years before you would have been lucky to obtain 200! Clearly changes in exchange rates have an impact on firms doing business abroad. *Foreign exchange transaction* costs arise because the firm that imports or exports from abroad is likely to pay and be paid in a foreign currency.

Economic growth

On the *benefit* side, economic growth increases the consumer's ability to buy more and different products. It provides an opportunity for the business to increase sales to the more affluent consumer. It also allows the government to increase expenditure on a wide range of services without increasing tax rates.

On the *cost* side, high economic growth may result in labour shortages and inflation as demand outstrips supply. More external costs, such as pollution, may result from higher growth. Rapid economic growth may also result in stronger competition from overseas firms.

Checkpoint 3

Despite the arguments for free trade many people argue for 'protection'. Briefly outline some of these arguments.

Links

For more on *scale economies* see pages 114–15.

Examiner's secrets

A *fall* in an exchange rate makes exports cheaper abroad and imports dearer at home! A *rise* will do the opposite.

Check the net

Sources of information on trade and exchange rates include
www.wto.org
www.imf.org
www.dti.gov.uk

Examiner's secrets

If incomes rise then products with high *income elasticities of demand* will gain most extra demand. Make sure you can explain 'income elasticity of demand'.

Exam questions   answers: page 26

1 Economic growth is expected to be high in the UK over the next three years. How might this influence the decisions taken by a firm? (20 min)

2 You are required to advise a local firm which is entering the export market for the first time. In particular, the firm wishes to know:
   (a) the additional costs it is likely to incur
   (b) the implications of exchange rate fluctuations. (30 min)

Examiner's secrets

Make sure you can explain how the macro-economic factors will affect an individual business.

Controlling the economy

Here we seek to understand the nature of the business cycle, how the government tries to control the cycle and the implications of the cycle for the businessperson.

The business cycle

Over the past 25 years the aggregate demand for goods and services has grown at roughly 2.2% per year in real terms. However the actual trend of business activity has moved above and below this trend line in a **business cycle** consisting of booms and slumps. Some observers suggest a distinct pattern to the cycle, with four different *phases*.

	Slump	Recovery	Boom	Recession
employment	low	rising	high	falling
skill shortages	few	starting	high	falling
inflation	low	low, rising	high, rising	falling
investment	low	rising	high	falling

In practice the four-phase cycle is quite complex. Not only can the length (period) of the cycle vary, the length of individual phases may also vary from cycle to cycle.

Expectations play an important part in the length of the cycle and the individual phases. If firms *believe* that aggregate demand is likely to fall in future, they are likely to reduce investment in capital equipment and stocks now. Equally, if firms *believe* that aggregate demand is likely to rise, they are likely to increase such investment.

You will find that there are a number of decision areas the firm has to consider apart from investment. These include

→ capital structure and gearing
→ market volatility
→ output break-even point
→ human resource management

The jargon

The *period* of the cycle is the time between successive peaks (or troughs), often thought to be 8 to 10 years.

Watch out!

Self-fulfilling expectations occur where a belief leads to actions which result in that belief actually happening.

Checkpoint 1

You should also be aware of the impact of the *accelerator* and *multiplier* on the business cycle. Try to explain these ideas.

Checkpoint 2

Fiscal policy may also have objectives other than stabilization. What are they?

The jargon

Marginal propensity to consume is the extra consumer spending from the last unit of income received.

Fiscal policy

The government uses its *budget* to influence aggregate demand. Taxes and government expenditure can be affected directly by the budget, but consumption and investment only indirectly. In general terms we can say that an important aim of the government is to *stabilize* economic activity. Thus in a recession the government would wish to increase the level of aggregate demand, perhaps by reducing taxes, increasing spending, or some of both. Aggregate demand could also be increased by redistributing income from those who have a low marginal propensity to consume (e.g. high income groups) to those who are likely to spend a greater proportion of any extra income (e.g. low income groups). Equally the government may encourage or discourage the consumption of certain goods through taxation or subsidies.

In determining the impact of fiscal policy upon a *single firm* you should consider both the overall effect of fiscal policy on the level of economic activity within the economy and more specific measures designed to affect demand in that firm's sector of operations.

Monetary policy ●●●

The economy may also be affected through monetary policy. In recent years the major weapon of monetary policy has been *interest rates* to control bank lending and therefore the supply of money in circulation. Movements in the level of interest rates may be used to encourage or discourage spending. This then would have an effect on demand for goods and services, potential levels of inflation, employment, exchange rates and foreign trade. In a situation where consumers have too much money to spend (from increased wages and credit) and where output is near its maximum (with the risk of inflation), interest rates will tend to be raised; and vice versa.

Supply-side policies ●●●

Some economists argue that the UK economy is not performing to full potential because there are 'supply-side' problems. In particular, they have focused on the labour market. They argue that output is restricted and unemployment raised by factors such as the power of trade unions, minimum wage legislation and the social security system. Other supply-side policies include efforts by governments to create more incentives for employers and employees through extra tax allowances, lower tax rates, etc. in the hope that such incentives will raise investment and productivity of both capital and labour.

Watch out!

The *Monetary Policy Committee* now sets interest rates independently of government.

Don't forget

Raising interest rates discourages firms and consumers from borrowing (and spending) money (and vice versa).

Example

Policies aimed at *reducing government regulations in labour markets* are also of this type.

Links

For more on supply-side policies see pages 48–9.

Exam questions answers: page 26

1   The table below charts the level of increase in GDP for a country over the last 5 years

1995	1996	1997	1998	1999	2000	2001
2.1%	1.2%	−0.2%	0.7%	1.2%		

(a) Estimate the GDP % values for 2000 and 2001. (5 min)

(b) Comment on the problems in estimating these figures. (5 min)

(c) Briefly explain two ways in which the government could encourage reflation (expansion of demand) in the economy. (10 min)

(d) Describe two problems that a manufacturing firm might experience from an increase in demand during an economic recovery. (10 min)

(e) How could a marketing department assist in the recovery of a business following a recession? (10 min)

2   The government is expected to use its budget to lower the level of economic activity through a reduction in real incomes. What will be the impact on

(a) an off-licence selling mainly cigarettes and alcohol

(b) a travel firm specializing in exotic holidays? (20 min)

Examiner's secrets

Make sure you can analyze and evaluate the impact of these government policies upon business organizations.

Examiner's secrets

Think about the policy instruments the government can use to raise or lower aggregate demand. Consider the impact of these measures on the individual firm.

Social and demographic influences

Firms operate in a dynamic and complex social environment. Social and demographic factors influence the firm, not only in terms of the types of product it produces but also in the ways in which it produces them. Conversely, the actions of the firm may also influence the attitudes and behaviour of consumers and of the wider society.

Demographic changes

Demography is the study of population in terms of its size and characteristics. Globally the population is expanding rapidly. The biggest increases are in the Far East and South America. Within Western Europe population growth has been very small, with some countries (e.g. Germany) experiencing a decline in population.

Within the UK, three important demographic trends have been taking place, namely

→ *An ageing population* The birth rate has been falling since the 1960s. As a result we have a declining youth population and an increasing proportion in the older age groups.
→ *Changing household structure* There are fewer married couples with dependent children and more married couples with no children. There has also been a *doubling* in the number of both one parent families with dependent children and one person households.
→ *Geographic distribution* The bulk of the UK population lives in the Midlands and the South of England. There is also a slow movement from rural to urban areas. Conversely there is a movement amongst affluent workers away from urban centres into the surrounding countryside.

These changes have many implications for businesses, and for public sector and the voluntary organizations. They will alter patterns of

→ consumption → production
→ savings → investment
→ employment → innovation

Social and cultural influences

Differences in the pattern of consumption cannot solely be explained by economic and demographic factors. Many more are explained by *social and cultural factors*. Whilst most of these are outside the control of the organization, an understanding of them is essential for it to be successful in that market.

By 'culture' we are referring to a set of values, attitudes, beliefs and customs which shape the way we view, and interact with, the rest of society. This culture is handed down through family, schools and other institutions.

Culture is important to the business because it determines

→ the *products* which are acceptable
→ the kinds of *promotion* which are acceptable

→ the *colours* which are acceptable
→ the *methods* that can be used for selling

One important determinant of an individual's pattern of behaviour (including consumption) is *social class*. A social class is made up of people who share certain common features. These would include occupation, income, education, wealth and lifestyle. The most widely used technique is to classify people into social classes according to the *occupation of the head of the household*. Evidence suggests that this has a major influence on consumers' buying behaviour. More importantly there is evidence that such buyer behaviour will change as individuals move from one social class to another.

Social and cultural *attitudes* change over time. In some cases the change is swift and can be the result of information in the media (e.g. fads and fashions). Such rapid changes in attitude may cause major problems for business organizations. In other cases the change is rather slower, with our attitudes broadly shaped by the experiences we encounter and the groups we belong to. Thus family, religious groups, leisure clubs, work and travel will all contribute to the shaping of culture.

The organization's response ●●●

Social and cultural attitudes have changed significantly over the last 20 years.

Changes	Firm responses
concern for healthy living	natural foods, low fat products, keep-fit centres
concern for the environment	recycled products, environmentally friendly products, better pollution controls in production processes
greater life expectancy	new ranges of products catering for the elderly
more single person households	smaller houses, singles holidays, smaller portions of pre-packed foods

Exam question answer: page 27

A local retailer of children's clothing obtains the following information from the census.

The total population in the town has fallen by 7%. The number of children aged 0–15 has declined by 17%; 15–35 years has fallen by 12%, 35–55 years has increased by 19% whilst pensioners have risen by 5%.

(a) What is the census? (5 min)

(b) For the retailer, what is the most significant piece of information? (5 min)

(c) What are the implications of these trends? (10 min)

(d) What other information would help the firm? (5 min)

(e) Explain what action you would expect the firm to take. (5 min)

Example

Group	Description	%
A	Upper middle class	3
B	Middle class	11
C1	Lower middle class	22
C2	Skilled working class	32
D	Working class	23
E	Pensioners and Unemployed	9

Links

You should be aware that there are other ways of classifying consumer behaviour – see page 63.

Watch out!

The organization may itself seek to change social attitudes through advertising and promotion, thus making the purchase of certain products acceptable.

Action point

Can you identify any other *firm responses* to these changes? Can you identify any other *changes* and likely firm responses?

Examiner's secrets

Make sure your answer takes into account the data presented and concentrates on the local retailer of children's clothing. Try to be specific.

13

Technological influences

Technology has had a major impact upon business in the last two decades. It has led to the development of new products and new processes for making these products together with new ways of distributing products and storing information. The adoption of 'new' technology has important implications for the success of the firm and for a country's rate of economic growth.

Technological change and business implications

At the heart of today's technological change is the *microchip*. This has transformed the computer industry and led to a tremendous growth in information technology. Combined with the development of the telecommunications industry, all aspects of business operations have been affected and new *opportunities* created.

→ *Planning and control* within an organization have been facilitated by the ability to store and rapidly transmit large quantities of information. This enables transnational companies to control subsidiaries more easily.

→ *Location* Large scale administrative or productive units can now be located away from the head office, in areas where the costs of buildings and labour are lower and without any loss of efficiency.

→ *Production* **CAD** will shorten the length of time to design and build a new product. **CAM** (e.g. robotics) has enabled some monotonous manufacturing jobs to be eliminated as well as enabling a movement from the production of standardized to customized products. Computerized stock control has resulted in the introduction of **JIT** management techniques.

→ *Administration* Many routine administrative tasks involving data processing and retrieval can be computerized, with cost savings. Similarly standard letters, financial statements and sales material can all be computerized, saving 'creation' time. There is also the possibility of 'delayering' within the organization with the computerization of many routine middle management processes.

You should be aware that the new technology may also be viewed as a *threat* to the firm as well as an opportunity, threatening the survival of an industry or destroying a market. There are many examples of firms which have failed to note changes in the use of technology within their industry until it was too late!

Technology and the workforce

The workforce has been just as affected as the firm by new technology. For example, we have seen

→ the deskilling of some high skill jobs, e.g. printing trades
→ a reduction in unskilled and semi-skilled jobs
→ a reduction in the number of supervisors and middle managers
→ a loss of jobs through the transfer of manufacturing or servicing operations to low cost centres overseas

Examples

Other technological changes include the development of superconductors, artificial intelligence, biotechnology, new materials.

Check the net

Use the search engines on the net to research e-commerce. Alternatively visit www.alti.gov.uk for more general information on technology.

Example

Most call centres are located outside London.

The jargon

CAD (page 132) refers to *computer aided design*, CAM (page 133) to *computer aided manufacturing* and JIT (page 117) to *just in time*.

Action point

Can you give any examples here?

Examiner's secrets

Technological change can also have *benefits* for workers such as better working conditions, more interesting jobs, greater job security.
Can you give some actual examples?

- → the transfer of tasks to homeworkers
- → an increase in demand for operatives with higher level skills
- → the need to undergo retraining several times in a working life
- → an increase in stress from greater flexibility, a faster pace of work, more job insecurity or a loss of status

Employee resistance to change ●●●

We have seen that technology can bring about considerable change within an organization – much of it affecting employees. Many employees fear change, even though they recognize its inevitability. There are many reasons

- → possible loss of job
- → transfer to another job
- → break-up of social groups
- → need for retraining
- → skills become redundant
- → need to make new friends

This fear of change may be heightened by poor communications (which allows rumour or gossip), an overly formal management style, etc. Resistance to change may manifest itself in industrial action or in low worker morale, reducing productivity and the standard of service given to the firm's customers.

However resistance to change can be contained and changes can more easily be introduced with a *proper strategy*. This should include

- → identifying the workforce changes needed and planning them
- → communicating the changes (and the reasons for them) as soon as possible to avoid the problems of the *grapevine*
- → involving the trade unions, so that the workers participate in the change process
- → ensuring that social groups are not disturbed
- → giving guarantees where possible (e.g. no compulsory redundancies) and retraining where necessary
- → introducing the changes slowly, where possible
- → explaining the benefits of change

Exam questions answers: page 27

1 The greater availability and the reducing cost of information technology (IT) have increased the number of people who are able to work from home rather than the office.
   (a) How has IT enabled this to occur? (10 min)
   (b) Assess why this development may, or may not, continue to grow in the future. (20 min)

2 Sandal Manufacturing Ltd, a medium-sized manufacturing company, introduced information technology into its manufacturing and administrative processes as a means of improving profitability. However, in the year of its introduction, far from improving profitability, profits have fallen.
   Explain why an organization might experience a reduction in profitability following the introduction of information technology. (30 min)

Checkpoint

Can you explain how new technology might actually create more jobs than it destroys?

Action point

Can you provide any actual examples to support these points?

Check the net

The human resource network has a number of brief guides on HRM issues www.hrnetwork.co.uk

Examiner's secrets

In a case study situation, ensure you analyze both the benefits and problems arising from the material. In evaluating the scenario you should be aware of the many unquantifiable issues in making your judgement.

Examiner's secrets

Try to give reasons and then apply them to particular situations. The production and administrative processes might be dealt with separately.

15

Business and the law

Business law exists to ensure that firms can engage in lawful activity without impediment and to restrain unlawful activity by that or any other firm.

Check the net

The Business Bureau provides information on legal issues facing businesses
www.u-net.com/bureau/

Checkpoint 1

How does *consumer legislation* affect these situations?
(a) An advertising agency running a series of advertisements for seaside hotels.
(b) A manufacturer of electrical plugs.
(c) A retailer holding a 24-hour sales bonanza.
(d) A retailer who refuses to accept liability because there is an exclusion clause in the consumer contract.

Action point

Identify a major recent merger proposal. Note down how the merger might influence competition in that sector.

Watch out!

The *Competition Commission* is the new name for the Monopolies and Mergers Commission (MMC). For information on the work of the Commission, go to www.competition-commission.org.uk

Consumer protection law

In the past the relationship between business and the consumer was best described by the legal maxim '*caveat emptor*' or 'buyer beware'. This indicated that the buyer had to use common sense when entering into a contract to purchase goods. The onus was on the buyer to ensure that everything was satisfactory and functioning as claimed. This, of course, left the consumer wide open to abuse, particularly as products became more sophisticated. Additionally the manufacturer or retailer was in a far stronger position to resist consumer complaints and had the financial resources to fight any legal action brought by a consumer.

Today the consumer is in a far stronger position and the supplier must abide by a series of Acts designed to protect the rights of the buyer. The consumer has also become far more knowledgeable as a result of the many 'consumer' watchdog programmes on TV and radio.

The major **consumer protection legislation** is as follows

→ *Trade Descriptions Acts 1968/72* make it illegal for a trader to give a false or misleading description of the goods on offer
→ *Consumer Credit Act 1974* requires that all credit brokers should be licensed and that the true cost of borrowing be disclosed
→ *Sale of Goods Act 1979* insists that the product should be of merchantable quality, fit for its purpose and as described
→ *Consumer Protection Act 1989* requires that manufacturers and retailers provide warnings, safety advice and instructions for all dangerous goods

Consumer protection legislation has

→ protected the purchaser against unscrupulous traders
→ ensured that all traders compete on equal terms
→ made traders more concerned about product quality and customer satisfaction
→ increased business costs

Competition legislation

The state is keen to encourage competition because of its beneficial effect on prices, quality, efficiency and innovation. Firms, however, may seek to *avoid* the problems caused by competition. Thus firms may merge rather than compete. Alternatively they may adopt restrictive practices such as making secret agreements with their competitors on prices and output, or restricting supplies to those retailers who are unwilling to maintain pre-set prices. Legislation has been introduced in both the UK and the EU to promote competition.

UK legislation: the *Monopolies and Mergers Act (1965)*, *Fair Trading Act (1973)* and *Competition Act (1999)* have given the UK government power to investigate monopolies (over 25% of market) and mergers which might be 'against the public interest'. The Director General of Fair Trading can refer monopolies to the Competition Commission. Restrictive practices must be registered and can be challenged.

EU legislation: applies to trade between member states. In the case of conflict between UK and EU law the latter has precedence. There are three broad categories outlined in the Treaty of Rome:

→ *Articles 92–94* forbid governments to give aid to firms or industries where the effect is to distort competition
→ *Article 85* bans restrictive practices which allocate markets, limit output or determine prices
→ *Article 86* bans an abuse of a dominant position, for example where a firm uses its power to impose unfair terms on suppliers, retailers, consumers or competitors

Employment law

Until the last 25 years **employment legislation** dealt with the relationship between trade unions and employers. Much of this legislation appeared in a series of *Trade Union Acts* between 1871 and 1927, often referred to as **collective labour law**. Trade unions are a major force in the labour market and the last Conservative government believed that they prevented the operation of free market forces and were the cause of high wage costs and low labour productivity. Thus between 1979 and 1997 a series of acts were passed which effectively limited union powers.

Individual labour law refers to legislation that guarantees individual workers a 'floor of rights'. This floor of rights has been considered necessary because of the imbalance of bargaining power between the employer and the employee. In 1999 the UK introduced a **national minimum wage (NMW)** for workers over 18 years of age.

In recent years UK employment law has become more closely aligned with that of the EU. The Labour government has abandoned the 'opt out' from the EU Social Chapter agreed in Maastricht in 1992. The UK has now introduced various EU directives aimed at improving working conditions, e.g. the *Working Time Directive (1999)* which places an upper limit of 48 hours per week (averaged over 17 weeks).

Exam question answer: page 28

Legal constraints upon business are designed to provide a so-called 'level playing field' which is fair to all parts of society.

(a) How does the law attempt to achieve this? (15 min)

(b) To what extent can this aim be achieved? (15 min)

(c) What are the implications of such legislation for a firm? (15 min)

Example

Few mergers have been investigated (less than 200 over 50 years) and even fewer prevented (less than 3% of those investigated).

Examiner's secrets

Make sure you can give practical examples of how both UK and EU legislation has worked.

Checkpoint 2

List three ways in which trade union power has been curtailed since 1979.

Example

The NMW was set at £4.50 per hour from October 2003, with a lower £3.80 rate for 18–21 year olds.

Links

For more on the NMW see page 49 and for more on the Social Chapter see page 23.

Take note

You may be required to
→ discuss the pros and cons of a certain area of law
→ explain the impact of law on a firm (and its strategy)
→ argue the case for government intervention

Examiner's secrets

Try to support your points with details of legislation and examples of how this has affected actual firms.

17

Business and society

A firm is both affected by its business environment and can influence that environment. It is the ability of firms to change their business environment that is causing increasing concern. If this power is not controlled then the 'public interest' might be damaged.

Social responsibility

There are two views of social responsibility.

In the **shareholder approach** the firm is responsible to its shareholders alone. Its sole objective is to serve the interests of its shareholders through the efficient production of goods and services. The firm should not be concerned with other issues. These are the responsibility of the government and other groups in society. The firm will ensure that all its activities are within the law but if the government wishes the firm to act differently it must legislate for this.

In the **stakeholder approach** the firm owes an obligation to many different groups in society. These groups are called *stakeholders* because they have some interest in the actions of the organization. Shareholders are one of many stakeholders in the company but at a given point in time may not be the most important. The objectives of the firm will then be a compromise based on the demands of these many different groups.

Benefits to the firm from taking the stakeholder approach to social responsibility include more loyal customers and employees and better relationships with suppliers and the local community. The firm is also less likely to become a target for a pressure group. Many investors are now targeting socially responsive firms because they believe that these are the firms more likely to earn above average long-term profits. Most organizations would accept that they have a social responsibility, but in many cases this has not been translated into action because of the conflict between social responsibility and profitability.

Business ethics

Ethics refers to the system of moral principles that guides our behaviour. It tells us what is right or wrong, what we should do and more importantly what we shouldn't do. As individuals our moral code has been influenced by many different people or institutions. The most important of these will be our families, our friends, our religion and more generally those groups and individuals we admire.

In business, managers must constantly take decisions. **Business ethics** provides a *code of behaviour* for managers, regardless of the cost or benefit to the firm. The basis of business ethics is twofold

→ Business consists of individuals who have their own *moral code* which will guide their business decision-making.
→ Business decision-making is also influenced by the *corporate culture* of the organization. This refers to the values, beliefs and norms of the organization, and includes the attitudes of senior management as communicated to other employees.

In the last 20 years people have become much more questioning about the ethics underpinning business activity. A number of high profile cases each year have drawn attention to how ethical standards may have been compromised. Many large firms are now introducing 'ethical codes of practice' as a means of making their ethical principles clearer.

The role of pressure groups ●●●

A **pressure group** can be described as an organization which sets out to influence the activities of others. Greenpeace is an example of a 'multi-cause' international pressure group whereas Action on Smoking and Health (ASH) is an example of a 'single-cause' group. Some pressure groups were created for other purposes but now find a need to act as a pressure group.

The success of a pressure group will depend on factors such as:

→ finance
→ organizational ability
→ public sympathy
→ access to business decision-makers
→ reputation
→ access to politicians
→ ability to raise awareness of an issue

It is likely that a firm targeted by a pressure group will have to change its activities in some way. Apart from the costs it incurs in doing this, it may also suffer from a tarnished reputation and lower sales.

Examiner's secrets

Make sure you are able to give examples of ethical business failure, e.g. Bhopal, Exxon Valdez, Maxwell Communications.

Example

Trade unions were created for other reasons but now often act as a pressure group, representing their members' interests to the government.

Don't forget

PEST analysis looks at the **P**olitical, **E**conomic, **S**ocial and **T**echnological threats and opportunities faced by the firm.

Check the net

Pressure group websites include:
www.foe.co.uk
www.tiwf.co.uk
www.greenpeace.org.uk

Links

A pressure group could also be considered as a 'stakeholder' – see pages 34–5.

Watch out!

Be aware that social or ethical decisions are often influenced by factors such as the market, competition and profitability.

Exam questions   answers: page 28

1 There is currently great concern about pollution and the destruction of the environment. Pressure groups such as Friends of the Earth have been formed in an attempt to raise awareness about this issue.
  (a) Give three forms of direct action which an environmental pressure group might take to influence both consumers and businesses. (5 min)
  (b) Identify two companies or organizations which have attempted to reduce the amount of environmental damage caused by their operations. Explain the type of action they have undertaken. (10 min)
  (c) A trade union can be described as a pressure group. How could it use its power in order to persuade an organization to take into account environmental issues, particularly those which affect the working conditions of the employees? (15 min)

2 (a) To what extent should government legislate to control business activity in a mixed economy? (10 min)
  (b) Define the term pressure group and give THREE examples of pressure groups, each with different interests, which might affect a business enterprise. (10 min)
  (c) What problems might a business experience when it is directly affected by the activities of a pressure group? (10 min)

Examiner's secrets

Be ready to use up-to-date examples of pressure group activity to support your points. Consider the issues involved from both the business and pressure group perspectives.

19

Business and the natural environment

There is an increasing awareness of the damage we are doing to our physical environment. There are now many pressure groups which closely monitor firms' actions in relation to the environment and both the UK government and the EU are prepared to intervene to protect the environment.

Markets and pollution

The problem with the environment is that it is a free resource. It is often difficult for society to charge for the use of the environment and so people are left unaccountable for the way they use it.

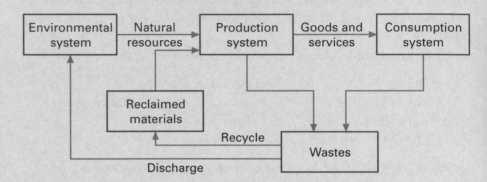

We can see from the diagram that the firm has a choice as to how it *disposes* of the waste products from production. One option is to *reclaim* them for future use. The other option is to *discharge* the waste into the environmental system. Unless the government intervenes, the firm will select the option which costs less. Thus firms have discharged toxic waste into the atmosphere and the sea because it was cheaper to do this than treat it. In economic terms this results in a **misallocation of resources** within the economy because the final price of the product to the consumer does not reflect the additional external costs that society has to bear.

Environmental issues

→ *Economic growth* Most countries want economic growth because it normally provides their citizens with higher standards of living. The problem with this is that faster economic growth is associated with more rapid depletion of natural resources and also with higher levels of pollution.

→ *Global problem* Unfortunately pollution does not respect national boundaries. Thus the acid rain from UK power stations affects Scandinavian forests and lakes. In circumstances such as this it is very difficult to 'make the polluter pay'. Equally whilst most people recognize that over-fishing the sea is wrong, they would not want to give up this free resource.

→ *The Third World problem* As these countries industrialize there will be greater depletion of natural resources (e.g. Brazilian rainforests) and more pollution. They are often unable to afford the more sophisticated environmental products (e.g. refrigerators using non-CFC gases etc.)

Don't forget

The environment provides *natural resources* (e.g. timber) and *amenity services* (e.g. recreation) as well as *receiving waste products* (e.g. dumps).

Don't forget

Different stakeholders may take different views on these environmental issues.

The jargon

Negative externalities exist whenever the firm imposes costs on society which it doesn't have to pay for.

Example

Real income (or *output*) *per head* is often used as a measure of the standard of living. UK real output per head has been growing at over 2% per annum since 1950.

Checkpoint 1

Can you explain why faster economic growth may increase pollution?

→ *A future problem*   Exploitation of the environment affects not only us but also future generations. Unfortunately the attitude of many firms and individuals is to ignore the future problems likely to be caused by current consumption patterns.

Possible solutions

→ *Regulation*   Both the UK government and the EU have introduced legislation. In the UK the *Environmental Protection Act* (EPA) of 1989 introduced the idea of integrated pollution control.

   Governments may also 'tax' polluters and give incentives to cleaner technologies (e.g. lower tax on lead-free petrol).

→ *Self-regulation*   Many large firms undertake an *environment audit* each year. The audit concentrates on items such as pollution levels and waste management (including recycling). They have also cultivated a 'green image' by changing existing products so that they are environmentally friendly.

→ *Recycling*   Where waste products can be recycled, the demand on natural resources and the impact on the environment may be reduced. It also has the advantage of reducing the amount of waste that has to be dealt with.

→ *Sustainable economic growth*   This is a level of growth that can be achieved without harming the resources on which future growth depends. Unfortunately, this restraint is unacceptable to many developing countries – particularly when the problem of overuse is thought to have been caused almost wholly by the developed nations. However individual firms may adopt policies consistent with this principle.

Exam question   answer: page 29

Bernard Bothey, Managing Director of Paling plc (the largest of Yorkshire's chemical companies), appeared in court yesterday to answer charges brought under the Water Resources Act of 1991. The charges relate to an emission of arsenic and zinc based chemicals into the local river. The firm admitted two such offences last year and was fined £5 000 plus costs on both occasions. Chris Barton, a local member of Friends of the Earth, said, 'This is ridiculous, why can't they install filtration equipment? The river will take years to recover.' The maximum fine is £20 000 but negligent directors may be sent to prison for up to two years.

(a) Using supply and demand curves, explain why firms do not want to install filtration equipment. (15 min)

(b) Discuss the reasons why firms continue to pollute and pay the fines rather than installing the filtration equipment. (15 min)

(c) Why might chemical firms prefer self-regulation to regulation? (15 min)

(d) Why do you think the legislation has been drafted so that directors may be sent to prison? (20 min)

Example

Nuclear waste may still be toxic in 20 000 years' time.

Action point

Make some notes on the Environmental Protection Act (1989).

Action point

Can you give some examples of such products? Why are firms doing this?

Example

Almost 80% of materials, by weight, in modern cars are now recycled in the UK.

Check the net

The issue of *sustainability* can be considered at www.sustainability.co.uk

Example

Body Shop seeks to replace any resources used. Use ten trees, plant ten trees!

Links

To revise supply and demand analysis see pages 4–5.

Examiner's secrets

Make sure you draw a clear diagram in question 1 and then use it to explain your answer. Remember that changes in costs will shift the *supply* curve and that profit is revenue minus cost.

The European Union (EU)

The environment facing European business is changing faster than ever before. It is important to understand the workings of the EU and its implications for the UK.

Example

There are around 400 million (high income) consumers in the current 15 EU countries.

Watch out!

As well as *scale economies* (see pages 114–15) the wider market has created opportunities for smaller firms in niche markets.

Action point

Can you name the 12 members of the Euro-zone?

Check the net

This site has a wealth of detail about the EU, its institutions and the Euro www.europa.en.int

Checkpoint 1

What are the convergence criteria the UK has set itself before joining the Euro?

The single market

A huge unified market of around 380 million people has been created through the abolition of *physical*, *technical* and *administrative barriers* in the heart of Europe. It is twice the size of the Japanese market and 15% larger than that of the USA. Not only is the market large but it is extremely prosperous. Many American and Japanese firms attracted by the size and richness of the market have created subsidiaries in Europe to avoid the **common external tariff**.

For the *consumer* the major advantages have been greater choice and lower prices (arising from fierce competition).

For the *firm* the major advantages have been the opportunity to expand into a wider market and in doing so to achieve **economies of scale**. There have been many **cross-border mergers** creating 'European champions' able to compete on equal terms with the biggest of international companies. However a disadvantage has been the increased level of competition in all markets. This has forced firms to place greater emphasis on efficiency in all areas of the business and also on new product modification and development.

The Euro

The **Euro** is the unified currency that took the place of many members' national currency in 2002. The three members of the EU that did not join were the UK, Sweden and Denmark.

The major advantage of the Euro to the *consumer* is thought to be **price transparency** which will lead to greater competition and therefore lower prices. *Firms* will also benefit by avoiding both **exchange rate costs** (e.g. currency conversion) and the **costs of forward contracts** to reduce uncertainty over future rates. It is also argued that a European-wide co-ordinated economic policy will result in faster economic growth and falling unemployment.

Some possible disadvantages of the Euro include the *loss of sovereignty*. Members of the Euro-zone can no longer have a wholly independent fiscal or monetary policy. Some believe this to be important in order to deal with *asymmetric shocks*. An asymmetric shock occurs when an economic event hits one country harder than others. With the UK trade cycle moving more in line with that of the USA than its European counterparts, this is a serious point. This is why the EU has set down some **convergence criteria** for joining (e.g. government deficits less than 3% of GDP).

The Social Chapter

The Maastricht Treaty of 1992 sought to bring members of the EU closer together and included the 'Social Chapter', which was meant to harmonize working conditions throughout the EU. It included *directives* which guaranteed workers the right to

- → join a trade union
- → consultation with the firm
- → a minimum wage
- → parental leave
- → take industrial action
- → equality of treatment
- → a maximum 48-hour working week
- → 4 weeks' paid holiday per year

Much of this ran counter to the then Conservative government's belief that labour markets needed to be deregulated for them to work better and consequently the UK negotiated an opt-out clause. However the Labour government of 1997 has declined this opt-out and joined the Social Chapter.

Enlargement of the EU

There are many Eastern European and former Soviet bloc countries which now wish to join the EU. There are two major attractions. From an *economic* point of view they gain access to one of the world's largest and richest markets. From a *political* point of view, their poorly developed commercial and legal systems and regulatory frameworks will be replaced by the tried and tested systems of the EU.

On the negative side there will be considerable dislocation to the economy as efficient EU firms compete against less efficient Eastern European firms.

From the viewpoint of the EU, Eastern European countries represent an extra 100 million people for the Single Market. However, the entry of several much poorer countries is likely to cause problems with budget contributions, regional transfers and the Common Agricultural Policy.

Don't forget

The aim of the *Social Chapter* is to create a 'level playing field' for all members of the EU as regards conditions of work. The EU had already taken many initiatives in this area before Maastricht.

Links

See also page 17.

Checkpoint 2

Can you explain why, say, Eastern European car making firms (e.g. makers of the Trabant) faced major problems in competing with Western European firms?

Exam questions answers: pages 29–30

1   Your manager has been asked to give a talk to the local Junior Chamber of Commerce on the advantages and disadvantages of the Social Chapter. He has asked you to prepare brief notes for him. (20 min)

2   Ace Electrical Components Ltd is a successful medium-sized firm. Up until now it has concentrated on the UK market. However it has now decided to export to other countries in the EU.

(a) What implications does this have for:
   (i)   the personnel department
   (ii) the finance department
   (iii) the production market? (15 min)

(b) What problems apart from price might arise from the firm's marketing mix? (15 min)

Examiner's secrets

You need to know some facts about the operation of the EU and then be able to relate these facts to the concerns of the individual firm.

Answers
The business environment

The market

Checkpoints

1 (a) Any of: rise in income of consumers, change of taste in favour of apples, rise in price of substitutes (e.g. oranges), rise in population, etc.
   (b) Opposite of all the above.

2 (a) Any of: fall in price (i.e. costs), production inputs, improvements in technology for producing/harvesting apples, fall in price of substitutes in production (e.g. plums so apples are more attractive), lower taxes or higher subsidies on apples.
   (b) Opposite of all the above.

3 (a) Increase in demand (shifts to right) raises equilibrium price and quantity.
   (b) Increase in supply (shifts to right), reduces equilibrium price but raises equilibrium quantity.

4 Sales revenue, growth, satisficing (i.e. reasonable levels of various objectives), etc.

Exam questions

1 The quantity of goods and services that people plan to buy depends in part on the price of related products. There are two types – substitutes and complements. We are concerned here with complements.

A complement is used together with some other product. If the price of a complement rises, the demand for both products will fall. Thus in the case of a sharp rise in petrol prices, the demand for cars will fall (decrease) from D to D_1, which, other things equal, will reduce the price of cars from P to P_1 and quantity sold from Q to Q_1.

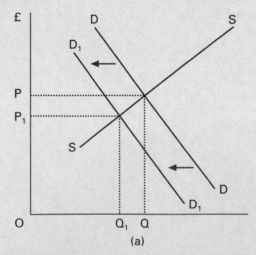

(a)

2 (a) Maximum price legislation is often used in times of shortage, for example during the Second World War. This was necessary to divert resources to military use. The diagram illustrates the situation. Here, at the maximum price P* a situation of *excess demand* exists. Firms do not find it sufficiently profitable to supply all that is demanded. Thus in order to ensure that all who want to buy this product are treated fairly a system of *rationing* is often introduced.

However as some people are willing to pay far more than the maximum price a secondary market, often termed a 'black market', develops.

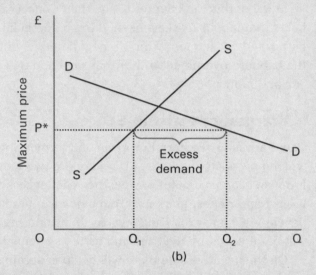

(b)

(b) Minimum wage legislation is designed to raise wages above the current market (equilibrium) level. The diagram illustrates the situation. Here, at the minimum wage W*, there exists *excess supply*. This arises because firms are having to pay more than the market rate for labour. Total costs and prices of finished products may rise. Therefore the demand for the finished product (and consequently labour) falls. Thus whilst the wages of some workers are raised as a result of this legislation, it may be at the expense of some other workers losing their jobs. For the government, therefore, minimum wage legislation is very much a two-edged sword, particularly as the newly unemployed will now have to rely on state benefits.

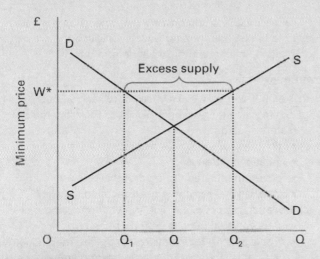

Examiner's secrets

Better candidates might refer to the UK government's recent introduction of minimum wage legislation and the fact that, as yet, it seems to have had little effect on levels of employment. They may also make the point that the short- and longer-term effects of such legislation may appear only when employers begin to introduce 'labour saving' technology.

Markets and competition

Checkpoints

1 Other barriers might include size (e.g. existing, large firms benefit from economies of scale), tariff barriers, geographical distance, exclusive contracts with suppliers/consumers, etc.

2 Other externalities might include pollution of air by private/public transport, damage to ozone layer by CFCs (Chlorofluorocarbons), etc.

Exam questions

1 Apart from any cost reducing strategies, a successful strategy for many small or medium-sized firms in very competitive situations is to analyze their market and through this identify different segments. It is then possible to target a small segment or niche market. These small segments, because of their size, are often not of interest to larger firms. The smaller firm, by concentrating on the needs of this small segment, may be able to provide added value and thus charge a premium price.

Examiner's secrets

Another approach could be to use the four Ps (see page 76) as a means of developing possible strategies.

2 A key factor that allows a firm to charge different prices for the same product (this is termed *price discrimination*) is market segmentation, which classifies buyers into different identifiable groups of people.

These segments often have different degrees of willingness to buy a product in response to price changes (elasticity of demand). Thus, for train journeys, it is easy to distinguish between businesspeople and students. Businesspeople value their time highly and are willing to pay a high price in order to reach their destination at a particular time. Students will not value their time so highly (they are also willing to consider other, slower forms of transport), nor are they willing to pay such a high price. It is therefore sensible for railway companies to charge more for the early trains to London which businesspeople use and less for the later trains.

The UK and European market for cars is also segmentable, first by geography and also by left- and right-hand drive models. Once again this allows car manufacturers to charge different prices. Although it is possible to purchase right-hand drive models on the continent, manufacturers and dealers make this as difficult as possible to maintain segmentation. Firms practise price discrimination because they know that they will get more revenue by charging people different prices based on their different price elasticities of demand rather than by having one price for the whole market.

Examiner's secrets

Although many students find 'elasticity' a difficult concept to come to terms with, you will find it is often used somewhere in an examination.

3 (a) The fact that some people cannot afford some of the things they would like to have is part of the economic problem of scarcity. For most people income is limited and choices have to be made on how to spend that limited income.

(b) Immediate needs, e.g. food, clothing and shelter, are usually the first to be demanded from a limited income. It is the longer-term needs that poorer people are more likely to go without. Thus the purchase of education and healthcare are most likely to be ignored.

(c) The government overcomes this problem by intervening in the market to avoid situations of gross inequity. Thus where people cannot afford important items such as housing, education or healthcare, the government will redistribute resources by providing these goods at a subsidized price or by giving cash benefits so that poorer people can purchase them.

Examiner's secrets

This is really about the idea of 'necessary' and 'luxury' products and that the demand for different products responds in different ways to changes in income.

Macro-economic factors

Checkpoints

1 'Cost push' inflation is where rises in prices can be linked to rises in costs of production. 'Demand pull' inflation is where a rise in aggregate demand (e.g. consumer spending) is the main cause of higher prices. 'Imported

inflation' is where a rise in the cost of imports (e.g. more expensive raw materials) causes prices to rise.

2 Check the definitions on pages 32–3.

3 Protection can help 'infant industries' to become established before facing international competition. It can safeguard jobs when competition is believed to be 'unfair', e.g. imports from countries with very low labour costs and little labour protection.

Exam questions

1 High economic growth means a rise in the standard of living (real GDP per head). Higher real incomes means extra spending is available – so demand curves shift to the right (increase) for most products. A firm can expect a rising demand for its products, so it may increase its production short-term, with higher capital utilization, overtime, etc. It may also plan to raise its production capacity (e.g. new investment in plant and equipment) in the medium term, recruit extra workers, etc.

Examiner's secrets

This question touches on the ideas of income elasticity of demand, i.e. the responsiveness of demand for products to changes in consumer income. Products with higher income elasticities will experience the greater rises in demand.

2 (a) The additional costs will partly depend on the individual firm. If it is using its own vehicles to transport product, then it faces extra distribution and transport costs. If it is sub-contracting these activities, then it must pay agency fees, etc. In any event it will be involved in more administrative costs, e.g. invoicing and other forms of documentation. Time costs of managers, etc. will also be involved in liaising with the export market.

(b) A fall in the exchange rate will make exports cheaper; a rise will make exports dearer. The impacts of exchange rate changes on the firm will be more significant if the product is price sensitive (i.e. price elastic demand). Dealing with foreign currencies also imposes transaction costs on the firm. Competitors in the Eurozone may not face these costs.

Examiner's secrets

This question asks you to apply your knowledge of international trade and exchange rates to the circumstances of an individual firm.

Controlling the economy

Checkpoints

1 The *multiplier* is where an initial change in spending (and output) leads to a greater final total of spending (and output). The *accelerator* links new investment spending of the firm to a rise in output beyond its full-capacity level.

2 Fiscal policy (taxes and government spending) may be used to bring about greater equality, reduce the pressure of inflation, influence the exchange rate, etc.

Exam questions

1 (a) An upward trend is likely, say 1.7% and 2.2%.

(b) Estimates are always problematic. They depend on factors such as
  • tightness in the labour market
  • inflationary trends
  • government action to control the economy
  • international factors, e.g. US economic policy

(c) Reflation means expanding the economy. There are various ways and you should mention two.
  • *Fiscal policy* – by injecting money into the economy (i.e. reducing taxes, increasing expenditure, transferring money from low to high spending groups) demand for goods and services is increased.
  • *Monetary policy* – by reducing interest rates or relaxing controls on the supply of money, consumption and investment will be encouraged.
  • *Supply-side policies* – these are designed to make the labour market work better. Increases in the numbers entering the labour market and their greater flexibility reduces the likelihood of inflation stopping the recovery.

(d) Various possibilities, e.g. bottlenecks in the production process caused by shortages of labour, materials or plant. A second might be cash flow problems arising from expanding production without increasing working capital, etc.

(e) You should mention the possibility of market research to identify where opportunities exist. This information could be on target markets, consumer preferences, assessing the need for producer modifications in the product, the prices to be charged or the channels to be used. The second possibility is a promotional campaign to raise awareness of the firm's products. You should indicate that this is based on prior market research.

Examiner's secrets

In this question you must relate a rise in economic activity to the impacts this might have on an individual firm. Sometimes even growth of the firm may bring with it certain problems and impacts.

2 (a) Cigarettes and alcohol are both habit forming and therefore people are likely to continue purchasing these products even though their incomes may fall.

(b) Firms selling expensive products that normally form part of our 'discretionary income' expenditure are likely to have a high income elasticity of demand. Thus any fall in incomes is likely to have a more than proportionate impact upon sales of exotic holidays.

Examiner's secrets

You should be aware that this question is looking at the impact of income elasticity of demand on two particular products.

Social and demographic influences

Checkpoints

1 (a) Teen market, 'baby boomers' (born after the Second World War), 'grey market' (old and retired), etc.
   (b) Male-orientated products, female-orientated products.
   (c) Certain foodstuffs, colours, etc. more acceptable to some ethnic groups than to others.
2 Extra supply of labour; often part-time, so less expensive and more flexible. Extra demand for products as incomes of women rise through employment, labour-saving products and foodstuffs.

Exam question

(a) A statutory investigation into facts about the nation. A full census occurs every ten years.
(b) The number of children has fallen by 17%.
(c) The population is getting older and more importantly the market for children's clothing has fallen substantially. Competition amongst existing retailers is likely to intensify within a contracting market.
(d) (i)   Does the census information for other towns and cities show a similar pattern?
    (ii) Is this demographic trend likely to continue?
    (iii) Is expenditure per child rising or falling?
    (iv) What are the reactions of the competitors? Etc. . . .
(e) There are several possibilities
   • look for ways to reduce overheads
   • look for new, cheaper suppliers
   • identify market niches that are less vulnerable to these trends, e.g. school uniforms, baby clothes
   • move into related markets, e.g. dress hire
   • cartel agreement with other clothing firms not to compete on price (illegal!)
   • identify other distribution channels, e.g. e-commerce

Examiner's secrets

The key issue is applying these demographic trends to the situation of the local retailer.

Technological influences

Checkpoint

If new technology lowers costs of production (and therefore price) or improves the quality of a product, then more might be demanded. Even if fewer workers are needed *per unit of output* as productivity rises via the new technology, so much more output might be needed that total employment actually rises.

Exam questions

1 (a) You should identify the forms IT takes, for example, computer work stations, mobile phones, teleconferencing, fax machines, e-commerce, etc. You should explain how these enable people to work from home and also their impact on cost.

(b) There are points both for and against this trend continuing.
   The points 'for' include
   • direction of relative cost trends will continue
   • reduces employer overheads
   • working from home gives greater flexibility
   • output is becoming less paper based
   'Against' this though
   • many people go to work for social reasons
   • there are difficulties in controlling the employee
   • technical barriers still exist
   • the paperless office is a long way off

Examiner's secrets

In order to obtain high marks you should be able to relate at least two points to each side of the argument. You should pay attention to developing a balanced and coherent answer for the future. In practice the conclusion you draw is less important than the arguments you use to reach that point of view.

2 You should define the term 'information technology' and perhaps briefly explain how the new system could be expected to improve profitability in the long term. However the core of the essay is taken up identifying factors which will, in the short term, reduce profitability These could include
   • consultancy costs deciding which system to buy
   • installation costs
   • costs of transferring data to the computerized system
   • costs of training new and retraining existing staff on new system
   • redundancy costs of staff no longer required
   • costs of mistakes made by staff in early use of the system
   • costs of maintaining back-up system in the short term
   • employment of computer services manager
   Your conclusion should emphasize that most organizations or functions within organizations that adopt a new system will incur additional short-term costs. One would expect these to disappear within a short period of time and for the organization to benefit from its investment.

Examiner's secrets

Although it is useful to show the examiner your breadth of knowledge, this should not be at the expense of developing your points. Each point you make should be in the form of a well explained paragraph.

Business and the law

Checkpoints

1 (a) See *Trade Descriptions Acts, 1968/72* (page 16).
   (b) See *Sale of Goods Act 1979* (page 16)
   (c) See Acts in (a) and (b) above and also *Consumer Protection Act 1989* (page 16).

(d) Retailer may still be overruled by provisions in the *Sale of Goods Act 1979* (page 16).

2 Any from: removing the 'closed shop' (only members of a particular union employed), preventing secondary action (i.e. a union taking action against another firm not a party to a dispute), secret ballot before any strikes, unions required to oppose unofficial action, etc.

Exam question

(a) You might define and give examples of legal constraints, e.g. consumer protection, employee protection, trade union legislation, environmental protection, investor protection, competition legislation.

You should take at least two examples from the above and use them to illustrate the concept of the 'level playing field' by explaining how the legislation works. Better candidates would probably put this in the context of 'stakeholders' and how their legitimate demands can only be met through legislation.

(b) You should discuss ideas such as
- lack of/cost of inspection powers
- powers to enforce rules
- cost of getting caught
- some firms will always try to bend the rules
- multinationals have the ability to move to avoid restrictions – hence the need for joint action by states
- the ethical climate is important

(c) You should make at least two major points
- within a country firms are competing on level terms if they obey the legislation
- the firm incurs costs to ensure compliance: this increases the price

Business and society

Checkpoints

1 Profit maximization may be attractive to shareholders, resulting in higher dividends and a higher share price (giving capital gains). Of course a longer-term view might lead shareholders to support market share or other strategies even if they reduce short-term profits.

2 Many possibilities here. The drive for profits might have led Monsanto to introduce GM crops before having fully consulted all the interested parties.

Exam questions

1 (a) Examples could include
- disrupting business operations
- boycott of products or services
- protests and demonstrations

(b) Relevant examples such as Shell, Monsanto, etc. Description of action taken.

(c) Examples include
- referring matter to Health and Safety Executive
- involvement of media and/or local MP
- negotiation
- threats of sanctions
- implementation of sanctions such as work to rule, strikes, go slow, etc.

2 (a) You could argue that it is necessary
- to protect consumers
- to protect employees
- to protect the environment
- to protect other businesses
- to further economic policy
- for social policy

Through the use of examples you should show that, without legislation, the interests of these groups may not be taken into account.

(b) They are organized groups which exist to promote a specific cause or interest by influencing business, government or society.
Examples could include
- Médecins sans Frontières – Third World medical issues
- Greenpeace – environmental issues
- Consumers' Association – consumer issues
- AA/RAC – motoring issues
- Chambers of Commerce – represent business interests

You should explain in some detail how each could affect particular types of business.

(c) You should discuss at least three of the following
- public image affected
- demand for products falls
- recruitment difficulties
- possible legal costs
- costs of changing bad image
- possible changes to production methods
- increased R&D into environmentally friendly products

Business and the natural environment

Checkpoint

Faster economic growth means higher incomes, higher demand and more output. This will mean more pollution as a by-product of production (e.g. more road transport to distribute extra output, etc.),

Exam question

(a) The diagram shows that should the firm install the filtration equipment it increases its costs so that the supply curve shifts vertically upwards (i.e. decreases) from SS to S_1S_1. Any given quantity will now only be supplied at a higher price. Thus prices rise (from P to P_1) and output falls (from Q to Q_1) – a situation the firm would like to avoid.

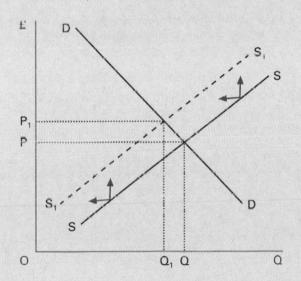

(b) Although the fines raise the costs of Paling plc it might be even more costly to install the filtration equipment. Firms will only install the filtration equipment when the expected cost of fines exceeds the cost of installation. The issue here is not only the fine applied but the likelihood of detection.

(c) Self-regulation allows the industry to decide how to respond to a problem and what the penalties for non-compliance will be. Experience has shown that self-regulation is far less likely to identify a satisfactory response to the problem or to penalize offenders sufficiently.

(d) Directors pursuing the interests of their firm may follow a policy which runs contrary to legislation and the public interest. As it is normally the firm which bears liability, directors are under no personal pressure. Legislation making directors personally liable for negligent acts is an attempt to change their attitude and the way they act.

The European Union

Checkpoint

1 (a) Are business cycles and economic structures compatible so that we could live comfortably with Euro interest rates on a permanent basis

   (b) If problems emerge is there sufficient flexibility to deal with them.

   (c) Would joining the EMU create better conditions for firms making long term decisions to invest in Britain.

   (d) What impact would entry into the EMU have on the competitive position of the UK's financial services industry, particularly the City's wholesale markets.

   (e) In summary will joining the EMU promote higher growth, stability and a lasting increase in jobs.

In 2003 the Treasury assessment was that the UK had made real progress toward meeting the five economic tests. But on balance, though there are clear benefits in areas such as investment, trade, financial services and growth, there is still doubt whether there is sustainable and durable convergence or the flexibility to cope with any potential difficulties within the Euro area.

2 Such producers from the previously 'command economies' have not faced competition. In particular they have not been forced to control costs, maintain high quality or 'market' their output.

Exam questions

1 Your notes should include an introduction explaining what the Social Chapter is and the background to it. For example,

The Social Chapter is part of the 1992 Maastricht Treaty. It is designed to harmonize working conditions throughout the EU. Under it workers have rights such as

- the right to join a trade union
- the right to take industrial action
- the right of consultation
- equal treatment for men and women
- minimum wages and maximum hours

The UK government, at that time, opted out. The 1997 Labour government however took the view that the UK should join.

Points for:

- level playing field argument – within UK and within EU
- workers better motivated
- better industrial relations and worker participation

Points against:

- raises labour costs
- less competitive in world markets
- sovereignty arguments

2 (a) The implications for different departments are
   (i) • recruitment of staff with language ability
        • training key employees in languages
        • where people are employed abroad they need a knowledge of employment law of those countries
   (ii) • increase in working capital
        • additional labour costs
        • additional marketing costs
        • dealing in foreign currencies
        • possible need to increase long-term capital if permanent presence required abroad

   (iii) • product modifications to comply with law or different tastes
         • increased production levels leading to changed production planning and control
         • increased maintenance
         • changes to purchasing requirements
         • product modifications to meet overseas markets tastes (also packaging)
   (b) Define marketing mix
        • identifying suitable ways of promoting abroad and also developing promotional material
        • identifying suitable distribution channels

Business objectives and strategies

The business environment provides opportunities and imposes constraints on organizations. It is important, therefore, for firms to have clear *objectives* for both the short term and the long term. Appropriate *strategies* are required for the successful attainment of these objectives. All of this needs to be monitored and reviewed as the market is constantly undergoing change. Firms that adopt a dynamic, proactive approach to the environment will have the opportunity to be the market leaders, but those that adopt a passive, reactive approach will struggle to remain competitive.

Exam themes

→ The nature and purpose of business activity.

→ The stakeholder approach to business decision-making.

→ The classification of business by size and sector.

→ The benefits, problems and methods of growth.

→ The importance of objectives, both short-term and long-term.

→ The methods and importance of strategic analysis.

→ The importance of strategic planning.

→ The causes and problems of change.

→ The management of change.

→ Governmental impacts on the business environment.

Topic checklist

O AS ● A2	AQA	EDEXCEL	OCR	WJEC
Nature of business	O	O	O	O
Stakeholders and their objectives	O	O	O	O
Size of business	O●	O	O	O
Business organizations	O	O	O	O
Business objectives	O	O	O	O
Strategic analysis	O●	●	●	O●
Strategic planning	●	●	●	O●
Management of change	O●	●	●	●
Government and business	O●	O	O	O

Nature of business

Business is simply the transformation of inputs into an output that is demanded by consumers. For a business to be profitable it must 'add value' during the transformation stage so that a price can be charged that is higher than the cost of the resources used.

Inputs and outputs

Inputs are the resources needed to produce marketable products and include the *four factors of production*: land, labour, capital and enterprise. These resources are then transformed into an **output**

→ **a consumer good** – this is either a *consumer durable*, which is long lasting (TV, washing machine, radio etc.), or a *consumer non-durable* to be consumed in the near future (foodstuffs, paper tissues, petrol etc.)

→ **a capital good** – a product needed by business in order to make further goods such as machinery, tools and vehicles

→ **a service** – activities such as banking, insurance, transport, warehousing that assist firms and individuals, together with all of the *personal services* (hairdresser, doctor, dentist, plumber etc.)

These activities are supplied either by companies on a profit basis in the private sector or by government in the public sector.

Private and public sector

The *private sector* is that part of the economy operated by privately owned firms, ranging from small sole traders to multinational conglomerates. In the UK and most of the Western world it is the dominant sector.

The *public sector* includes all those activities and organizations that are owned and/or financed by government, such as public corporations (nationalized industries), national public services (e.g. NHS) and local government services (leisure centres, swimming pools, libraries). As well as describing business according to ownership it can be classified according to the type of product.

Primary sector

Most goods start their life as some form of *raw material*, either in the ground, the seas or the fields. The activities associated with extracting minerals from the ground, harvesting fish from the sea or growing crops and rearing animals are known as **primary sector** activities, and include the following

→ *mining and quarrying* mainly quarrying for stone products and the mining of coal

→ *mineral oil and natural gas extraction* mainly the output of oil and natural gas from the North Sea

→ *agriculture, forestry and fishing* agriculture has declined continuously since the 1960s. By 2000 it contributed less than 2% of the UK's GDP

Action point

List three consumer durables that you own and three consumer non-durables that you have bought recently.

Links

For more on the types of firm see pages 38–9.

Don't forget

Here we are classifying business according to *ownership*.

Check the net

You can find more about these types of business on the Department of Trade and Industry website at www.dti.gov.uk

Example

The *primary sector* has generally declined since the 1960s. In 1964 it provided 5.8% of the UK's total output but by 2000 it produced only 3.9%, of which nearly half was provided by oil and gas. In terms of employment it created 5.1% of all jobs in 1964 with over 1.2 million employed. By 2000 this had fallen to just 1.3% of all jobs, with 417 000 employed.

The future for many small farming units, particularly low productivity ones such as hill farms, is not very promising. The long-term trend is for the primary sector gradually to become less important as a generator of output and employment in the UK.

Percentage share of GDP in UK

Sector	1964	1979	2000
Primary	5.8	6.7	3.9
Secondary	40.4	36.7	25.8
Tertiary	53.8	56.6	70.2

Secondary sector

The conversion of the raw materials produced by the primary sector into products involves either processing or manufacture. This is known as **secondary sector** activity. Output from the secondary sector has grown slowly in recent years but its *relative share of GDP* has fallen from 40.4% in 1964 to 25.8% by 2000. In 1964 the secondary sector provided around 47% of all employment (i.e. 11 million jobs). By 2000 this had fallen to below 21% of employment with a little over 5 million employed. Not all industries, however, suffered the same decline. Chemicals, electrical and instrument engineering, transport equipment and food have all seen output grow in absolute and relative terms through the 1980s and 1990s.

Within the secondary sector, manufacturing industry has experienced particularly rapid decline, falling from 38% of employment (9 million jobs) in 1964 to only 15.6% of employment (just under 4 million jobs) in 2000.

Tertiary sector

The products of the primary and secondary sectors need to be distributed to *consumers*. The services of transport, wholesaling and retailing perform that function. In turn *industry* needs support from banking, insurance, education, communications and administration. All of these make up the **tertiary sector**. In 1964 the tertiary sector accounted for almost 54% of all UK output but by 2000 this had expanded to over 70%. This is also reflected in employment, which has grown from just over 11 million in the tertiary sector in 1964 to around 19.7 million in 2000. The major contributors to this expansion were 'communications' and the 'finance, insurance, banking, business services and leasing' groups of businesses. This last group now accounts for around 20% of all UK output.

Checkpoint 1

Why do you think the *primary sector* employs fewer people than it used to?

Don't forget

The *secondary sector* includes manufacturing, construction, energy and water supply.

Example

The output from the energy industries has grown at almost 3% per year since 1981.

The jargon

This relative decline in manufacturing output and employment is often referred to as *de-industrialization*.

Watch out!

Some people also speak of a *post-industrial* (or *quaternary*) *sector* involved with creating, processing and distributing information.

Checkpoint 2

Why do you think the *tertiary sector* employs more people than it used to?

Exam questions answers: page 50

1 What have been the main causes of de-industrialization in the UK? (20 min)

2 From the table above calculate the percentage change in output for each sector from 1964 to 2000. How has this structural change affected the labour force? (30 min)

Examiner's secrets

It is important to be able to describe these structural changes *and* to understand the impacts they are having on businesses and regions as industries decline or expand.

33

Stakeholders and their objectives

All businesses operate within an environment and as such they deal on a daily basis with customers, suppliers, employees and the local community. Each of these groups has its own objectives that might not agree with those of the firm. Modern firms must recognize these objectives and determine how significant they are for their own operations.

The 'shareholder' v 'stakeholder' concept

The 'shareholder' concept – a traditional view of a firm whereby all of its actions are designed to increase the wealth of the business for the benefit of the owners or shareholders. Management's main task is seen as being to maximize profits, but this may result in conflict with the other groups interested in the business.

The 'stakeholder' concept – any individual or group that has an effect on, or is affected by, a business or organization is known as a 'stakeholder'. Some management theorists believe that it is beneficial in the long run for firms to recognize the views of these groups and to include their objectives in the decision-making process. A business holding such stakeholder views might be expected to

→ improve working conditions for its employees
→ support local community projects
→ build long-term 'partnerships' with suppliers
→ adopt environmentally friendly policies

   In this way the firm would obtain benefits such as

→ more committed, loyal staff with lower labour turnover and absenteeism rates
→ improved productivity from better motivated personnel
→ increased loyalty from customers who are more likely to resist the temptations of competitors
→ less local opposition to items such as planning permission

   In a modern economy a firm cannot just rely on advertising and marketing to build up customer loyalty, but must look to the building of more long-term relationships with its 'stakeholders'.

Individual objectives

A business is made up of *groups of individuals* who might be pursuing their own set of objectives.

→ *Employees* – who desire to have a just reward for their services, not only in terms of salary and working conditions but also in job satisfaction.
→ *Customers* – who may not necessarily want the cheapest item but one that they perceive as 'value for money'. They are also concerned about service, both during the buying process and after sales.
→ *Owners or shareholders* – who want an income in the form of dividends and the prospect of a capital gain through an increasing share price. They have to balance the prospect of pursuing

The jargon

Stakeholders is the collective term used to refer to all these groups.

Action point

Contrast the objectives of an *employee* with those of the *employer* under profit maximization.

Action point

Identify the stakeholders of your school or college. Have they any shared objectives? How do their objectives differ?

Checkpoint 1

What *strategies* do
(a) the Body Shop and
(b) the Virgin group of companies
adopt in order to appeal to their respective customers?

Check the net

Visit the *Body Shop website* for material on human rights and environmental issues www.thebodyshop.com

Action point

Compare your objectives with those of your teacher. Do they always agree?

short-term profits against the need to build long-term growth and customer loyalty.

→ *Managers* – although they are paid to represent and promote the shareholders' interests they might possess objectives of their own. These could range from building good working relations with employees in order to avoid workplace conflict to enhancing their own position in the firm by rewarding themselves with high salaries, luxury offices and expensive company cars.

Business objectives

The business itself might have a number of objectives that change as time and performance dictate. The most common objectives are:

→ *survival* – to reach a sustainable sales level that allows the firm to break even
→ *profit maximization* – to maximize the difference between total revenue and total cost
→ *growth* – which may be in terms of market share for each product (or a group of products) in order to decrease the risk of failure

It is easy to see that even these limited business objectives could cause *conflict* at some stage. For example the quest for more market share might entail cutting prices, which reduces profit margins and possibly overall profit.

Conflict of objectives

It appears, therefore, that a firm's responsibilities to its shareholders may directly conflict with its responsibilities to the other stakeholders. For example a significant wage rise will benefit the *employees* but only at the expense of lower profits for the *owners*. All of the groups are competing for a slice of the rewards generated by the business. It appears as though one group can only benefit at the expense of another. This is the traditional 'shareholder' view.

The 'stakeholder' view envisages all groups benefiting through increased *co-operation* that leads eventually to higher rewards for all. For example higher wages might lead to higher productivity, reduced unit costs and higher profits. **'Satisficing'** is the acceptance of a strategy that is satisfactory for all instead of pursuing a policy that is in the interests of only one group. Although this might be viewed as a compromise it can have extremely beneficial effects on the long-term prospects of a business.

Don't forget

When the (profit related) objectives of the owner shareholders (*principals*) conflict with those of the managers (*agents*) we say there is a *principal–agent problem*.

Links

See the discussion of *Business objectives* (page 40) for a more detailed treatment.

The jargon

Spreading risk by producing a greater variety of products is called *diversification*.

Don't forget

Be aware that some companies might support stakeholder objectives in public but are not so enthusiastic when large amounts of money are required to put them into practice, e.g. pollution controls or higher wages.

Checkpoint 2

Why might the profit and growth objectives conflict?

Exam questions   answers: pages 50–1

1   To what extent do firms have to take notice of consumer pressure groups? (15 min)

2   Outline two arguments in favour of the shareholder concept and two arguments against it. (20 min)

3   Identify the stakeholders in a charity or a hospital. (15 min)

Examiner's secrets

To obtain high marks it is important not only to correctly identify the stakeholders in a business but also to assess their relative strengths in the decision-making process.

Size of business

One feature of industrial development in recent periods has been the growth in the size of the firm. It is important to understand the reasons for this, the problems associated with growth and why small firms continue to exist.

Small firm survival

Links

For more on *economies of scale* see below and also pages 114–15.

Economic theory suggests that large firms should be more efficient than small firms due to the existence of **economies of scale**. Despite this *small firms* continue to survive for the following reasons

→ *supply a small (niche) market* either geographically (e.g. corner shop) or by producing a specialist item or service (art restorer)
→ *provide a personal or more flexible service*, e.g. local builder erecting a house extension
→ *allow entrepreneurs the opportunity to start their own business and to test their ideas in the market place*; many of these people are dissatisfied with working for large companies and desire to be their 'own boss'
→ *the owners have made a conscious decision not to grow* because they do not want to undertake the inherent risks and workload associated with growth

The jargon

The *1985 Companies Act* defines a company as *small* if it satisfies two of the following
Turnover less than £2m
Net assets under £975 000
Less than 50 employees

In 1998 there were 3 708 000 businesses in the UK, of which 3 676 000 or 99.2% were classified as 'small'. Despite this superiority in numbers they accounted for only 44.7% of employment and 39.5% of turnover. In other words less than 1% of businesses provide over half of all employment and more than 60% of all turnover.

Reasons for growth

The jargon

Economies of scale are the factors that reduce average costs as firms expand, such as discounts for bulk buying, greater productivity via more specialization and the increased application of machinery, the availability of cheaper finance, etc.

Here are some of the main reasons for firms wanting to expand

→ *cost savings* – firms can benefit from economies of scale
→ *diversification of product* – reduces the risk of dependence on one product or service
→ *diversification of market* – reduces dependence on one economy and one set of customers
→ *market power* – increased power in the market allows firms to influence prices and to obtain better margins through reduced competition
→ *risk reduction* – larger firms are less likely to suffer in market downturns and are less likely to be taken over by competitors

Action point

Examples of mergers/takeovers include Walmart and ASDA, Royal Bank of Scotland and NatWest, Halifax and Birmingham Midshires, HSBC and Midland Bank. Can you add three more?

In an increasingly competitive market firms are pressured into continually reducing costs and improving efficiency. One way of achieving this is to expand either *organically* or by means of *takeovers* and *mergers*.

Methods of growth

→ **Internal growth** – this is when the firm expands without involving other businesses. It is *organic growth* achieved by increasing sales of its existing products to a wider market.

→ **External growth** – this can be achieved by either a *takeover* (gaining at least a 51% share in another firm) or a *merger* (two firms agreeing to join in creating a new third company).

There are four other types of growth depending on the *direction* taken:

→ **forward vertical integration** – towards the final consumer
→ **backward vertical integration** – towards the raw material supplier
→ **horizontal integration** with a firm in the same business and at the same stage of production (e.g. Cadbury-Schweppes)
→ **conglomerate integration** involving firms in a totally unrelated business

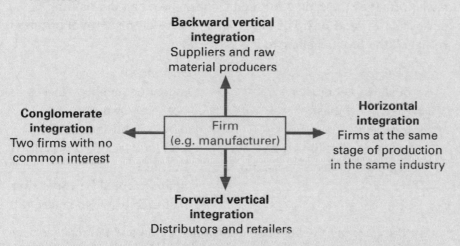

Backward vertical integration
Suppliers and raw material producers

Conglomerate integration
Two firms with no common interest

Firm (e.g. manufacturer)

Horizontal integration
Firms at the same stage of production in the same industry

Forward vertical integration
Distributors and retailers

Problems of growth ●●●

Growth, especially when it is rapid, is very difficult to manage.

→ *Financial* – the firm might require significant increases in both its capital and its cash holdings in order to finance the increased volume of production and sales. This will involve either a further injection of permanent capital from shareholders or extra borrowings. In both cases the gearing and liquidity ratios will be affected.
→ *Operational* – ensuring that the increased market is supplied with the required goods on time and within budget. This is particularly difficult where two or more production processes are being merged.
→ *Managerial* – i.e. the problems of co-ordination and control, especially where merging firms have different corporate cultures. In takeovers, two boards of directors and two sets of management have to be replaced by one. This will lead to periods of uncertainty and speculation among the workforce.

Despite these problems the current trend is for firms to expand towards being multinational with operating plants all over the world. The global economy calls for global firms that can operate on a world scale.

Exam questions   answers: pages 51–2

1 Why are small firms considered to benefit an economy? (15 min)

2 Why might mergers fail to increase efficiency? (15 min)

3 Compare and contrast internal and external methods of growth. (30 min)

Checkpoint

Compare the methods of growth in the banking industries with those in the airline industry. What are the major differences?

Check the net

The government provides help for small business growth. Visit www.businesslink.org

Example

Walmart's takeover of ASDA is an example of horizontal integration that provides the US retailing giant with an opportunity to enter the highly profitable UK market.

Links

See *ratio analysis* and the importance of *gearing* to shareholder and market confidence (page 155).

The jargon

Glocalization is the attempt by multinationals to produce on a global basis but customizing to take account of local conditions.

Examiner's secrets

The better answers to questions on growth will consider *both* the benefits and drawbacks of expansion. This demonstrates 'evaluation'.

Business organizations

There are many types of business in the commercial world. Each type of business has a role to play in the modern economy with its own unique benefits and drawbacks.

Sole trader

A **sole trader** is the simplest form of business unit as few legal formalities are needed to start and little capital is required. Sole traders are often found in activities where personal service is important and where large-scale production would be uneconomic. In general, the sole trader provides the capital for the business, bears all the risk and makes all the decisions. The principal incentive of this form of business is that all the profits belong to the sole trader.

Advantages
- → business kept private
- → easy to establish
- → independence
- → receives all of the profit
- → flexibility of decision-making

Disadvantages
- → unlimited liability – losses borne by owner
- → may lack business skills
- → potential lack of continuity of business
- → limited capital for expansion
- → historically a high failure rate

For the *customer* the benefit can be a dedicated and personal service specifically targeted at individuals. There are still many consumers who prefer doing business with small, well-known, local traders.

Partnership

Many of the difficulties associated with being a sole trader may be overcome by forming a **partnership**. As the partners still have *unlimited liability* (each partner is liable for the debts of the other partners) it is common for partnerships to exist in family businesses or in professional areas such as law, insurance and accountancy. The rights and responsibilities of each partner may be written down in a **Partnership Agreement**. This states the capital supplied by each partner, the sharing of profits and losses, the voting rights and the arrangements for enlarging or dissolving the partnership.

Advantages
- → injection of extra capital
- → division of labour – specialists can be brought in, e.g. accountant, sales manager, purchasing manager, etc.
- → shared responsibility therefore can cover for illness, holidays, etc.
- → business affairs still kept private

Disadvantages
- → unlimited liability
- → disagreements over decision-making and control
- → limited to a maximum of 20 partners except for solicitors, accountants and other specially exempted groups

Examples

Typical local examples would include *local retailers* (tobacconists, grocers, butchers, newsagents, florists), *local services* (hairdressing, window cleaning, restaurants, garages) and *local manufacturers* (self-employed craftspeople, small engineering companies, etc.).

Watch out!

Sole traders are the most common form of business organization (68%) but account for only a small percentage (5%) of the total output and sales in the UK. They are, however, important sources of employment (14%), particularly in remote and rural areas.

Example

Approximately 40% of all new businesses fail in the first two years.

The jargon

A *partnership* is a legal form of business organization where two or more people trade together under the *Partnership Act of 1890*.

Action point

Find out whether your doctor or dentist is in a partnership.

Companies

Private limited company

The purpose of forming a **private limited company** is to encourage people to invest in larger enterprises with relatively little risk. The owners are responsible only for the amount invested in the company (*limited liability*) rather than risking their entire personal wealth.

Advantages	Disadvantages
→ limited liability	→ can't sell shares to the general public
→ continuity of existence	→ transfer of shares has to be approved by all members
→ easier to raise capital	
→ economies of scale	→ public access to accounts at the Registrar of Companies

Public limited company (plc)

Most plcs start life as *private companies* that go 'public' in order to raise further capital for development and expansion. Although small in number they account for most of the turnover, employment and capital investment in the UK. The principal purpose of creating a plc is to raise large amounts of capital to fund future expansion. This necessitates offering shares to the general public through a listing on the Stock Exchange. The plc (and Ltd company) must issue a **Memorandum of Association**, defining its relationship with the outside world, and **Articles of Association**, defining its internal government.

Advantages	Disadvantages
→ limited liability	→ costly to establish
→ easier to raise large amounts of capital	→ accounts must be published
→ shares transferable on the Stock Exchange	→ risk of takeover by other firms buying shares on the Stock Exchange
→ greater economies of scale	
→ continuity guaranteed	→ greater size may lead to slower decision-making

Public sector organizations

The **public sector** is made up of public corporations (nationalized industries), government departments (e.g. Department of Health) and local government services (e.g. council-run leisure centres). The emphasis here is not on making a profit but on providing a service for the community. Increasingly this objective has become more commercialized, with government agencies having to operate within strict budget guidelines and to rely on cost savings for extra funding rather than on increased government subsidy.

Exam questions   answers: pages 52–3

1   What distinguishes a private limited company from a plc? (10 min)

2   What does the term 'limited liability' mean and why is it so important? (10 min)

3   How is a franchise (see page 75) different from other forms of business organization? (15 min)

The jargon

The *private limited company* must have at least two shareholders. They are not allowed to sell shares to the general public but must offer them on a private basis. There are over half a million private limited companies.

Don't forget

Incorporation is the process of becoming a corporate body, i.e. establishing a business as a separate legal entity. The name of the *private limited company* must be registered with the Registrar of Companies and it must have the designation 'Limited' (often abbreviated to 'Ltd') at the end.

Action point

British Telecom, Glaxo, Sainsburys, Royal Bank of Scotland are all plcs. Can you add ten more plcs to the list that produce products or services that you use?

Watch out!

Both Ltd and plc companies must publish accounts, but they must be more detailed for a plc.

Examiner's secrets

Many students are surprisingly weak at distinguishing between the different forms of business organization, particularly plcs and Ltd companies and between the private and public sector. Accuracy with terminology will avoid losing marks.

Business objectives

Business objectives are a statement of what an organization wants to achieve, through its operations, both in the short and long term. Some people refer to these as aims or goals but whatever term is used, it is important to stress that the objectives provide direction for all of the firm's actions. Different companies will have different objectives depending on their size, their age, their market and the sector in which they are operating.

Survival

All new firms face enormous problems in trying to establish themselves profitably in the market. At the beginning, the owner may be satisfied for the company merely to *survive* its early problems while building a reputation and a guaranteed market share. Large profits may be of secondary importance. Survival may involve offering goods and services at highly competitive prices that do not (at least initially) provide optimum profits. The initial objective might be to reach a sustainable level of sales that guarantees break-even.

Links

For more on *break-even analysis* see page 158.

Profit maximization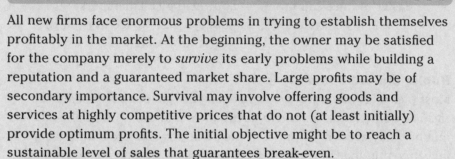

For most firms *profit making* is the major concern of the business. This is often the principal reason for the original formation of the company. The traditional economist's view is that firms in the private sector are profit maximizers where each business decision is based on the need to increase profits. This may be the case for small operations that are under the direct control of the owner, but large companies may be equally concerned with objectives such as market share or growth. Profit, however, remains an important objective because

→ it ensures the long-term survival of the business
→ it provides a source of finance for future investment
→ it provides rewards for stakeholders (dividends for shareholders, wage increases for employees, price reductions or improved products for the consumer, etc.)
→ it provides a measure of the efficiency and effectiveness of management policies
→ it allows comparison with other forms of investment

Don't forget

H. A. Simon, the Nobel prize-winning economist, used the term 'satisficing' to describe the situation where a firm seeks *reasonable* (not maximum) outcomes for various targets, e.g. for sales, market share and profit.

Action point

Check the mission statements of some well-known companies for their overall long-term aim, e.g. Walt Disney World's mission statement is 'To make people happy'.

Growth

Once established many firms pursue **growth** as their main objective. Growth is seen as a means of limiting risk because

→ expansion of output will allow *economies of scale* which in turn will improve competitiveness through cost and price reductions
→ a firm can *diversify in terms of product* so that a fall in demand for one item can be compensated by growth in other products
→ a firm can *diversify in terms of market* so that recession in one market is balanced by sales in a more buoyant market

Links

For more on *economies of scale* see pages 114–15.

Despite these obvious advantages many smaller firms are hesitant to follow an aggressive policy of growth due to the risks involved in investing more capital.

Alternative objectives

In larger firms there is the possibility for a *range of objectives* to be pursued such as

→ **Managerial objectives** – where managers have considerable power in an organization they may aim to maximize their own salaries, fringe benefits, pensions, department budgets, the number of subordinate staff and leisure time. This is true in firms where there is considerable divorce (separation) between control and ownership.
→ **Sales revenue maximization** – this is often the case where managers' salaries are linked to sales and not to profit levels.
→ **Corporate image** – with the growth of consumer pressure groups it is important for firms to be seen to be environmentally and socially responsible, even if this entails earning lower profits.

In the final analysis it is the *group* that dominates a business that will determine its objectives, but in most cases it will be a mix of the above.

Public sector objectives

Public sector organizations include public corporations (nationalized industries), government departments (e.g. DSS) and local government services. In the past the nationalized industries were required to provide a service and where possible to break even or at least make a rate of return sufficient to fund new investment. When they failed to do this many of them were *privatized*.

Government departments, both national and local, are now required to operate on a more commercial basis. They must work within much tighter budget guidelines and rely on cost savings and efficiency gains for future extra funding. Local authorities have been forced to introduce charges for many of their services, relying on means testing to identify those not capable of paying. Many of the services must now be put out to *tender* so that government departments are forced to compete directly with private sector businesses.

Exam questions answers: page 53

1 Under what circumstances might survival be the overriding objective? (15 min)

2 Identify three advantages and three disadvantages of pursuing growth. (20 min)

3 What are the advantages and disadvantages of the public sector adopting more commercial objectives? (20 min)

Examiner's secrets

Evaluation can be shown when you balance the benefits of growth against the risks involved. Remember to come to a conclusion about the overall outcome as you see it but based on the data provided.

Checkpoint 1

Can you explain what is meant by 'a separation between ownership and control'? How might this affect the business objectives?

Action point

Think! Is it ethical for directors to award themselves larger pay rises than those offered to the ordinary employee? Under what circumstances would you agree?

Checkpoint 2

Define *privatization*. Can you briefly list the points for and against privatization?

Examiner's secrets

Ensure that you differentiate between long-term aims (as indicated in mission statements) that are predominantly *qualitative* in nature and objectives which should be *quantified* and set within a time frame.

41

Strategic analysis

An organization lays down certain *strategic objectives* and develops *strategic plans* to achieve these objectives. However, in doing this it must first undertake a strategic analysis of the position it finds itself in.

The strategic analysis model ●●●

This is an attempt to ensure that an analysis of the firm's situation is undertaken properly and that alternative strategies are considered. The model shows that there are two major areas to audit.

→ *External environment* This is the environment which provides the *opportunities* that the firm would like to exploit and the *threats* that it needs to avoid. Obviously, there are many factors which will affect the firm but you will find that there are three or four which are critical to the success of the firm. These are termed 'key success factors'.

→ *Internal environment* This involves looking inside the organization to identify the firm's *strengths* and *weaknesses*. You should be able to identify the firm's 'key competences' from this audit.

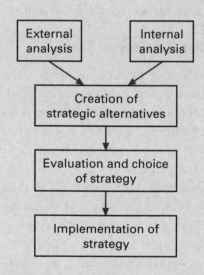

The external audit ●●●

This is a means of identifying the *opportunities* and *threats* facing the firm. Firms operate in a business framework which is affected by changes in political, economic, social and technological factors.

→ *Political factors* Government *legislation* may have a major impact upon organizations. Thus new legislation to protect workers or consumers may push up a firm's costs. Equally changes in monetary and fiscal policy may affect the firm's costs and revenues.

→ *Economic factors* The firm must be aware of the general direction of the whole economy. The *business cycle* has important implications for the opportunities and threats the firm faces. Of equal importance is the *state of the markets* within which the firm operates, e.g. the nature and intensity of competition.

→ *Social factors* Changes in *tastes* and *fashion* may have a direct effect on the firm in the short term. *Demographic changes*, increasing

The jargon

The term *SWOT* analysis is often used here: **s**trengths, **w**eaknesses, **o**pportunities, **t**hreats.

Don't forget

The firm can also develop *strategic alternatives* for evaluation from these audits.

Don't forget

Make sure you read a good newspaper each week so that you can comment on the dynamic nature of the external environment and its recent changes.

The jargon

The term *PEST* is often used to refer to **p**olitical, **e**conomic, **s**ocial and **t**echnological factors.

Example

For firms with overseas subsidiaries (i.e. multinationals such as BP) *political stability* is of major importance.

Links

For more on the *business cycle* see page 10.

Checkpoint

Select two *demographic trends* in the UK and outline the impact of these upon the leisure industry.

environmental awareness and *pressure group* growth will affect firms in the longer term.

→ *Technological factors* Advancements in science mean that no firm can be complacent about the product or service it is operating. *New technology* may render existing products or the methods of making them obsolete. Technology may also provide the firm with opportunities to improve its product or produce something entirely new.

Example

Toffler in his book *Future Shock* argues that the rate of technological change is accelerating.

The internal audit ●●●

This is a means of identifying the *strengths* and *weaknesses* of a firm. It is important this is done within the context of the industry within which the firm works. Thus the fact that a firm has modern efficient machinery is not a strength if every other firm in the industry uses the same technology. The aim is to identify those areas in which the firm has some *competitive advantage* over other firms. The areas include

Area	Characteristics to consider
People	skills, training, attitude
Organization	structure, relationships
Systems	formal, informal, technology based
Products	quality, costs, life cycle, portfolio
Production	efficiency, nature, capacity
Finance	profitability, liquidity, controls, raising of finance
Credibility	reputation, goodwill, security, customer perception
Knowledge	technical, competition, market

Watch out!

The internal audit must be *objective*. For example if competence is claimed in a particular area, *evidence* must be provided to back up that claim.

Presenting the results ●●●

The information you have obtained from the external and internal audit must be summarized in a way that busy managers can absorb.

Strengths
→ high quality products
→ efficient production system

Opportunities
→ raise finance from sale of town sites
→ new export markets in Asia

Weaknesses
→ workforce motivation
→ cash flow problems

Threats
→ increased competition in EU
→ stricter health and safety legislation

Examiner's secrets

The two upper quarters of the table give the results of the *internal audit*, the two lower quarters the results of the *external audit*.

Watch out!

Be aware that you may be required to assess and evaluate the overall effectiveness of the strategic analysis process.

Exam question answer: page 54

(a) How can benchmarking (see page 129) help in strategic analysis? (20 min)

(b) Explain the term SWOT analysis. How can it be used to develop a firm's strategic plan? (20 min)

Strategic planning

Strategic planning is the long-term planning dealing with an organization's mission, objectives and plans on how to achieve those objectives. Underpinning the decisions made regarding objectives and strategic plans will be the *strategic analysis* already considered.

Strategic direction

Michael Porter argues that there are two factors which will determine a firm's **strategic direction**.

The first factor to consider is the nature of the firm's **competitive advantage** over its rivals. Porter sees two ways in which a competitive advantage can be gained

→ providing goods and services at a *lower price* than other market players; this enables competitive prices to be charged and greater profits to be earned

→ using *product differentiation* to create a situation whereby the firm can charge a higher price because the consumers believe the product or service is in some way unique

The second factor the firm has to consider is the **scope of the market** in which it wishes to operate. Again there are two possibilities

→ to compete in *all sectors* of the market; achieving and holding on to a major part of a mass market will always be difficult, but if successful is highly profitable

→ to focus on *certain segments* of the market rather than the whole; whilst this is unlikely to be as profitable as the first option, it is far easier to defend

Porter combines these two sets of decisions in a *matrix* which suggests there are four separate strategic positions the firm could adopt.

		Competitive advantage	
		Low cost	**Differentiation**
Competitive scope	**Industry-wide**	Cost leadership	Differentiation 'Pig in the middle'
	Narrow segment(s)	Cost focus	Focused differentiation

→ **Cost leadership**   This has come to prominence in recent years with the growth of continent-wide or even global marketing to support massive new production plants which permit large economies of scale.

Links

For more on business objectives see pages 40–1.

The jargon

Competitive advantage refers to the means by which the firm seeks to create and sustain a superior performance.

Watch out!

A choice may have to be made between *cost leadership* and *product differentiation*.

Example

This has been the Japanese approach in attacking many EU markets. They have been willing to accept large losses in early years to build up a *strategic position* in specific market segments.

- **Differentiation** This enables the firm to avoid competing head-to-head on price by creating a sense of uniqueness that persuades consumers they are buying something different or better than the competitors have to offer.
- **Cost focus** Within the segments targeted, the firm concentrates on providing value for money, for example through superior purchasing of inputs or providing fewer (unnecessary) additional features.
- **Focused differentiation** As with differentiation above, but involving a limited number of market segments.

Strategy implementation

Once the strategic direction of the firm has been established it is then the responsibility of senior managers to set the parameters within which subordinate managers will act. In practice such **strategic implementation** means establishing time periods or *planning horizons* within which certain specified and measurable activities should occur. It is the responsibility of these middle and junior managers to develop medium- and short-term tactical plans which move the firm from the position where it is now to the desired position in, say, five years' time.

Strategic gaps

A **strategic gap** may be revealed by the ongoing external and internal audits undertaken by the firm, when they suggest that changes in the market or inside the firm are such that a previously planned objective is not now going to be achieved. The strategic gap which has been identified may be *closed* by modifying the strategic direction and objectives of the firm – though in reality this is the last thing senior management will want to do. A more likely response, at least initially, is that functional departments will be asked to develop alternative plans which contribute more effectively to achieving the existing overall objective.

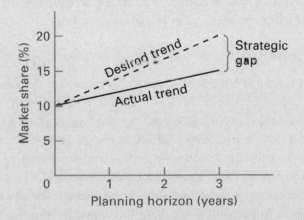

Exam questions answers: pages 54–5

1 Consider three ways in which functional managers might help in closing a strategic gap. (20 min)

2 How important do you consider planning to be in achieving the firm's objectives? (30 min)

Management of change

In the modern economy *change* is a constant feature and firms must address its implications or risk losing out to competitors. Unfortunately not all change can be foreseen and in any case is not always within the firm's control. Despite these drawbacks a policy of **change management** allows firms to deal systematically with the impacts of change, especially those involving the human resources of the firm.

Causes of change

Businesses today face a market place where products, production methods and customers are constantly changing. The causes of such changes may include the following

→ *Technological development* – there have been rapid changes in production processes, communication methods and materials which have forced firms to revolutionize their operations.

→ *Consumer preferences* – customers are better informed and more willing to use their spending patterns to support their views about the environment, animal testing or the exploitation of labour.

→ *Market opportunities* – new markets have developed, such as Eastern Europe and China. Older markets have become more competitive, requiring firms to be more innovative (product differentiation) as well as more efficient.

→ *Legislation* – the government (including the EU) has imposed stricter measures to curb pollution and to safeguard the interests of consumers.

→ *Demographic change* – population changes affect the age profile and hence the demand patterns of consumers. Many *industrialized economies* are faced with ageing populations whereas *developing nations* have increasingly younger populations.

Whatever the causes of change, a firm needs to recognize the problem and where possible take appropriate action.

Type of change

The firm's reaction to change will depend on whether the change was foreseen or unforeseen and whether it is within its power to control.

Foreseen change – predictable changes such as gradual sales growth should be met by *planned* organizational change. Failure to plan for such change is really the result of poor internal management. It is within the firm's power to control such events.

Unforeseen change – unpredictable changes are more problematic. A sudden increase in demand might lead to rushed production, soaring costs in overtime payments, a reduction in quality control and a declining reputation as dissatisfied customers return unsatisfactory products.

External change – factors such as customer tastes, new legislation, increased competition and the general state of the economy are largely outside the control of a firm (i.e. *external change*). Advertising and the

Action point

List some of the *impacts* that the following changes have had on businesses (try to be specific): plastics, silicon chip, Internet, e-commerce, pollution controls, break-up of the Soviet Union, banning of CFCs.

Links

For more on demographic change in the UK, see page 12.

Checkpoint 1

The BSE crisis is an example of unforeseen change. Consider how the banning of beef exports affected the UK beef and dairy industries.

Checkpoint 2

Identify *two* pieces of legislation that have either increased the costs of business or altered how the business can be operated.

lobbying of politicians might help, but the outcome is not certain. In these cases the firm must prepare itself to respond quickly. *Contingency planning* and *scenario analysis* are both useful tools to apply.

Resistance to change

People implement change, but they also form the most significant *barriers* to change, both individually and collectively.

Individual resistance – individuals resist change because they prefer to deal with existing processes and procedures. People do not like being pushed or forced out of their 'comfort zone'. They prefer to protect existing jobs, status and working groups. To individuals, change is often viewed as a threat, as highlighted by the theories of Maslow.

Collective resistance – sometimes there is organizational resistance because the change requires a new type of corporate 'culture'.

For these reasons a well designed change management programme is required if the firm is to make a successful transition.

Change management programme

A change management programme is relatively simple to design but extremely difficult to implement, involving the following stages

→ *Planning* – this stage includes recognizing the need for change, identifying the current position of the firm and devising a suitable method to reach the desired outcome.
→ *Implementation* – this is often the hardest stage. First resistance can be overcome by *involving all personnel affected* by the changes in the decision-making process. This will help build ownership of the changes. Second it is important to keep everyone *informed* about each aspect so that fear of the unknown is not allowed to impair the judgement of the workforce.
→ *Control* – targets must be set so that management and the workforce can measure progress towards the desired outcome.
→ *Evaluation* – the final state is to review the changes and to assess their success against the original objectives.

The *review process* should lead to the examination of new initiatives as firms that stand still risk losing market share in a constantly changing economic environment.

The jargon

Contingency planning means preparing for unwanted or unlikely possibilities such as a prolonged fall in sales or bad publicity. It involves the process of asking and answering 'what if' questions.

Links

See *Maslow*'s views about human psychology and the need for security, social groupings and self-esteem (page 92).

The jargon

Corporate culture is simply the 'accepted way of doing things' within a company.

Examiner's secrets

In a discussion of change it is vital to stress the importance of good communication between management and employees. Are the leaders of the organization imparting a clear vision of what is expected from the change?

Examiner's secrets

There is no simple solution to the problems created by change. Each case will need to be considered on its merits. In general, consider whether the change is *incremental* and therefore can be carefully planned or *radical*, requiring more dramatic action.

Many firms used *business process re-engineering* (BPR) in the recession of the 1980s to reinvent themselves in the face of falling demand. Not all of them were successful. Others used the incremental or '*kaizen*' approach.

Exam questions   answers: page 55

1   What are the key questions that management should ask when considering change? (20 min)

2   Why is change considered to be a continuing process? (20 min)

3   Contrast BPR with kaizen as a means of bringing about change. (30 min)

Government and business

Government attempts to influence the business environment as part of its overall economic strategy. The aim is to create a *stable business sector* where firms can compete on an equal basis and where workers and consumers are not disadvantaged. The government also acts as *provider* in situations where it believes the private sector would be inappropriate as the only source of supply.

Government as entrepreneur

The government, through its departments, nationalized industries and local authorities, is a major user of resources and supplier of goods and services. The privatization of the 1980s and 1990s has removed a lot of direct production from government control but it is still a major provider of employment through the NHS, education, armed forces, police and social services sectors.

The manner in which the government deals with spending levels and wage negotiations in the public sector is a significant influence on the rest of the economy. Many private sector firms also rely on government contracts for the majority of their sales.

Government as planner

The government seeks to provide a suitable *framework* within which business can operate efficiently. To this end the government establishes long-term **plans** for energy, transport, communications, regional aid, overseas trade, training and research and development. An example of this long-term view was making the Bank of England solely responsible for the conduct of monetary policy and the setting of interest rates in 1997. The objective was to make the control of inflation independent of political issues and to assure the business community of the government's intention to establish a long-term inflation target of $2\frac{1}{2}\%$. Arguably, low inflation will help to convince businesses to adopt long-term views for investment, improvement and expansion.

Government as regulator

In order to ensure equity and fairness the government regulates the market place in the following manner

→ *Competition policy* – the *Office of Fair Trading* prevents restrictive practices (which reduces competition between firms) and the *Competition Commission* investigates proposed mergers (to ensure that they do not act against public interest). For newly privatized industries a series of regulatory bodies or 'watchdogs' has been established to oversee pricing and competition in the market.

→ *Health and Safety* – the *Health and Safety at Work Act 1974* ensures that employers provide a safe working environment, adequate safety equipment and appropriate training.

Check the net

Visit the *Department of Trade and Industry* at www.dti.gov.uk

Example

The *nationalized industries* now account for only around 2% of total output. However the broader *public sector* accounts for around 40% of all spending and over 30% of total employment.

Check the net

See how inflation has changed by viewing the Monthly Inflation Report at www.bankofengland.co.uk

Links

See the discussions on *competition policy* on page 16. You can use the net to find out more, e.g. www.oft.gov.uk

Checkpoint 1

Name some of these 'watchdog' bodies.

Action point

Make brief notes on the following consumer laws
- Sale of Goods Acts 1893 and 1979
- Weights and Measures Acts 1963 and 1985
- Trade Descriptions Act 1968
- Food Safety Act 1990
- Consumer Protection Act 1989

- *Consumer law* – various acts protect the consumer from shoddy goods, short measure, false or misleading descriptions and claims, and unhealthy food products.
- *Labour law* – various acts protect the worker from discrimination on grounds of sex, religion, disability, race and unfair dismissal. Since 1999 a national minimum wage has been introduced to prevent excessively low wages.

All of these regulations impose constraints and costs on firms but they do provide workers and consumers with confidence about the market, without which business might be more difficult to conduct.

Government as promoter

The government has taken positive action to *promote* the interests of business and to provide it with new opportunities.

Research and development (R&D) – government encourages R&D by the provision of direct grants, by joint ventures and through financing university research.

Small firms' assistance – the government has helped in three ways

- *improving access to equity and loan capital* – various initiatives exist to help small firms obtain new capital
- *tax allowances and grants* – a reduced corporation tax for small firms, extra allowance for new investment in plant and machinery
- *training and advice* – Training and Enterprise Councils (TECs), Chambers of Commerce, Local Enterprise Agencies (LEAs) and Business Links all provide advice or training

International trade – the government promotes the sale of British goods overseas through its network of embassies and high commissions and subsidizes UK participation in major international trade fairs. The government also promotes trade by providing *export credit guarantees*, i.e. it takes on the risk of default by an overseas purchaser of UK exports.

Employment and training – the *Jobseekers Allowance (1996)* and the *New Deal Initiative (1998)* encourage, respectively, the unemployed to find gainful employment more quickly (via restricting benefit) and firms to provide more jobs (via wage subsidies).

Regional policy – help is provided for areas of high unemployment (*Development Areas*) through discretionary grants awarded under the Regional Selective Assistance (RSA) scheme.

Exam questions answers: page 56

1. How does a lower tax rate assist small firms? (20 min)

2. Identify three reasons why nationalized industries were privatized by government in the 1980s and 1990s. (20 min)

3. What are the costs and benefits to business of the health and safety legislation? (20 min)

Action point

Make brief notes on the following labour laws
Equal Pay Act 1970
Sex Discrimination Act 1975
Race Relations Act 1976
Employment Act 1982
Disability Discrimination Act 1995

Checkpoint 2

Can you be more specific in outlining some of these initiatives?

Example

In 1999 *Business Links* advised over 72 000 businesses. You can visit the national Business Links centre at www.businesslink.org

Example

RSA grants helped to guarantee the production of the X400 Jaguar car at Halewood, safeguarding 2 400 jobs.

Examiner's secrets

There is always some form of market failure that, if left untouched, would disadvantage weaker groups such as workers and customers. The government seeks to remove or prohibit these failures by legislation, education or self-regulation.

Answers
Business objectives and strategies

Nature of business

Checkpoints

1 Productivity has risen dramatically in agriculture (mechanization, etc.) and other parts of the primary sector, so fewer people are needed. Output has been growing less rapidly in this sector than elsewhere (hence declining share of GDP).

2 Many possible responses, e.g. high income elasticity of demand for many services, so as real incomes rise people spend a higher proportion of their income on health, education, leisure, etc.

Exam questions

1 Start by defining 'de-industrialization' as the long-term decline in Britain's secondary or manufacturing sector relative to the other leading industrialized nations.

  Use data to show the extent of the decline, making sure you identify the time period, e.g.

   In the secondary sector employment fell from 11 m to 5 m from 1964 to 2000.
   Output fell from 41% of the UK total to 26% over the same period.
   Having set the scene, identify *causes*, expanding each point to obtain development marks. Causes regularly accepted include

- lack of competitiveness of UK companies
- lack of investment
- unhelpful government policy
- poor education and training
- restrictive trade unions
  Point out that not all secondary industries have declined, e.g. chemicals.
  Close by commenting on the relative importance of the changes. Alternatively set de-industrialization in the context of the globalization of trade where firms are actively transferring manufacturing to lower cost economies.

2 Use the equation

$$\frac{change}{original\ value} \times 100$$

  The percentage changes in output from 1964 to 2000 are
  Primary sector – 33% decline
  Secondary sector – 36% decline
  Tertiary sector – 30% rise
  Briefly refer to the structural change as an opening comment, emphasizing the impact it has had on the demand for labour both in terms of quantity demanded and in terms of quality.

The main changes have been
- increase in service sector jobs, decrease in agricultural and industrial jobs, particularly in manufacturing
- location of manufacturing industry, etc. is regional in nature therefore some areas have suffered more job losses than others
- a significant fall in demand for unskilled labour and semi-skilled labour in the traditional heavy industries
- rise in demand for highly skilled labour particularly in the service sector
- growth in long-term unemployment especially in the older age groups
- modern technology has made many skills redundant therefore need for retraining
- female and part-time labour has risen in service sector
  These changes have produced an economy that requires a labour force that is more flexible, highly skilled and more mobile.

Stakeholders and their objectives

Checkpoints

1 Many possibilities here.
  (a) Body Shop stresses ethical/environmental considerations as well as wholesome, natural products.
  (b) Virgin stresses access to quality services/products at affordable prices, innovative design/presentation, etc.

2 Many possibilities here, e.g. growth might require a low price strategy (penetration pricing), at least initially, to gain market share. This may be unprofitable in the short run but may give the opportunity for higher profits in the longer run.

Exam questions

1 The opening paragraph should briefly explain what pressure groups are and what they attempt to achieve. Provide a couple of examples such as the Consumers' Association and Friends of the Earth. The reaction of a firm to consumer pressure groups will depend on
- the purchasing power of the pressure group
- the media coverage of their views
- the reaction of competitors
- the relative costs and benefits of adopting the demanded changes
- the views of shareholders
- current public opinion

- resources of the firm
- the attitude of management

Where there is keen competition, wide media coverage and general public support, the demands of pressure groups are likely to be more effective. For example, Shell had to reverse its decision to sink the Brent Spar oilrig at sea because of adverse publicity and the significant drop in its sales of petrol in the UK.

2 Arguments for
- the shareholders have provided the risk capital and as such they fully deserve the best return on their investment
- the managers' task is to maximize shareholder value otherwise the long-term future of the business might be jeopardized, thus risking the interests of all stakeholders

Arguments against
- social responsibility might attract more customers, e.g. the Body Shop, i.e. it can be used as a positive marketing tool
- social responsibility can lead to cost savings, e.g. reduced waste through recycling or increased awareness of waste among the workforce

3 The stakeholder concept can be applied to all types of organization, including your own school or college. This question calls for you to identify the various interested groups and then to state their particular viewpoints.

For example, a hospital will have the following stakeholders
- patients – interested in the quality of service
- relatives – concerned about the safety and comfort of the patient as well as access and services available during visiting hours
- administrators – the efficient use of the hospital's scarce resources
- government – the efficient use of resources and the reduction of waiting lists
- employees – security of employment, working conditions, remuneration and future prospects
- local community – the future of the hospital and the standard of services offered as well as employment opportunities
- suppliers – the level of demand for goods and services

A similar list can be created for charities or any other non-profit organization.

Size of business

Checkpoint

Certainly the banking industry has been marked by conglomerate integration as well as horizontal integration, e.g. banks now offer insurance, mortgages and many other forms of personal finance services. Of course banks have also merged horizontally (e.g. Hong Kong and Shanghai Bank merging with Midland Bank to form HSBC). The airline industry has been far more focused on horizontal integration, with small airlines going bankrupt or being taken over by large airlines.

Exam questions

1 Virtually all businesses start small. The majority of firms remain small but some grow and prosper while others fail. Examples of small firms expanding to become internationally known businesses in recent times include Microsoft, the Body Shop, Apple computers, IKEA and the Virgin group.

Small firms benefit an economy because
- they are an important source of new jobs: not only do they provide employment for the owner, they also account for 30% of all employees
- they are the traditional breeding ground for new industries, e.g. the rapid growth in e-commerce
- they are quick to identify new market opportunities
- they serve 'niche' markets, too small for large firms to service profitably
- they are willing to invest time and money in speculative opportunities
- they often provide services that larger firms require at a more economic rate (outsourcing)
- they provide an opportunity for new entrepreneurs and new ideas
- they have a 'competitive advantage' in many personal services

Small firms are the seed bed from which larger firms emerge as well as being the testing ground for new products, processes and ideas.

2 It is always assumed that the main reason for mergers is to take advantage of economies of scale and thus improve efficiency. In fact most mergers occur for reasons other than economies of scale. In some cases a merger might not lead to efficiency improvements for the following reasons
   • rationalization has left the workforce in a demoralized state
   • key employees have left rather than stay with the larger concern
   • the two firms have different management cultures that lead to conflict
   • management have concentrated on the problems of the merger and have neglected the core business
   • personality clashes at both the operational and managerial level as rival groups of employees seek to secure their future
   • incompatibility of production systems
   The situation is made more difficult if the merger involves vertical integration as the two firms have little experience of each other's business.

3 The opening statement should highlight that growth can be achieved in a variety of ways and at various speeds. The choice of method will depend on the rate and direction of growth required by the firm.
   Comparisons might include
   • direction of growth (vertical or horizontal)
   • speed and extent of growth
   • risk reduction and growth
   • reasons for growth, e.g. diversification, market share, etc.
   Contrasts might include
   • direction of growth – vertical tends to be external, horizontal could be either
   • speed and extent of growth – external growth tends to be more rapid and extensive
   • financing of growth – external growth is often funded by outside agencies
   • risk involved – external growth often involves borrowing
   • the involvement of outside parties, e.g. financiers, venture capitalists, etc.
   • loss of some management control with external growth

The method, direction, speed and extent of growth should relate closely to the firm's overall strategic objectives.

Business organizations

Exam questions

1 Both organizations are examples of limited liability companies in that the shareholders are only risking the amount invested in the business. There are, however, some significant differences.
   • The shares of a private limited company cannot be purchased on the Stock Exchange. They can only be sold privately and with the consent of the other shareholders.
   • The maximum value of shares is restricted to £50 000 whereas a plc has no restriction placed upon it.
   • Plcs must publish far more detailed accounts than private limited companies.

2 Limited liability means that the owners are only financially responsible for the amount that they have invested in the business. Their personal wealth is protected from creditors in the event that the business becomes insolvent.
   Limited liability is important because it encourages entrepreneurs to accept the risk of investing in a business. The extent of any loss is known in advance. This results in a larger pool of finance being available to industry.

3 A franchise is different from other forms of business because
   • the franchisee is buying only the use of the franchiser's name, logo and trading methods

- the franchisee is limited to a defined geographical area
- the design of the premises is strictly laid down
- all supplies must be purchased from the franchiser
- an annual fee must be paid to the franchiser based upon the annual turnover
- the franchisee is never the complete owner of the business

It is extremely popular, especially with those who have limited business skills but who desire to run their own operation.

Business objectives

Checkpoints

1 The owners (shareholders) of medium/large plcs may not be in control. The shareholding may be spread across many investors, giving management some freedom to control the business in the ways they see fit. This may be to pursue objectives such as corporate growth, which may not necessarily mean the highest profits for shareholders, at least in the short term.

2 Privatization is difficult to define, but basically means the transfer of assets or economic activity from the public sector to the private sector. Arguments for include supply-side benefits (greater efficiency), wider share ownership, reductions in PSBR (Public Sector Borrowing Requirement), greater managerial freedom, etc. Arguments against include public interest, 'natural monopoly', taking better account of externalities, etc. (See also answer to Question 2, page 56)

Exam questions

1 There are three occasions when firms might consider survival as the overriding objective.
   In the early stages of trading – this is because
   - the firm will have initial fixed costs to pay
   - there is no recognized customer base
   - management lacks experience
   - there are limited cash reserves
   - there is competition from established businesses
   - the firm might have to offer low prices in order to attract customers

   In difficult trading periods – during recessionary periods general demand falls, causing price competition as firms struggle to maintain sales levels. The profit margins are squeezed and unit costs might rise as output falls and economies of scale are lost.

   When faced with the threat of a take-over – if the management view the take-over as hostile they will recommend that the shareholders resist the take-over and keep the firm in its present form.

2 Advantages of pursuing growth include
   - obtaining economies of scale, especially in the purchase of raw materials and capacity utilization
   - improved competitiveness through lower costs and lower prices
   - diversification of the product base
   - market diversification reduces risk by selling to customer groups in different areas
   - increase in profit potential as sales rise
   - lower financial charges from banks and other lenders who recognize that large firms are less of a risk
   Disadvantages of pursuing growth include
   - greater capital investment therefore higher risks
   - management burden increases
   - increase in gearing if financed by borrowing
   - competitors might perceive a growing company as more of a threat and adopt a more aggressive trading policy
   - original owners might lose some control as the management and shareholder base expands

3 Advantages of the public sector adopting more commercial objectives include
   - reduction in wasted resources
   - increased provision of services to the general public via higher productivity
   - lower burden on government finances
   - self-financing of future investment
   - increase in productivity
   - more sensitive to customer views and opinions
   The disadvantages include
   - increased bureaucracy
   - reduction in 'free' services
   - closure of 'unprofitable' units, e.g. expensive libraries, rural bus services, etc.
   - reduction in labour and increased use of computers produces a more depersonalized service
   - rationalization increases unemployment

Strategic analysis

Checkpoint

Many possibilities here. Ageing population. More leisure facilities and opportunities (holidays) provided geared to the interests/preferences of older people. Single-parent families. More crèche and other facilities provided to meet the needs of this growing segment.

Exam question

(a) Most organizations are concerned about the efficiency with which they carry out operations. The measures used may vary but the most important ones are cost, quality, speed, dependability and flexibility. Each of these can be broken down further, thus quality may be measured by

- number of defects per unit
- level of customer complaints
- scrap levels
- warranty claims

Traditionally performance standards were set by using historical standards, target performance standards or absolute performance standards.

Another approach though was developed by the Xerox corporation in 1979. This it called *benchmarking*. It was described as 'a process used by the manufacturing function to revitalize itself by comparing the features, assemblies and components of its products with those of competitors'.

Since then benchmarking has been developed so that

- it covers all functional areas of a business
- it is widely used in service organizations
- staff as well as experts may be involved in the benchmarking process
- comparison is made with both competing and non-competing firms.

The key to benchmarking is to identify the most important needs and preferences of customers (the order winning factors!). The firm then sets out to provide these requirements through benchmarking those organizations whose operations in these areas are superior. Thus British Rail reduced the time to clean its trains to eight minutes after studying British Airways' methods. Rover reduced the time it took to test products by 50% after benchmarking Honda. Similarly Rank Xerox benchmarked itself against the RAC and British Gas when trying to improve the way it answered telephone calls.

(b) As part of its strategic analysis a firm will conduct a SWOT analysis. SWOT stands for strengths and weaknesses (the internal environment of the firm) and opportunities and threats (the firm's external environment). The analysis of the external environment is meant to identify opportunities for the firm to exploit and threats to avoid or counter. The internal analysis is meant to identify the firm's strengths and weaknesses. Benchmarking, for example, enables the firm to undertake this process in an objective manner.

Strategic planning

Exam questions

1 A strategic or planning gap is the difference between the predicted performance of the organization and what is desired. Where a strategic gap is expressed in terms of a financial objective, all functions are able to contribute to its reduction. It is unlikely that any one function will be able to identify ways to eliminate the gap but together their 'plans' may achieve the target. For example, all functions may seek *cost savings*.

- Thus the *personnel function* may look at ways of reducing employee turnover through training or the *finance function* may identify ways of reducing the cost of borrowing.
- The *production function* may consider different methods of stock control or introduce a JIT system. The production function could also consider changes in processes or quality systems.
- The *marketing function* will have a major role to play through analyzing ways to sell existing products more effectively (the 4 Ps!). They might also consider the closure of marginal product lines, the introduction of new products or the opportunities of diversifying into new products and markets.

2 This is a question which requires you to consider the importance of planning in the context of other management functions.

Your introduction should identify the various management functions – planning, organization, direction and control – giving a brief explanation of each.

The main body of your answer should explain the importance of each of these functions in contributing to the achievement of organizational objectives. In this sense all functions are equally important and contribute to the achievement of objectives. A failure in any area will lead to the failure of the desired objective. However you should draw the attention of the examiner to the primacy of *planning* in that if planning is wrong then the firm's objectives will never be achieved, however effective are the other functions involving organization, direction and control.

Management of change

Checkpoints

1 BSE is an example of unforeseen change. Sudden loss of markets, especially export, meant fall in demand for beef and dairy products. This in turn led to a fall in prices, the need to cull cattle (both to reduce supply and to eradicate BSE), switches of production away from beef and dairy cattle to other activities (e.g. arable farming, etc.).

2 Many possibilities here. EU Social Chapter adoption by UK of EU directives such as 'Working Time Directives' means that the working week must be reduced for many employees (e.g. 48 hours per week now the maximum).

Exam questions

1 The three questions that should be asked when considering change are
- *Where are we now?* This requires management to assess realistically and objectively the firm's current market, its position within it and the strengths and weaknesses of the organization. Using management models such as SWOT or PEST analysis is a good starting point, especially if this is done on a wide basis throughout the business.
- *Where do we want to be?* This is a strategic question with a long timescale. Brainstorming techniques can be used to 'imagine the impossible' so that all alternatives are considered and not just those that are safe and obvious. Contingency planning and scenario analysis may play a part here.
- *How do we get there?* This is often the hardest part as it involves implementing the change needed. The business needs to do a resource audit so that it knows what resources it has and to match these against the needs of the envisaged future position. Shortfalls have to be remedied by training, investment, new work practices and recruitment. The implementation will be easier if the workforce has had some input into the decision-making process so that they have some 'ownership' of the planned developments.

At all stages the business must monitor and review the changes and where necessary adapt.

2 The business environment is constantly changing as new technologies are developed, new competitors arrive on the scene and consumer tastes develop. Any business that stands still will soon find its sales being affected by new products or new suppliers. In recognition of this, firms must strive constantly to develop their products, their production techniques and the ways they sell and market their output. Change, therefore, is not a one-off occurrence but a mind-set that must be adopted as a way of doing business. The Japanese have encapsulated this with their kaizen approach, which seeks for infinitesimal improvements. The sum total of many small improvements can have a radical impact on the competitiveness of a business.

3 Business process re-engineering is a radical approach to changing a business. It attempts a complete reinvention of how work is carried out, involving everything from the type of machinery used to factory layout and employee requirement. It involves massive change in a short period of time. Kaizen, however, involves continuous improvement in small steps rather than one-off improvements. It is carried out on a daily basis with the full co-operation of the workforce. Many of these improvements, unlike the expensive overhauls associated with BPR, are relatively cheap to implement, as they are often simple shop floor practices.

The major differences, therefore, involve the time span, the cost and the impact on the workforce.

Government and business

Checkpoints

1 OFTEL, OFWAT, OFGAS, OFFER, etc. See the net linkage on page 48.

2 Many possibilities here.

Loan Guarantee Scheme Government guarantees 70% of each loan to companies trading for less than two years, and 85% to companies trading for over two years.

Lower corporation tax for small firms (e.g. 20% instead of 30%).

Enterprise Investment Scheme Offers income tax relief to those investing up to £150 000 a year in small, unquoted companies.

Enterprise Initiative Grants provided for firms employing less than 25 people in the Development Areas.

Exam questions

1 A lower tax rate will help small businesses by
* increasing the amount of profit available to the firm for future investment ('ploughed back profits')
* acting as an incentive for entrepreneurs to start their own businesses
* attracting outside investment
* improving cash flow by reducing the outflow to government

Examiner's secrets

These points apply only to businesses that are or are expected to be profitable. Don't assume that all businesses are profit makers.

2 Nationalized industries were privatized in order to
* make them more efficient and productive
* make them more market-orientated
* raise much needed capital for investment from the private sector
* reduce the drain on public sector finances and to release funds for other spending priorities
* reduce the monopoly power of the industries
* allow the private sector to remedy the politically sensitive over-manning and low productivity problems

Examiner's secrets

Be ready to argue the case 'for and against' privatization.

3 As an introduction briefly outline the health and safety legislation referred to in the question without going into too much detail.

The body of the answer should reflect the relative costs and benefits, which should include the following

Costs
* the provision of safety equipment
* the safe design of business premises
* the provision of adequate training
* the regular maintenance of all machinery and equipment
* payment for regular inspections and certification of equipment

Benefits
* a safe working environment within which employees feel comfortable
* reduced labour days lost to accidents
* avoidance of litigation for negligence
* lower insurance costs
* a better public image as a caring employer
* lower labour turnover

Examiner's secrets

Health and safety is a two-edged sword. It has benefits as well as costs. Few candidates consider both sides of the argument and therefore fail to gain evaluation marks.

Success in business today is very much dependent on an organization's marketing activities. In today's crowded market place an organization has to understand its customers' requirements and satisfy them in a way that gives the organization a *competitive edge* over other firms in the same market. The firm has to offer the right mix of product, price, promotion and place to its customers. The marketer works in a rapidly changing environment; customers are not loyal, they modify their needs and wants constantly, competitors alter their strategies and the whole of the external environment is subject to change.

Exam themes

→ Production, sales and marketing orientations.

→ The relationship between marketing and other functional departments.

→ The importance of marketing research.

→ The use of sampling and sales forecasting, together with the problems associated with each technique.

→ The link between corporate and marketing objectives.

→ The product life cycle, extension strategies and portfolio analysis.

→ Market segmentation, the benefits and limitations of niche marketing.

→ The importance of mass or global marketing.

→ The elements of the marketing mix and the importance of blending them.

→ The evaluation of plans for product development, pricing, promotion or distribution.

→ The uses and limitations of the concept of elasticity of demand.

Topic checklist

O AS ● A2	AQA	EDEXCEL	OCR	WJEC
Marketing objectives	O●	O●	O●	O●
Defining the market	O	O	O	O●
Global marketing and segmentation	O	O●	O●	O●
Market research	O	O●	O●	O●
Sampling and sales forecasting	O●	O●	O●	O●
Product	O	O	O●	O
Price	O	O	O●	O
Promotion	O	O	O●	O
Place (distribution)	O	O	O●	O
Marketing strategy	O	●	O●	O●

Marketing objectives

Many factors help to determine the marketing objectives of a firm. Two important influences are the external environment in which the firm is operating and the situation within the company.

Market orientation

Businesses used to operate on the basis of 'selling what they made'. The decision-making process started with the product and it was the marketing department's job to persuade customers to buy this product. Such a firm is said to have a **product orientation**. Firms are more likely to be product orientated where

→ there is high emphasis on technical quality or safety
→ those in charge have a technical background
→ there is little competition

As the customer has become more discerning this approach has arguably failed. Today companies are faced increasingly with the situation that they must 'make what they can sell'. Such a firm is said to have a **market orientation**. Firms are more likely to be market orientated where they

→ undertake market research continuously
→ develop products that the market wants and in the right quantities
→ price the products at an acceptable level
→ promote the products effectively to the target market
→ distribute the products in ways that meets consumer needs

Marketing objectives

You will find that **marketing objectives** are decided at the very highest level in the organization. They state where the company expects to be at a specific time in the future. The most important marketing objectives include the following.

To maintain or increase market share
This implies that the firm's sales will be a constant or rising *proportion* of the industry total. Being the leader or a large player in a market gives the firm a degree of *market power*. It might then be able to dictate pricing policy to smaller firms or to influence the price and quality of items provided by suppliers. Equally, it may be able to make cost savings as a result of growing in size.

To improve profitability
Improved profitability ensures shareholder satisfaction and helps to provide the funds for supporting new product development or entering new market segments.

To enhance product image
This is often identified as a way to protect sales and increase profit margins by strengthening consumer allegiance to the product. For

Example

The Concorde aircraft project is often used as an example of *product orientation*.

Don't forget

The consumer is central to everything the firm does under *market orientation*.

Watch out!

Marketing objectives should be precise, measurable and achievable.

Checkpoint 1

Can you provide examples of firms using market power in this way?

Example

Various studies suggest that *branded products* can charge prices around 10% higher than unbranded products.

example, consumers may be willing to pay a higher price for a product with a positive image.

To target a new market

Once a firm has achieved a high market share it is often difficult and extremely costly to increase that share. Moreover, being in a too dominant position in one market may result in the unwelcome interest of the competition authorities. In these circumstances it is logical to identify other market opportunities for the product.

Constraints on achieving marketing objectives

The environment

Environmental factors can be broadly defined to include **p**olitical, **e**conomic, **s**ocial or **t**echnological (**PEST**) factors and may act as a *constraint* on the achievement of marketing objectives. For example, the desired level of sales or profitability may not be achieved when the level of economic activity is less than predicted. Equally, the introduction of a new product may not be successful as a result of consumer resistance. Finally, there is considerable legislation that protects the consumer and prevents the unscrupulous firm from making extravagant or false claims about its products and prices.

The internal organization

Marketing objectives may not be achieved because of difficulties *within* the firm. For example, sales levels may not be achieved as a result of problems with the production line or the supply of raw materials. Equally, problems in raising the necessary finance or finding the right R&D staff may prevent a new product being launched on time.

The marketing budget

Task based costing is the most effective method of determining the marketing budget. This is because it identifies the *marketing activities* necessary to achieve *marketing objectives*. These activities, when costed out, become the basis for the marketing budget. In practice many other, less accurate, methods may be used and in many cases the marketing department will be left with an inadequate budget.

Watch out!

Make sure you are able to distinguish between a marketing objective and a marketing strategy.

Examiner's secrets

PEST analysis is a useful way for a firm to try to identify the environmental factors.

Action point

Look for company results in any newspaper's business section. Environmental factors are often blamed for a firm's failure to achieve its objectives!

Example

In 1999 Marks and Spencer blamed internal wrangling as one reason for not achieving the predicted levels of turnover and profits.

Checkpoint 2

Suggest some other ways of setting such a budget.

Exam questions   answers: page 78

1   Enhancing corporate image is often seen as a marketing objective. What benefits does a firm gain from trying to improve its corporate image? (20 min)

2   (a) Explain the term marketing budget. (5 min)
      (b) Assess the benefits and problems which may arise from the use of marketing budgets within a firm. (15 min)

3   List five points that might affect the size of the marketing budget. (5 min)

Examiner's secrets

Candidates regurgitating large chunks of data in response to stimulus material fail to gain many marks. For high marks you are required to analyze and interpret the data.

Defining the market

We have noted the importance of the successful firm being market-orientated (page 58). In practice this means that through market research the firm has made considerable efforts to understand and define the nature of the market it is in.

The market

Defining the market

Most organizations would accept that they have **core competencies** in a specific market area and in normal circumstances would only want to diversify into *related* market areas. However, defining the market is more difficult than is often realized. Let us take a firm that brews beer and runs pubs. Such a firm could define its market as being the hospitality industry or the leisure industry. In each case the related activities the firm might want to enter into are different.

Market size and trend

Market size is obtained by adding together the sales of all firms in the market. It can be measured in *money terms* or *volume terms* (the number of units sold). Market size is important because it allows individual firms to calculate their own market share and also acts as a base for determining trends.

There is very little that a firm can do to influence market trends. However by understanding the *causes* of the trends, the firm may be able to make better marketing decisions.

→ *Position in business cycle*, e.g. from past experience firms know that when the economy is in recession the demand for 'meals out' will fall and consumers will demand cheaper holidays.

→ *Social changes*, e.g. the growth in the number of 'single' family units has resulted in above average growth for one bedroom homes and apartments and 'singles' holidays.

→ *Changes in taste*, e.g. when designer jeans were in fashion people not only bought more (volume) but were prepared to pay more (value).

Market share

For many firms **market share** is the most important marketing objective. It measures the success of a firm's marketing strategy against that of its competitors.

Where a firm is a *market leader*, its competitive advantage is likely to be one of

→ product superiority   → low production costs
→ branding   → patents
→ aggressive marketing   → better knowledge of market

This competitive advantage will be used by the market leader as part of its strategy to defend or improve its market position.

Check the net

Sources of information on the market include
www.keynote.co.uk
www.euromonitor.com

Checkpoint 1

How have football clubs defined their market and what related activities would this allow them to enter into?

The jargon

Moving into related market areas is often described as *lateral integration*.

Don't forget

Divide sales value by sales units and you have the *average price per unit*.

Checkpoint 2

Can you think how this relates to *income elasticity of demand*?

Examiner's secrets

An understanding of these social changes and changes in taste may enable a firm to *anticipate* market trends by developing new products and services.

The jargon

A *brand manager* is responsible for the success of the product.

Challengers to the market leader will try to gain competitive advantage over that firm through strategies such as

→ product innovation   → quality improvements
→ price discounts   → aggressive promotion
→ new production or distribution techniques

Consumer buying behaviour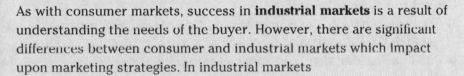

The decisions and actions of consumers in purchasing and using products is termed **buyer behaviour**. It is important for firms to analyze consumer buying behaviour in order to discover the main influences underlying what, why, where, when and how consumers buy. This is sometimes not as easy as you might imagine. For example, why do people buy toothpaste? There are three obvious possibilities: to make their breath fresh, to clean their teeth or to give whiter teeth. A marketing-orientated firm will want to know this information so that it can provide for customer needs more effectively. It also helps in the formulation of successful marketing strategies. The information not only ensures more satisfied customers but enables firms to compete more effectively in the market place.

Industrial markets

As with consumer markets, success in **industrial markets** is a result of understanding the needs of the buyer. However, there are significant differences between consumer and industrial markets which impact upon marketing strategies. In industrial markets

→ many products are 'custom-built'
→ the buyer is better informed about the product
→ the buyer usually acts more rationally, basing the purchase decision on quality, service, delivery and price
→ many products are sold direct rather than through intermediaries
→ the decision to buy is often taken by persons other than those seen by the sales force
→ the number of potential customers is much smaller
→ the average order is much larger

> **Checkpoint 3**
>
> A housewife buys a ready-to-cook meal for her family. What motives might she have for this purchase, and how could a marketer use that information?

> **The jargon**
>
> An *industrial market* exists where a business sells to another business.

> **Watch out!**
>
> *Sole sourcing* is becoming more popular, i.e. where a firm purchases all its requirements from one supplier.

Exam questions   answers: pages 78–9

1   Noreen Hussain has just completed a Higher National Diploma in Catering. She has returned to her home town and believes there is a gap in the market for an 'Indian takeaway'. What information could market research provide which would help her come to a decision about whether or not to start this new business? (20 min)

2   Construct a market map (based on price and quality) for national supermarket groups.
    (a) Explain what it shows.
    (b) Explain how it might be used. (30 min)

> **Examiner's secrets**
>
> Candidates are frequently criticized for failing to 'contextualize their answers'. Make sure the market research referred to is applied to the catering industry and, more especially, to an 'Indian takeaway'.

Global marketing and segmentation

Check the net

Interesting material on global marketing and segmentation strategies can be obtained from www.marketing.week.co.uk

Action point

List some more global brands in the following areas: electrical equipment, soft drinks, rock music and cosmetics.

Example

In terms of *economies of scale*, in a period of 20 years Coca-Cola saved $90 million on the production costs of commercials through global marketing.

Links

For more on *product life cycles*, see page 68. For more on *payback period* see page 164.

Checkpoint 1

List three ways in which trade could be restricted by government.

There are two very distinct trends in marketing today. The first is to identify and produce those products which have a universal appeal throughout the world. At the other extreme there is the attempt to divide the market into smaller segments with different characteristics and needs.

Global marketing

The basis of **global marketing** is to identify products or services for which similarities across several markets enable a single, global marketing strategy to be pursued. Examples today include

- → Coca-Cola
- → McDonalds
- → Heinz
- → Marlboro
- → Kellogg's

All the examples given are of *consumer* products but the potential for globalization in *industrial* markets is also great. In particular where there is little or no need to adapt a product to meet local needs, global opportunities exist. Thus, a global market exists in areas such as

- → telecommunications
- → construction machinery
- → computers
- → bio-engineering
- → pharmaceuticals

Global marketing benefits

- → *It increases the size of the market* and, if successful, will improve profitability dramatically.
- → *Domestic markets* may have reached saturation point.
- → *Economies of scale* in production and advertising can be made.
- → *Product life cycles* are shorter. Global marketing can help compensate for this by reducing the payback period.

Global marketing problems

Marketers have found that whilst it has been possible to standardize brand name, product characteristics, packaging and labelling, *economic*, *cultural* and *social differences* make it difficult to standardize promotion, distribution outlets and price. For example, McDonalds adopts different prices in different countries, reflecting consumers' different buying power and different sensitivities to changes in price. It also has had to adapt its product offerings to take account of local tastes and culture (e.g. beef is not eaten in some cultures).

Marketing on a global scale may also be prevented by the actions of *governments*. Thus in an attempt to protect local firms or to prevent the outflow of capital, governments may *restrict* free trade. High levels of inflation and fluctuating exchange rates may also make it difficult to price goods profitably in foreign markets.

Market segmentation ●●●

Producers tend to define markets broadly, but *within* these markets are groups of people who have more specific requirements. **Market segmentation** is the process by which a total market is broken down into separate groups of customers having identifiably different product needs. Segmentation allows the marketer to differentiate between groups and produce a marketing strategy appropriate to these individual segments. The most popular ways to segment markets include

Characteristic	Example
age	clothing
sex	cosmetics
income	home ownership
ethnicity	music

You should be aware that there are many different methods of segmenting a market. One widely used technique is to classify people according to the *occupation* of the head of the household. This is because there is evidence that this has a major influence on a family's buying behaviour. Market research suggests that this buying behaviour will change as individuals move from one class to another.

The concept of the family life cycle is another attempt to predict consumption and spending patterns. These are the stages

1. bachelor – young, single, away from home
2. newly married – typically young, no children
3. full nest 1 – at least one child under 6
4. full nest 2 – youngest child 6+
5. full nest 3 – older couples, older children
6. empty nest 1 – older couples, children left home
7. empty nest 2 – retired couples, children left home
8. solitary survivor 1 – working
9. solitary survivor 2 – retired

By defining the market in this way we can target the groups which are most relevant to the firm.

Segmentation has allowed the growth of small specialist or 'niche' markets. As people have become more affluent they have been prepared to pay the higher price for a product that meets their precise requirements. The growth of niche markets has also been important in supporting the existence of *small firms*. In many cases the large firm has found many of these segments to be too small to service profitably.

Exam questions   answers: pages 79–80

1   Distinguish between the following forms of marketing (20 min)

   (a) undifferentiated marketing   (b) niche or concentrated marketing

   (c) differentiated marketing   (d) custom based marketing

2   In what circumstances will a market niche be attractive to a small firm? (20 min)

Checkpoint 2

Give *two examples* of the ways in which these characteristics can be used to identify a market segment.

Examiner's secrets

Many candidates frequently confuse segment with 'geographical area'.

Links

See page 13.

Checkpoint 3

Explain the terms: benefit segmentation, behaviour segmentation, geo-demographic segmentation, lifestyle segmentation.

Links

For more on *small firms* see page 36.

Examiner's secrets

Candidates who are able to give examples to illustrate their explanations of terms will gain high marks.

Market research

Market research is the collection, collation and analysis of data relating to the purchasing habits, lifestyle, consumption and attitudes of current and potential customers.

The need for market research

Markets are constantly changing. As a result there is a regular need for market information for the following reasons

→ *sales prediction* – data is needed about future buying patterns in order to determine output levels and to design new products and services
→ *market analysis* – to determine the extent of the market, who the actual customers are, who the potential customers are and what factors influence consumer buying habits
→ *new opportunities* – exploring the market either to test newly designed products or to identify new wants and desires among the customers

Market research aims to reduce the uncertainty about the launch of new products or the development of existing ones.

Primary research

This is the process of gathering *original* data directly from the target market. This data does not already exist and as such should provide, if correctly designed and collected, a new insight into the market. This alone could provide the business with a marketing advantage over its competitors. Various methods can be used to collect primary data.

→ *Personal interviews* – face-to-face interviews using either *structured questions* in a predetermined order or *open questions* to obtain detailed responses. Expensive and time consuming.
→ *Telephone interviews* – cheap to conduct and easy to cover a wide geographical area. May be biased towards higher income groups who own a phone.
→ *Postal surveys* – cheap to conduct but suffer from poor response rates (often well below 10%).
→ *Direct observation* – looking at how customers behave in shops or how they react to certain displays.
→ *Test marketing* – selling a product in a restricted area and assessing market reaction before launching on a wider geographical basis.

Secondary research

This involves the unearthing of data that *already* exists. It is available from either within the business or from outside agencies.

Internal

→ sales figures
→ previous market reports and analysis
→ stock movements
→ sales representatives' reports from customers

External

→ *Government publications* – such as *Social Trends*, *Economic Trends*, *Census of Population* and *Annual Abstract of Statistics*, published by the Office of National Statistics.

→ *Trade associations* – information/data from organizations set up to represent the interests of, and to lobby on behalf of, all companies within an industry.

→ *Trade journals/magazines* – produced for all the major trades, e.g. *The Grocer*.

→ *Commercial data specialists* – organizations that collect and publish data on a fee basis, e.g. Dun and Bradstreet, Mintel, the Economist Intelligence Unit.

Questionnaires

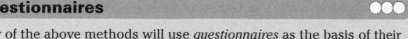

Many of the above methods will use *questionnaires* as the basis of their information gathering. These must be carefully designed and tested in order to eliminate bias and ambiguity. They can consist of

→ *closed questions* – which allow only a limited response, often from a predetermined list of alternatives

→ *open questions* – which allow a more detailed response and therefore investigation of the interviewees' attitudes

For the questionnaire to be effective it must

→ have clear, unambiguous questions
→ not rely on calculations or on the subject's memory
→ be easy to understand and avoid jargon
→ not contain leading questions that suggest a particular answer or opinion
→ be reasonably short
→ be easy to complete and tabulate

Of course the process must be conducted in a polite manner.

Problems of market research

In order to obtain a full picture of the market it would be necessary to ask all of the customers (known as the *population*). As this is extremely expensive only a small number are asked (a *sample*). This introduces a measure of uncertainty into the validity of the findings. This is further compounded by the unpredictability of human nature.

Check the net

A useful starting point is www.globalweb.co.uk or try The Market Research Society at www.marketresearch.org.uk

Don't forget

The reasons for market research can be remembered as DEEP.
Describe the market
Explain consumer behaviour
Explore reactions to new products
Predict future changes

Links

For more on sampling, see page 66.

Test yourself

Use the information on these pages to draw up a table with five benefits and five drawbacks of market research. Write a paragraph balancing the argument for increased spending on market research. Doing this will demonstrate the skill of evaluation.

Exam questions

answers: page 80

1 What are the advantages and disadvantages of field and desk research? (20 min)

2 Outline three ways in which market research data might be inaccurate. (20 min)

3 Distinguish between qualitative and quantitative research. (10 min)

Examiner's secrets

Always compare the *costs* of gathering more data with the *benefits* from using it. The extra expense might not lead to any further insights than those obtained from a small sample.

Sampling and sales forecasting

Market research can involve data which is either *qualitative* or *quantitative*. As it is extremely expensive to ask the entire population of a market, only a sample is chosen. This sample data can then be used to forecast likely demand.

Qualitative research

This is research into the *motivations* that lie behind consumer attitudes and behaviour. Psychologists may conduct these sessions in a relaxed environment and often without pre-set questions. The objective is to explore the *emotion* behind purchases rather than the logic behind them. This type of analysis often discovers unexpected influences that can be used to gain a competitive advantage. The main forms of this type of research are *group discussions* or *in-depth interviews*.

Quantitative research

This type of research relies on asking a small sample of the target market. The main problem is to identify the best sampling method and the appropriate sample size.

Sampling method

One of the following types will usually be selected

→ *Random sampling* – selecting respondents to ensure that everyone in the population has an equal chance of being chosen. This is difficult to do in practice. To avoid any bias, names are often chosen from the *electoral register* and interviewees are contacted at home. This is obviously an expensive method.

→ *Quota sampling* – to overcome the expense of random sampling, businesses often resort to selecting respondents *in proportion to* the consumer profile within the target market.

→ *Cluster sampling* – respondents are drawn from a small *geographical area* chosen to represent a particular aspect of the target market. Often used for sampling political opinion.

→ *Stratified sampling* – involves interviewing only those respondents with a *particular characteristic*, for example those within a certain age range, such as teenagers. Within this stratum individuals are usually selected randomly or by quota.

Sampling size

One of the major problems in sampling is to determine the number of respondents to ask. Asking only a few (five or ten) might result in a biased opinion, as there is the possibility of chance variations. The researcher would not have any 'confidence' that the sample represented the views of the population. Many surveys ask approximately 100 people, a sample size which gives the researcher enough confidence in clear-cut results such as 60/40% splits. Only with larger samples can the results be statistically significant for marginal differences of opinion. The problem with larger samples, e.g. 1 000 people, is one of cost.

Sales forecasting ●●●

Businesses are very keen to know about what might happen in the *future*. A number of techniques exist to help estimate future events, such as likely sales levels, but these must be treated with great care.

Qualitative techniques

The **Delphi technique** is a form of subjective long-range method that relies on a panel of experts achieving a consensus of opinion. It is generally used where no historical data is available.

Quantitative techniques

→ **Extrapolation** – simply plotting known data such as sales figures on a graph and extending a line through the points into the future. This method assumes that the past is a good guide to the future, which is not always the case.

→ **Time series analysis** – a more scientific method is to use *moving averages* to compute the **trend**, which is the underlying movement in the data. This can be plotted on a graph and a *line of best fit* extrapolated into the future. Unfortunately the trend data is distorted over a year by **seasonal variations**. These can also be calculated by finding the average difference between the trend data and the actual data for each of the given periods.

→ **Index numbers** – these provide a convenient way of showing change in a set of data over a period of time. A typical year is chosen as the *base year* and the data for that year is given a value of 100. All the rest of the data is altered relative to this value (see example below). The sales value £250 m for 1998 has been given the index number 100 and the remaining sales data altered accordingly. It is now easier to see that sales have increased by 20% from 1998 to 1999 and 60% from 1998 to 2000. The average annual increase is 30% on the base period value. This annual increase could be used to predict the sales value for 2001 as being approximately £475 m.

Year	Sales £m	Index No
1998	250	100
1999	300	120
2000	400	160

Exam questions   answers: page 81

1 Why might a business want to predict the future? (15 min)

2 Explain how you would choose the number of periods in a moving average in order to identify the underlying trend. (15 min)

3 Identify three possible sources of bias in primary market research. (15 min)

Example

The Delphi technique was used by electronics companies to predict the demand for luxury consumer goods in the newly emerging markets of Eastern Europe.

Watch out!

Over a number of years there may be also a 'cycle' of highs and lows which is often caused by the cyclical effect of changes in general economic activity associated with booms and slumps.

Examiner's secrets

The *seasonal* variation can be used to adjust any future estimate for the likely seasonal effect, giving a more realistic forecast for the period concerned.

Examiner's secrets

Moving averages are a popular exam question. Data given in an even number of periods (four-quarterly or twelve-monthly) needs to be 'centred'. Revise this aspect carefully!

Be extremely sceptical about any prediction that is more than six months into the future as the economy is dynamic and subject to rapid change.

Product

The term is used to cover not only goods but also services. Indeed, even pop stars can be 'products' in that we can buy their CDs and go to their shows. Here we look at how the marketer plans the portfolio of products to ensure the continued success of the firm.

Product life cycle

This is an extremely important concept which suggests that all products brought to the market follow a **life cycle**, with four stages.

→ *Introduction*   This is the stage when the product is relatively unknown and when sales are low, outlets few and losses often made.

→ *Growth*   During this stage of rapid growth the first signs of competition emerge. The search begins for *product modifications* and other ways to extend the life of the product and also *new products* to eventually replace this one.

→ *Maturity*   The majority of sales are *repeat orders* rather than first time purchases. Although prices may be reduced because of competition, *economies of scale* resulting from high volume production help to keep costs low and profits high. The firm may be looking to sell the product into other markets and to introduce product modifications in this stage.

→ *Decline*   As sales decline costs are cut wherever possible (e.g. less promotion) in order to reduce prices. The product will normally be withdrawn when it moves into a loss-making situation.

Extension strategies

The aim is to prolong the life of a product by extending the maturity stage. This is often a far safer option than introducing a new product to the market.

Extension strategies include

→ finding new markets for existing products
→ finding new uses for the product
→ developing the number of products in the product line
→ modifying the product (changes to features, quality, style, image)

New product development

It is often difficult to distinguish between *product modification* and *new product development*. It is estimated that less than 10% of profits come from major innovations, involving entirely new products.

The diagram illustrates the process of new product development. Of the 100 new product ideas only two make it to the market place. Most ideas will not even pass the *screening* stage. This is because costs begin to rise significantly after this stage. New products may fail because of

→ product inferiority   → unrealistic demand forecasts
→ inadequate promotional budget   → consumer resistance
→ technical problems   → poor timing

Checkpoint 1

Draw a diagram to represent the product life cycle.

Watch out!

Although most products have a life cycle it is likely to be *different* for every product.

Example

An example of problems of *new product* development was when Ford replaced the very successful Cortina with the Sierra. It took Ford over five years to re-establish leadership in that market segment.

"The most successful new product development typically revolves around the revitalization of existing products."

Mercer

Example

In America it is estimated that one in three new products is a failure or near failure.

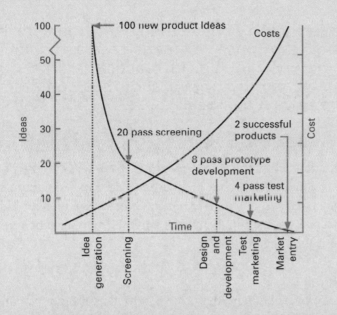

Product portfolio analysis ●●●

The longer-term survival of the organization requires it to have a number of different products at different stages of development and preferably in different markets. The **product matrix** is an attempt to assess the firm's *product portfolio* in terms of sales growth and market share. There are four segments.

→ **Question marks**   Products where the market growth rate is high but the market share is low. Firms will invest large amounts of money in these products hoping they become stars/cash cows.
→ **Stars**   These products have a high market share in a fast growing market. However the cash needed for development and promotion means that these products may do little more than break even.
→ **Cash cows**   These products have a high market share in a low growth market. As market growth has slowed down, development and promotion costs are low, so these products are highly profitable.
→ **Dogs**   Both market share and growth rate are low.

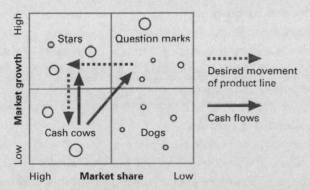

Exam question
answer: page 81

In the 1990s certain confectionery producers decided to develop ice cream brands based on their best selling products.

(a) For what reasons might the manufacturer develop the product in this way? (15 min)

(b) Suggest reasons why this strategy was successful. (15 min)

Check the net

Interesting information on product launches, modifications, etc. can be found at www.marketing.week.co.uk

Action point

Whatever element of the marketing mix you are discussing, make sure you can give examples of how it may change through the product life cycle.

The jargon

The *product matrix* is sometimes called the *Boston Matrix* after the Boston Consulting Group in the USA which developed this approach.

Checkpoint 2

Give an example of a product in each of these segments.

Example

The diagram shows a *balanced* portfolio. It is hoped that today's question marks become tomorrow's stars and cash cows. The investment needed for these products is provided by today's cash cows.

Watch out!

Not all 'question marks' become 'stars' and 'cash cows'!

Examiner's secrets

If you have a choice of questions spend some time making your choice. Do your best questions first, so that you build up confidence for the harder questions to follow.

Price

In a perfectly competitive market the marketer's ability to exploit the 'price' element of the marketing mix would be very limited. In practice, markets are less than perfect so the organization has some discretion over the price it charges.

New product pricing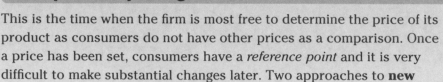

This is the time when the firm is most free to determine the price of its product as consumers do not have other prices as a comparison. Once a price has been set, consumers have a *reference point* and it is very difficult to make substantial changes later. Two approaches to **new product pricing** have evolved.

Skimming

This is an approach where the price is initially set high to 'skim' as much revenue and profit out of the product as possible. It is most appropriate for products which have a monopoly with no competition having emerged. Prices will later be lowered as the competition develops. The lower profit margin from a reduced price may be partly offset by the *economies of larger-scale production* reducing average costs.

Penetration

A low price is set so as to reach as large a market as is possible in a short period of time. It is often used where products are price sensitive or when a firm wishes to discourage competitors from entering the market. In the longer term the firm may hope that market domination will ensure greater control over prices.

Pricing methods

There are three major ways in which price can be determined.

Cost-orientated pricing

Under the **mark-up** method the average cost per unit is calculated, on which a mark-up for profit is added. Alternatively, **target return pricing** involves calculating a selling price which yields a particular return on the capital employed in the activity.

Demand-orientated pricing

Many retailers adopt **psychological pricing**. Goods will be charged at £199 rather than £200 as consumers will tend to *band* it in the £100 to £200 price range. Consumers also use price as an indication of quality. Manufacturers of 'luxury' products such as perfumes may, therefore, set prices far in excess of their cost.

With **discriminatory pricing** different prices are charged for the same product. For discriminatory pricing to work the total market must be segmentable, some segments being willing to pay a higher price than others and the higher-priced segments being unable to obtain the 'product' at the lower price.

Don't forget

Under perfect competition firms are *price takers* and so have no control over market price.

Watch out!

The danger is that high prices may encourage competitors to enter the market.

Don't forget

Other firms, wishing to avoid a price war, may be 'price takers' following the lead of the dominant firm.

Watch out!

These methods take no account of market demand.

Example

Demand for perfumes has been known to rise when prices have been increased!

Checkpoint 1

Give three examples of *discriminatory pricing*. Identify the *barriers* which allow such pricing to take place.

Competition-orientated pricing

Here the prices charged by the **competitors** are the major influence on the firm's pricing strategy.

In 'follow my leader' pricing, the dominant firm in the market sets the market price which other firms will subsequently adopt. The logic is that to do otherwise might start a *price war* (and these follower firms doubt their ability to survive).

In 'destroyer' pricing one firm sets a price which is designed to drive the other firms out of the market. In the short term this may benefit the consumer but in the longer term the reduced competition may result in higher prices.

In the building, construction and engineering industry 'tendering' for a contract is often used. Here, sealed bids for a contract are submitted by interested parties. The contract is awarded to the lowest bidder.

Price sensitivity

Some products are far more *sensitive* to price changes than others. The **price elasticity of demand (PED)** is a measure of this sensitivity.

$$\text{PED} = \frac{\% \text{ change in quantity demanded of product}}{\% \text{ change in price of product}}$$

Where PED is greater than 1 we say that demand is *price elastic*. So if a supermarket faced with a PED of 2 were to reduce prices by 5% it could expect sales to expand by 10% (5% × 2).

Conversely, where the PED is less than 1 then demand is *price inelastic*. So if a cigarette manufacturer faced with a PED of 0.4 were to raise prices by 10% it could expect sales to contract by 4% (10% × 0.4).

We can summarize the impact of PED upon a firm as follows

Price change	Type of elasticity	Impact on total revenue
increase	elastic demand	falls
	inelastic demand	rises
decrease	elastic demand	rises
	inelastic demand	falls

Thus a firm wishing to raise prices may be constrained by the fact that with a *price elastic demand curve* any price increase is going to result in a fall in total revenue.

The degree of price sensitivity will depend on

→ uniqueness, status or prestige of the product
→ consumer awareness of substitutes
→ ratio of expenditure to total income
→ whether the product is habit forming

Exam questions
answers: page 82

1   An economist would tell us that supply and demand determine price, however firms employ numerous strategies when determining price. How do you account for this apparent contradiction? (30 min)

2   Discuss the extent to which a firm's price elasticity of demand can be calculated with accuracy. (20 min)

Don't forget
Competition based pricing is likely to occur where there is
→ a product difficult to differentiate
→ a mature market
→ spare capacity
→ an oligopolistic market structure

Checkpoint 2
What factors might make the demand for a product *more price sensitive*?

Check the net
The Business Owners Toolkit has a section on pricing and elasticity
www.toolkit.cch.com

Links
To refresh your memory on supply and demand analysis see pages 4–5.

Test yourself
Give examples of products with different price sensitivities.

Examiner's secrets
The examiner is looking for answers which express points concisely. Try to be familiar with the idea of price elasticity of demand and its links to total revenue of the firm.

Promotion

Promotion is necessary to make consumers aware of what a firm has to offer. The old saying 'build a better mousetrap and the world will beat a path to your door' has a flaw. If the world *doesn't find out about* your new improved mousetrap no one will be beating a path to your door.

The major elements of promotion

Personal selling

This is person-to-person contact between buyer and seller. Whether over the phone or face-to-face, **personal selling** is the most flexible means of delivering a promotional message. It is used extensively in business-to-business marketing. It is also used in consumer sales where technical information has to be understood by the purchaser. As a method of promotion it is very effective but also very expensive.

Advertising

The ability to communicate to a large number of people at once is the major benefit of **advertising**. Whilst advertising is cost effective in reaching a targeted large group of people, it is non-personal and does not allow discussion or feedback.

Advertising may be *informative*, *persuasive* or *institutional*. Most advertisements are *informative*, providing some information about the product. Nevertheless, the majority of advertising, particularly in mature markets, is going to be *persuasive*. Persuasive advertising aims to create an element of *brand loyalty* for consumer goods, particularly in mature markets where there is spare capacity in the industry. An economist would say that the aim of the firm is to make the firm's demand curve *less price elastic* than before.

Institutional advertising aims to improve the standing of the firm in the community rather than to sell a particular product. The aim is to persuade different groups of people that this is a firm they wish to be associated with. Nevertheless the message, although not primarily directed at them, may influence consumers.

Advertising benefits include

→ firm gains through economies of scale
→ encourages competition
→ public informed of new/improved products
→ high sales result in greater employee security and investor confidence

Publicity and public relations

Both of these are similar to advertising in that the aim is to deliver a message – often using the same mass media. However the information provided for the media is believed, by the firm, to be newsworthy and therefore likely to be transmitted free. Often the precise nature of the message will be determined by a third party (e.g. a journalist).

Check the net

The Advertising Standards Authority provides information on non-broadcast advertising complaints at www.aga.org.uk

Checkpoint 1

Sponsorship and *direct mail* are also considered to be promotional tools. Give examples of when these are used.

Don't forget

Informative advertising is particularly important when new products are brought to the market or products are very technical.

Links

See the work on *price elasticity of demand*, page 71.

Don't forget

Advertising can also be criticized because it raises costs, can be misleading or may be used as a barrier to new firms entering the industry.

Watch out!

The emphasis here will be to promote positive items about the firm and play down negative material.

Sales promotion

This is a short-term activity designed to achieve

- → trial purchases
- → repeat business
- → extra volume
- → point of sale impact

Sales promotion is widely used in both the consumer and industrial markets. Despite there being little evidence of firms gaining any long-term benefit from sales promotion, more money is now spent on promotion than on advertising. There are a wide variety of sales promotion techniques available.

The promotional mix

Where an organization combines several different promotion methods to promote a product, the combination used constitutes the **promotional mix** for that product. For some products all methods may be used, for others it may be just two or three. The promotional mix may vary over time as the marketer changes the promotional objectives. Whatever the nature of the promotional mix, marketers must ensure that the elements of the mix are integrated and promote the same message. The phrase **integrated marketing communications** is sometimes used to emphasize this point.

Push and pull policies

In planning a promotional mix the marketer should also consider whether to use a *push or pull strategy*.

A **push strategy** would emphasize personal selling and advertising by each channel of distribution. A product manufacturer, for example, may offer wholesalers and retailers strong incentives to 'push' the product. Given the incentives offered it will be to the benefit of wholesalers to promote the product strongly to the retailers, and to the benefit of the retailers to promote the product strongly to the consumer.

The term 'push' strategy emphasizes that here it is the efforts of the members of the channels of distribution that push the different stages of the distribution process.

A **pull strategy**, in contrast, is aimed at the final consumer. Promotional efforts will generate extra demand at the retail outlets, encouraging the retailers and wholesalers to stock (or stock more) of the product. In short it is the demand at the retail end of the distribution channel that *pulls* the product through the other channels.

Some organizations – for example Mars – will adopt both a *pull* and *push* strategy at the same time.

Exam questions   answers: page 82

1   A manufacturer of double-glazed window units who has previously sold direct to large DIY firms is considering setting up its own sales force. Discuss the merits of this idea. (20 min)

2   Sales promotions now account for up to 60% of a typical marketing budget. Assess their effectiveness as a promotional tool. (20 min)

Checkpoint 2

Draw up a list of sales promotion techniques.

Watch out!

For many organizations though there will be one *dominant* promotional method.

Examiner's secrets

Promotion is expected to move the potential customer through the following processes: brand ignorance, awareness, knowledge, liking, preference, conviction, purchase, brand loyalty.

Watch out!

A *pull strategy* will emphasize advertising and sales promotion.

Examiner's secrets

Avoid repeating points. There are a specified number of marks for each point. Repeating information does not gain extra marks.

Place (distribution)

The place ingredient of the marketing mix looks at the distribution channel decisions that are required to ensure that the target market has easy access to the product in a way that is acceptable to the supplier of that product.

Channels of distribution

Channels of distribution provide the link between production and the market place. In choosing a particular channel the firm will seek to ensure that

→ it gives access to the customer segments targeted
→ it meets the firm's objectives (e.g. market share)
→ it is relatively cost-effective compared to other channels
→ it enables the firm to compete effectively against other products

There are three broad choices of channel network.

→ **Intensive distribution**   The aim here is to obtain as many retail outlets as possible. This strategy would be suitable for impulse purchases.
→ **Exclusive distribution**   Prestige products wishing to retain their image of up-market exclusivity will grant sole dealerships in each area.
→ **Selective distribution**   A situation where the producer wishes to retain some control over the way a product is sold.

Direct selling

This method is popular with industrial products – particularly those which are expensive and where there is a limited number of buyers. Although this channel is the simplest it is not necessarily the cheapest or most efficient distribution channel. Its *advantages* include

→ sales staff ensure the product is properly promoted
→ sales staff establish good relationships with customers
→ sales staff are a good source of marketing research information
→ direct selling cuts out the middlemen

Producer to retailer

Apart from direct selling, this method has the advantage of minimizing the loss of contact with the customer and maintaining control over the retail outlet. Thus the producer and the retailer may co-operate over matters such as store display, promotional activity or training of sales assistants. This is a channel that is often adopted by large firms with several products being sold through the same retail outlets.

The major problem associated with this form of distribution channel is that new products may not be promoted sufficiently. This may be because they do not generate the turnover per unit of floor space that is expected or because the retailer is more committed to other brands (e.g. those with higher mark-ups).

Check the net

Many interesting articles are appearing in newspapers on e-commerce. This may become a popular exam topic! Try
www.economist.co.uk
www.ft.com
www.telegraph.co.uk
www.times.co.uk
www.guardian.co.uk

Watch out!

In practice there is no reason why a firm should limit itself to just one distribution channel. In fact by using *different* distribution channels the firm may be reaching different segments of the market.

Checkpoint 1

How might a toy manufacturer 'distribute' its products?

Example

PYO fruit is an example of direct selling to the consumer!

Example

Retail outlets such as Tesco or Marks and Spencer sell both food and non-food items that they have purchased direct from the producers.

Producer to wholesaler

This channel tends to be chosen by smaller firms which cannot afford an extensive distribution network or a large sales force. The main advantage is that it avoids high selling costs of the two previous methods.

The other advantages include

→ wholesaler breaks bulk, selling in smaller lots than the firm may be prepared to provide
→ wholesaler has more contacts than many firms
→ reduced stockholding costs and more prompt payment
→ wholesaler may bear other costs, e.g. promotion

There are, however, disadvantages. The firm doesn't know who is going to stock its product or how it will be displayed. New products may not be promoted as aggressively as the firm might like. Profit margins may be lower than for the other distribution channels.

Franchising ●●●

This is a contractual arrangement between the owner of patents for goods or services (the **franchiser**) giving another person (the **franchisee**) the right to produce or sell those products or services. It is considered under the 'heading' of distribution because it is a way of increasing the number of outlets providing the product or service. A typical **franchise agreement** will contain the following terms

The *franchiser* agrees to

→ assign an exclusive sales territory
→ allow the use of (and promote) the trade name
→ provide training and advice on running the business
→ provide financial advice and assistance
→ sell goods to the franchisee

In return the *franchisee* agrees to

→ invest capital in the business
→ pay royalties to the franchiser
→ conform to specified standards
→ make all purchases from the franchiser
→ only sell the franchiser's products

The British Franchise Association claims that franchising is the safest way to set up in business. Put simply, the majority of business start-ups fail within three years, whereas the majority of franchises survive.

The option of franchising is also attractive to the franchiser. He can expand his activities with very little capital investment. In many cases franchising actually results in an injection of cash into the business.

> **Don't forget**
>
> This is the distribution channel most closely associated with *intensive distribution* – a situation where the producer wants to maximize the availability of the product.

> **Don't forget**
>
> When entering an overseas market an agent may be used. He offers marketing services that the firm would find too expensive to undertake itself. An agent does not take ownership of the goods and is paid commission.

> **Examples**
>
> *Franchising* is said to be the fastest growing part of the retail market. Well-known franchises include: the Body Shop, Burger King, Dynorod, Kwikprint, Pronuptia.

> **Don't forget**
>
> The *franchisee* may find these limitations irksome, but it has the advantage of being part of a well-known group.

Exam questions   answers: page 83

1   Outline the criteria you would use in selecting channels of distribution. (20 min)

2   'Cutting out the middleman' is often suggested as a way of reducing prices. In the light of this statement assess the value of distribution channel intermediaries. (20 min)

> **Examiner's secrets**
>
> When you are required to write an essay, always prepare a plan before you start writing.

Marketing strategy

Marketing strategies are the *means* by which marketing objectives are achieved. They are generally concerned with the '4 Ps' of the marketing mix.

Checkpoint

Can you remember the '4 Ps' of marketing?

Watch out!

Marketing objectives must always be consistent with the firm's overall corporate strategy.

Examiner's secrets

The process of determining *marketing strategy* includes: identify marketing objectives, review environment, develop strategy, implement plan, review outcomes.

Examiner's secrets

In evaluating any marketing strategy make sure you consider the implications for the other business functions – particularly finance.

Links

For more on the *product life cycle* see page 68.

Watch out!

Research has shown that in most cases the 'pioneer' firm retains the market lead in the longer term, whichever strategy is chosen.

Check the net

www.bized.ac.uk has information on the marketing strategies of various companies.

Evaluating marketing strategy

In practice there are many different **marketing strategies** that can be pursued to reach a given corporate objective. For example, an objective to improve profits may be achieved by developing new products, modifying existing products, varying pricing policy, devising a promotions policy and/or changing distribution channels. Criteria for evaluating individual marketing strategies include

→ does it conform to *overall corporate strategy*?
→ does the firm have the *correct organizational structure*?
→ does the firm have *sufficient resources to see strategy through*?
→ does it *make use of strategic strengths*?
→ does it *reduce organizational weaknesses*?
→ does it *exploit market opportunities*?
→ does it *reduce major threats*?
→ does it *agree with the firm's idea of ethical behaviour*?

In practice marketing strategy is a continuous process. This is because the situation facing the firm is continually evolving. As new opportunities and threats emerge, the successful firm must adapt to the changed situation with new strategies – and perhaps even objectives.

Marketing strategy and the product life cycle

When we looked at the **product life cycle** we noted that each of the *stages* had very different characteristics. The marketer's response is to devise a strategy to meet the needs of each stage.

Introduction stage

At the **introduction stage** the product is relatively unknown. The producer can choose one of two strategies.

Price skimming strategy – here the idea is to obtain maximum short-term profit potential by targeting early adopters willing to pay a high price for this product. Such a strategy enables the firm to recoup its development costs quickly, though the high price may quickly attract the attention of would-be competitors. Allied to such a strategy will be informative promotion, frequent product modifications and a *selective* distribution policy.

Penetration pricing strategy – here the idea is to gain as much market share as quickly as possible through setting much lower prices. The firm would hope that *economies of scale* might help offset the low price. This strategy is an attempt to dominate the market from the start and hopefully to retain that control in the longer term. Allied to this strategy will also be informative promotion and frequent product modifications, but in this case an *extensive* distribution policy.

Growth stage

At the **growth stage** consumers are now aware of the benefits of this product and the market is growing rapidly. The first signs of competition are beginning to emerge. Assuming the firm has initially adopted a skim pricing strategy, prices will now be lowered. The 'pioneer' firms will probably have to invest in extra production capacity and promotional campaigns to protect their market share. These investments are likely to absorb whatever profit is being made. The distribution network will also be expanded, which may also be costly.

Maturity stage

In the **maturity stage** there is a lot more competition, including price competition. Attempts will be made to develop product lines and to more clearly differentiate the products from those of the competitors. As competition increases and profits fall some minor brands may leave the market.

Decline stage

Porter suggests four potential strategies for this stage

→ *Leadership* – where the market is still profitable, invest to become the market leader before 'harvesting'.
→ *Niche* – identify market segments which are still profitable and will decline slowly.
→ *Harvest* – often termed 'milking the brand', i.e. minimizing costs and maximizing price in order to improve profitability. Product is withdrawn when it moves into a loss-making situation.
→ *Divestment* – sell the business at the end of the maturity stage.

Product strategy ●●●

There are four basic strategies for growth in unit sales and profit

→ market penetration   → product development
→ market development   → diversification

These are often shown in the form of a matrix. You will see that some strategies are more risky than others. *Market penetration* is the safest because both market and product are known. Both *market development* and *product development* carry a significantly higher degree of risk as the firm is moving into new areas. *Diversification* is the most risky strategy of all, as both markets and products are new.

Exam question   answer: page 83

ABC plc is a large carpet retailer with outlets in many town centres. Each January it holds an annual sale.

(a) Explain how the marketing mix it operates for the period of its January sale might differ from that used during the rest of the year.

(b) What are the benefits to the firm of holding the January sale? (30 min)

Watch out!

Nevertheless there will be relatively little price competition as the market is growing fast.

Don't forget

The market is now growing a lot more slowly. Many sales will be repeat purchases.

Examples

UK brands disappearing in the last 20 years include: Spangles, Treets, Farley's Rusks, Formula Shell, Munchies as well as *Now*, *Riva* and *Nova* magazines.

Check the net

Use the search engines to visit companies such as Unilever, Procter and Gamble and other major consumer product manufacturers for information on product strategy.

The jargon

This matrix is sometimes known as the *Ansoff matrix*.

Examiner's secrets

Where a question asks you to explain or justify, you are expected to provide a reasoned and developed answer examining all points of view.

Answers
Marketing

Marketing objectives

Checkpoints

1 Many possibilities, e.g. M & S and other major retailers are well known for imposing strict conditions as to price and quality on suppliers. The threat is that huge medium- to long-term contracts will be withdrawn if these conditions are not met.

2 Other ways of setting budgets include
   - competitor parity budgeting – financial allocation matches major competitors
   - sales related budgeting – allocating expenditure by reference to a percentage of sales revenue
   - incremental budgeting – last year plus a bit!

Exam questions

1 Corporate image is the view of the organization in the eyes of customers, employees and the public at large. Corporate image is particularly important for consumers. In many cases consumers have only limited product knowledge, particularly so in the case of long-term purchases. As the cost of a mistake is high, many customers will rely on the reputation of the company as a major determinant in the purchase decision. Where a company loses that reputation for fairness to the consumer, sales will suffer. In one case – the jewellers, Ratners – the company eventually had to change its name as a result of damage to its reputation.

   A good corporate image may also have a beneficial effect in other areas. Thus individuals may be more attracted to work for that firm. Equally, it may be easier to raise money to finance expansion.

> **Examiner's secrets**
>
> Corporate image is particularly important for large firms in the public eye. For smaller firms the pressure to maintain a positive corporate image may not be so great. You should try to give examples of organizations which have a good corporate image and what they have done to achieve that image.

2 (a) The marketing budget is the amount of money allocated to the marketing function in order to undertake its activities over the next financial year. In practice senior management within the marketing function will have submitted a detailed plan of the activities to be carried out and the expenditures necessary for this purpose.
   (b) There are both benefits and problems arising from the use of budgets. The *benefits* include
   - provide a target for staff to achieve (motivation)
   - setting budgets requires proper planning to be carried out
   - it is a means of controlling expenditure
   - it is a means of measuring performance
   The *problems* include

   - budgets make no allowances for changed circumstances
   - budget preparation is time-consuming
   - managers may feel that they have to spend full allocation of money.

> **Examiner's secrets**
>
> Your final paragraph should attempt to evaluate the importance of the points that you have put forward. Generally, you will find that the benefits of budgeting outweigh the problems that arise from budgeting.

3 The level of marketing expenditure will be determined by the precise circumstances the firm finds itself in. Key factors would include
   - nature of the product
   - level of competition
   - stage in product life cycle of product
   - number of products in portfolio
   - need to increase market share
   - need to obtain new markets
   - level of market research required
   - need to maintain or improve corporate image

> **Examiner's secrets**
>
> Note the key word 'list'. No development is required.

Defining the market

Checkpoints

1 Football clubs could define their market as sport, entertainment or leisure.

   As a *sports*-based organization they might be looking to develop other sporting activities, e.g. rugby, women's football, sports clothing and equipment.

   Where the market is defined as *entertainment*, opportunities include corporate hospitality and pop concerts.

   Finally, in the *leisure* market, opportunities might include keep-fit, catering firms and books.

2 The demand for some products is very responsive to changes in consumer income, e.g. leisure activities such as eating out or going on holiday. We say that such products have a high income elasticity of demand.

3 To give herself a break from domestic routine or to enable her to spend more time with her family. Having established *why* a group of housewives buy the product, the information might be used in a promotional campaign emphasizing these benefits.

Exam questions

1 Information which market research might provide includes
   Occupants   who are the customers?
   Opposition   who are the competitors?

Objects   what do consumers buy?
Occasions   when and how frequently do they buy?
Organization   who is involved in the buying
               decision?
Objectives   why do they buy?
Operations   how do they buy (distribution
               channels)?

2 (a)

Market mapping is an analytical tool which allows a business to identify the area of the market it is targeting. The map is created by comparing competing organizations in terms of two factors that are valued by the consumer. In practice this often means *price* and *quality*. The map (which is based on the perceptions of some students) shows two clusters of firms, one providing for consumers buying on the basis of quality (at a price), the other buying mainly on the basis of price (and accepting lower quality).

(b) By identifying that blend (or mix) of price and quality which is important to a firm's customers, the firm is able to promote its product offering to these groups more effectively. An alternative would be to use promotion to move the consumer nearer to what the producer is offering; however this is very difficult to achieve.

In the longer term, a firm may use a market map as a tool to measure the success of a repositioning strategy. Suppose, say (and it is only an example), Tesco wishes to raise its quality image. Market maps over a period of time would help to show whether this had been achieved.

Global marketing and segmentation

Checkpoints

1 Tariffs, quotas, technical requirements, financial bonds, voluntary export agreements.

2 • *Age*: holidays, insurance, magazines
  • *Sex*: magazines, alcohol, cars
  • *Income*: meals out, holidays, jewellery
  • *Ethnicity*: food, clothing, magazines

3 • *Benefit segmentation* looks at the benefits consumers want from the product. Thus toothpaste may be bought to obtain white teeth or a fresh mouth taste. A drink may be bought because it has a great taste or fewer calories.
  • *Behaviour segmentation* is based on individuals' behaviour patterns and consumption habits. Thus some people will only buy clothing from speciality men's or women's shops, whilst others will use department stores or discount stores. These shopping habits may be used as the basis for segmentation.
  • *Geo-demographic segmentation* is used where there are noticeable differences in people's habits based upon geography. For example, urban versus rural, hot versus cold or North versus South.
  • *Lifestyle segmentation* is based upon how individuals spend their time and money. Many magazines segment their market by lifestyle. These magazines provide other firms which wish to reach the same segment with the opportunity to advertise to and reach that target market.

Exam questions

1 (a) *Undifferentiated marketing* occurs where a firm believes that there is little diversity amongst customers and that it is more efficient *not* to distinguish between different market segments. The attempt to appeal to everyone, though, may make a firm extremely vulnerable to competition. Thus even the salt market can be segmented and Kellogg's found that it was worthwhile to treat the 2.6 million deaf Americans as a separate market segment!

(b) *Niche or concentrated marketing* is where a firm believes that different users have different needs and that it is appropriate to target these markets separately. Where a firm directs its marketing efforts towards one segment, this is termed concentrated marketing.

(c) *Differentiated marketing* occurs where the firm identifies a number of different market segments which it wants to target. Differentiated marketing requires the firm to produce a different marketing mix for each of these segments.

(d) *Custom based marketing* is a situation where the market is so diverse that it is difficult to identify meaningful market segments. In such a situation the firm must attempt to satisfy each customer's unique set of needs. A manufacturer of industrial robots may be faced with this situation, as might service industries as diverse as architects, tailors, hairdressers and lawyers.

2 Your introduction should define the term market niche and explain its relationship to segmentation. You might also explain what you mean by a small firm. Try to provide examples to illustrate your answer. The body of your answer should indicate that there are four tests which are used to identify viable market segments. They are that the segment should be
- *measurable* – easy to identify and measure
- *substantial* – large enough to justify developing and maintaining a separate marketing mix
- *accessible* – easy to reach in terms of promotion and distribution strategy
- *stable* – the segment must not be transient or temporary

Market research

Exam questions

1 There are two approaches possible with this type of question. You can either treat each type of research separately dealing with its own peculiar advantages and disadvantages. Or you can compare and contrast the two types. The latter tends to give a more powerful argument and one likely to lead to more analysis and evaluation rather than just description.

The content should include

	Advantages	Disadvantages
Field	• Questions are designed to answer your specific research objectives • Research is available only to you • The data gathered is current and up to date	• It is extremely expensive • Unless designed by professionals it is easy to introduce bias • It is a time-consuming task
Desk	• Can be obtained quite cheaply • Samples can be much larger • Market-wide data and international comparisons can be made for very little cost • Based on actual figures such as sales	• Data might be out of date compared with current customer needs • Data not specifically designed for the research objectives • Not able to measure the accuracy of collection

2 Market research can be inaccurate in the following ways
- *Poorly designed questions* Questions that are ambiguous, that rely on people's memories or that require calculations by the respondent often produce inaccurate and biased data.
- *Sample too small or incorrectly gathered* The sample must be large enough in order to eliminate the 'outlying' or 'rogue' answers.
- *False replies* These can either be deliberate lies or the respondent providing answers they believe are wanted.

3 • *Qualitative research* is in-depth research into the psychology of the consumer. It investigates the reasons behind buying behaviour. It is interested in how respondents reply as well as in what they actually say.
- *Quantitative research*, however, uses pre-set questions, often in the form of a questionnaire, in order to obtain a large pool of statistical data. It is more interested in determining concrete facts than attitudes of consumers.

Sampling and sales forecasting

Exam questions

1 There are two main reasons why a firm wants to predict the future
  - to reduce the uncertainty associated with a dynamic economy
  - to allow the company to plan more accurately
  Predictions are based on current data, therefore the data must be as accurate as possible. The types of prediction required include
  - future sales levels
  - future cash flow requirements
  - changes in major cost items such as labour and raw materials
  - changes in general economic performance
  - changes in demography

2 In order to identify the underlying trend you need to smooth out the raw data. The first step is to recognize any regular pattern occurring in the figures such as a peak in sales every four weeks (coinciding with the end of the month and many workers' pay day) or sales associated with the seasons (holidays). The next step is to choose the same number of periods for the moving average as there is in the pattern. The most common are four quarterly and twelve-monthly.

3 Primary research might be biased in the following ways
  - the questions are phrased as to invite a particular response
  - the interviewer, intentionally or unconsciously, encourages a particular response by tone of voice, facial expression or body language
  - the sample selected for questioning might not be representative of the desired population, e.g. wrong age group, incorrect gender mix, inappropriate income levels, etc.

Product

Checkpoints

1

2 Many possibilities. *Question mark* – e-commerce; *Stars* – mobile phones; *Cash cows* – Dyson vacuum cleaners; *Dogs* – vinyl records.

Exam question

1 (a) A producer might develop a market in this way because
  - natural extension of existing product
  - separate but sizeable segment
  - good knowledge of the market
  - present market saturated
  - increases revenue
  - counter-seasonal product
  - better use of existing resources
  (b) It was successful because
  - revitalized a mature market with a new product
  - product had a good reputation already
  - effectively marketed
  - caught consumer interest

Price

Checkpoints

1 Examples of discriminatory pricing include student railcards, pensioner bus passes, matinee theatre tickets, prices of domestic (as opposed to business) electricity, etc.
2 Price sensitivity might be raised by
  - more substitutes available
  - more awareness of substitutes
  - fall in status of product
  - product taking a higher proportion of income (consumers notice price changes more)
  - product becomes less habit forming

Exam questions

1 Your introduction should briefly explain how supply and demand determine price (perhaps using a diagram). It should also briefly detail some of the pricing strategies available, for example, skimming, penetration, discriminatory, cost-plus, psychological, competitive, promotional, etc.
   The body of your essay should make points such as
   * supply/demand analysis is an aggregate
   * supply/demand analysis assumes perfect knowledge, etc.
   * markets are segmented and subject to producer influence
   * price is only one factor in the purchase decision
   * consumers may be influenced by fashion or image

2 First of all define the term. Your answer could include difficulties such as
   * there are a number of variables affecting demand: difficult to isolate the effect of one (price)
   * elasticities change over time as competition changes
   * for new products estimates rely on accuracy of market research and test marketing
   * impact of price change on sales varies over time

Promotion

Checkpoints

1 *Sponsorship* is often used in sports events, e.g. football. Schools taking students abroad for study purposes may also seek sponsorship from local companies.
   Direct mail is often used to sell insurance, pensions, books, magazines, theatre tickets – the range of products is endless!

2 Sales promotion techniques include
   price reductions, coupons, competitions, buy one get one free (bogof), free gifts, trial offers, trade-in offers, savings stamps, loyalty cards, etc.

Exam questions

1 Your introduction should make the point that direct marketing may be considerably wider than using your own sales force to sell direct to the consumer. It could also involve the use of advertising, telephone sales, catalogue retailing, direct mail or e-commerce.

Points *for* direct selling include
* your staff will ensure the product is properly promoted
* can establish good relationship with customer
* sales staff can be a good source of marketing research information
* it cuts out the cost of middlemen
Points *against* direct selling include
* direct selling costs are likely to be high
* difficult to display goods as effectively as a retailer would
* stiff competition from other manufacturers marketing in the same way
* some people don't like buying on the basis of catalogue descriptions and pictures

2 Your introduction should define and give examples of promotional tools, e.g. advertising, public relations, exhibitions and direct marketing. You should then define the term 'sales promotion' with the aid of examples.
   Sales promotions can be used to
* increase sales
* target specific groups, retailers and/or their customers
* target specific objectives such as trial purchase or repeat purchase
* widen distribution or improve point of sale impact
Against this
* there is rarely any lasting increase in sales
* there are hidden costs including management and sales force time
* promotions may conflict with brand image
* price cutting (a particularly important technique) can persuade consumers to hold off repeat purchases until the product is once again on offer
* unless used in conjunction with advertising and other marketing techniques, sales promotions have often been found to be ineffective

Place (distribution)

Checkpoint

In practice a toy manufacturer could use any form of distribution channel. Toys could be sold direct to the public through a direct mailshot, a catalogue or e-commerce. They could sell direct to larger retailers or to smaller shops through a wholesaler.

Exam questions

1 Decisions relating to *channels of distribution* revolve around two factors, cost and control. If the option taken is to make all sales directly to the consumer there may be unacceptable cost implications. However using intermediaries may significantly reduce the level of control over how the product is sold. The choice will depend on factors such as

- the image of the product
- the creditworthiness of the distributor
- the complexity of the product
- the perishability of the product
- the location of customers

2 Your introduction should define the word middleman – that is, a business which handles goods or services in the distribution chain between producer and end user.

Middlemen have a number of important functions including

- breaking bulk
- stockholding
- after-sales service
- storage
- delivery
- promotion

For many firms you will find that using middlemen reduces costs and increases sales.

Marketing strategy

Checkpoint

Price, product, promotion, place.

Exam question

(a) You should define the term marketing mix. You should draw attention to any assumptions that you make. Thus it is likely that the retailer is covering the full range of product types rather than trying to satisfy specialist niches.

Marketing mix throughout the year

Product

The firm will offer a wide range of products, e.g. natural and man-made fibres. There will also be a wide range of qualities and designs. There will be a carpet delivery and fitting service available.

Price

A wide range of different prices depending on the quality and other features of the carpets. There will be credit facilities available.

Promotion

The store will be brightly lit and well laid out allowing customers to view the product ranges to their best advantage. Products will be promoted through local, and perhaps national, advertising. The media used will reflect the interests and reading matter of the target markets. The emphasis will be on quality, durability and style of the product as well as the reputation of an old-established high street store.

Marketing mix in January

Promotion

The target market for the sale will be people who aspire to the quality the firm's products provide but who are normally unable to afford this. Promotion will be aimed at this target market and will emphasize value for money and getting a bargain.

Products

Items on special offer will include surplus stock, ends of ranges and specially purchased stock (again possibly ends of ranges and surplus stock) some of which may be of a lesser quality than normally stocked.

Price

Surplus stock and end of ranges will be priced so as to ensure it is sold. This may be at less than cost price. Stock specially purchased for the sale will be priced competitively but at a price to yield some profit. Normal stock will be reduced in price but again the discount given will still allow the firm to make a profit.

(b) January sales are advantageous because

- provide cash flow at a quiet time of year
- surplus stock, etc. sold
- opportunity to try out new designs and producers
- provide space and cash to buy new season's products
- may attract new customers, who if satisfied may return

People in organizations

For most organizations success is dependent upon the efforts of their employees. Yet employees are the most difficult resource to manage. Employees will differ in terms of ability, aspirations and motives for working. Employees must not only be paid a wage, the employer has also to accept other financial burdens associated with their employment including National Insurance contributions, meeting the provisions of health and safety legislation, etc.

Since in many organizations the wages bill exceeds 75% of total cost there is great pressure on the Human Resources Department and line managers to ensure that labour is used effectively by the organization. At the same time workers are becoming more aware of their contractual and statutory rights and are also demanding a greater say in the way their work is organized.

Exam themes

→ The need for, and nature of, workforce planning.

→ Employment law; rights and duties of employer and employee.

→ Organizational design concepts including decentralization, span of control, chain of command, delegation.

→ The relationship between structure, objectives and culture.

→ Management functions – planning, organizing, directing, controlling.

→ The work of the main motivational theorists. Monetary and non monetary motivation.

→ The relationship between motivation and the achievement of business objectives.

→ Leadership style and its implications for the achievement of business objectives.

→ Managing change within organizations.

→ Communications media and their effectiveness in differing situations.

Topic checklist

○ AS ● A2	AQA	EDEXCEL	OCR	WJEC
Workforce planning	○●	●	○	○●
Workforce performance	●	●	○	●
Organizational structure	○	○	○	○●
Motivation in theory	○	○	○	○●
Motivation in practice	○	○●	○	○●
Leadership	○●	○●	○	○●
Communication	●	○	●	●
Collective bargaining	●	●	●	●
Industrial democracy	●	●	●	○●
Trends in employment	●	●	●	●

Workforce planning

Workforce planning is important to the organization to ensure that it has the employees necessary to carry out its activities. In undertaking this activity the Human Resource Department (HRD) has to be aware of the organization's corporate plan as well as the opportunities and constraints created by the business and legal environment.

The workforce plan

The process of **workforce planning** can be shown using a diagram.

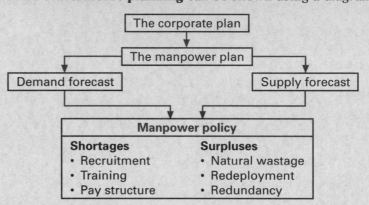

The precise manpower requirements of the organization will be determined by the organization's longer-term objectives – as laid down in the **corporate plan**. Assumptions are made regarding the goods/services to be produced, the technology to be used in providing the goods or services, how the goods will be marketed and what management information systems are required. Assumptions also have to be made about workers leaving the organization through retirement, ill health, dismissal or obtaining alternative employment. All these have implications for the future workforce plan.

Recruitment

This is a major part of the work of any human resource department. Selection of the right person for the job is vital to the firm's success. One major decision which has to be taken is whether to recruit internally or externally. The benefits of each are as follows

Internal
→ known to the firm
→ reduced recruitment costs
→ improves employee motivation

External
→ provides new blood
→ internal promotion causes friction
→ internal promotion transfers recruitment problem elsewhere

Interview is the most common form of selection procedure. However, it is not always a good indicator of candidate suitability. For this reason the interview is often supplemented by various tests. These may examine

→ competence in a task
→ personality
→ aptitudes
→ ability to work in groups

Tests also have problems – they are difficult to use objectively and are often distorted through the candidate being under stress.

The jargon

Workforce planning is sometimes called human resource planning.

Check the net

Many human resource issues of interest to business students are covered at www.hrnettwork.co.uk
www.lpd.co.uk

Watch out!

These *assumptions* are critical to the future workforce plan.

Checkpoint 1

Explain the importance of the *job description* and *person specification* in the recruitment process.

Examiner's secrets

You may be asked to assess the benefits and problems associated with different recruitment methods.

Training and development

All organizations will undertake some form of training. Training is seen as necessary because it

→ helps employees learn job
→ increases staff flexibility
→ reduces labour turnover
→ improves productivity
→ reduces likelihood of accidents
→ aids internal promotion

Termination of employment

In a majority of cases **termination** is the result of the employee finding another job or retiring. However an employer may terminate a contract of employment on the grounds of redundancy, misconduct or unsatisfactory work.

Redundancy

This occurs when the business, or part of it, is closed down and the employer no longer needs certain employees. For the employer to avoid a claim for unfair dismissal they must consult with the unions and give notice of their intention to make people redundant. Where not all the employees are being made redundant, the employer must ensure the method by which workers are selected is fair. Employees affected by redundancy must be allowed a reasonable amount of time off work to seek another job.

Misconduct

Not all misconduct is such that the employer can dismiss an employee. However an employee could be dismissed where he/she

→ plays practical jokes
→ ignores employer instructions
→ physically abuses another employee or customer
→ steals from the firm
→ is rude to customers

Unsatisfactory work

Where an employee is unable to perform his job satisfactorily the employer must go through a *formal process* to avoid a claim for unfair dismissal. This process is designed to allow employees sufficient time to improve their performance. The process has four stages:

→ *informal* – the employee is counselled and warned
→ *formal* – with no improvement a first written warning is given
→ *final* – again no improvement so final written warning is given
→ *dismissal* – where still no improvement is shown

Exam questions
answers: page 106

1   (a) give TWO reasons why on-the-job staff training might be more effective than off-the-job training. (5 min)

   (b) What criteria might a firm use to assess the effectiveness of a training programme? (10 min)

   (c) Why should staff training be a continuous process? (10 min)

2   Some firms appoint executives solely from their graduate trainee schemes while others promote from the shop floor. Evaluate this situation. (20 min)

Example

Induction training is designed to welcome new employees and familiarize them with the organization, their department and their job.

Checkpoint 2

Outline other forms of training undertaken by firms.

Checkpoint 3

How could a firm needing to lose workers avoid compulsory redundancies?

Example

'Last in – first out' is often used for selecting those to be made redundant.

Watch out!

Unfair dismissal claims not only cost the firm time and money but can also damage the firm's reputation.

Examiner's secrets

Questions may ask you to evaluate manpower strategy. Make sure you consider issues such as cost, turnover, motivation, public image, business ethics.

Examiner's secrets

In question 2 you must put forward the 'pros' and 'cons' of each method before attempting any form of judgement.

Workforce performance

In a market economy where firms are competing directly against one another, workforce performance (or productivity) is especially important. The firm that has an efficient and productive workforce is the one that is able to supply goods and services to its customers at a lower price than its competitors, helping its survival and profitability.

Labour productivity

Labour productivity shows the relationship between the output of the organization and the number of employees. Output may be measured in units of production, for example cars, or its monetary value. Another variation is to measure the productivity of a group of workers.

Productivity data can be used

→ to detect trends in productivity over time
→ to detect differences in productivity between various plants
→ in negotiations with trade unions
→ in negotiations with management over extra resources

Labour productivity is an important element in an organization's level of competitiveness. If an organization can produce the same level of output with fewer employees, then the cost per unit of output falls. This is particularly important where labour is a major cost of the firm.

Labour turnover and absenteeism

Labour turnover measures the rate at which a firm changes its workforce. It is calculated as follows

$$\text{labour turnover} = \frac{\text{number of staff leaving per period}}{\text{average number of staff}}$$

Although a high labour turnover is commonly thought to be adverse for the firm, it can be beneficial in that it allows the firm to recruit other employees with different ideas and enthusiasms. Nevertheless there are significant costs associated with the recruitment of new workers, which arise from

→ recruiting replacements
→ training replacements
→ lost productivity

Levels of **absenteeism** are another way of assessing how effectively an organization is using its labour force. Absenteeism is calculated as

$$\frac{\text{number of working days lost per period}}{\text{total potential working days in period}} \times 100$$

By monitoring absence over time, trends can be identified. At an *organizational or departmental level* increasing absenteeism may suggest low morale and job dissatisfaction. At an *individual level* you often find that a small number of workers are responsible for the majority of any absenteeism.

Check the net

Search under 'productivity' for interesting information.
www.dti.gov.uk

The jargon

Labour productivity is

$$\frac{\text{total output}}{\text{number of employees}}$$

Examiner's secrets

Labour productivity (worker efficiency) can also be gauged through
→ spoilt production
→ speed of service
→ customer complaints

Checkpoint 1

Explain the following terms for labour turnover
voluntary
involuntary
management action

Checkpoint 2

Suggest ways in which high absenteeism could be tackled.

Action point

Try using Herzberg's 'hygiene' factors to explain absenteeism!

Improving productivity

Improvements in productivity may enable the firm to reduce the selling price of its product. Alternatively the firm may maintain prices and enjoy a higher profit margin.

Using capital more effectively

It is often possible to use existing equipment more effectively. For example in many firms machines only run for part of the day. Rather than investing in new machinery it may make better sense to use existing capital more intensively. Improved maintenance to reduce breakdowns will also improve productivity.

Kaizen

This is a Japanese term meaning *continuous improvement*. Changes to working practices, often suggested by the workers themselves, enable firms to raise productivity. Although individually these improvements may be small, taken together they can have a significant effect on productivity.

Investment

Many firms improve labour productivity by buying new machinery. Much of this machinery is very sophisticated and requires far fewer workers than before. For example the use of information technology to control machine processes (robotics) may do away with most production line workers. Equally stock control in the retailing industry has been transformed by the use of microelectronics in the form of bar code readers at the till.

Improving motivation

Most people are capable of improving their personal productivity whilst at work. It is the role of the manager to unlock this potential. Motivation can be raised by ensuring that the working conditions are right and also by designing jobs with the employees' needs in mind.

Checkpoint 3

How might *price elasticity of demand* be important here?

Don't forget

As most of these improvements are suggested by the workforce there is no problem with 'resistance to change'!

Watch out!

As well as raising labour productivity, other benefits of IT include immediate analysis of sales patterns and automatic reordering of stock.

Don't forget

Training itself often improves motivation as well as raising productivity. For more on motivation, see pages 92–5.

Exam question   answer: pages 106–7

You are the Human Relations Officer for a large financial call centre in the North of England. Recent statistics have shown that over the last year labour turnover has risen from 5% to 15%. You know from previous experience that this rate is far higher than at similar financial call centres. You have decided that you must inform senior management of this problem.

Using a suitable form of communication you are required to

(a) summarize the facts (5 min)

(b) comment on potential causes of labour turnover (10 min)

(c) comment on the consequences of high labour turnover (15 min)

Examiner's secrets

Marks will be awarded for a suitable form of communication, e.g. memorandum. Then be specific in using that form to answer the question.

Organizational structure

The structure of an organization describes the role people undertake in an organization and their relationships with other employees. This formal structure is very important so that people can identify their role within the organization, who and what they are responsible for and also to whom they are responsible.

The work of management

Management is best seen as a unifying resource that brings together all the resources used by an organization so that its **objectives** are achieved efficiently.

Although there are different levels of management within an organization you will find that all managers will use the same skills namely

conceptual, technical, decision-making, human, communication

Similarly you will find that when we look at **managerial functions** we find that all managers undertake the same tasks, namely

planning, organizing, directing, controlling

Mintzberg suggested a third way of looking at the work of a manager which involves looking at the **roles** they perform for an organization, namely

interpersonal, informational, decisional

In practice all these different ways of looking at the manager's jobs aid our understanding of their work. The conclusion should be that the work of a manager is complex and requires the ability to act in many different ways over a short period of time.

Organization charts

Most organizations will describe their structure pictorially through an **organization chart**. This is because people find it easy to understand.

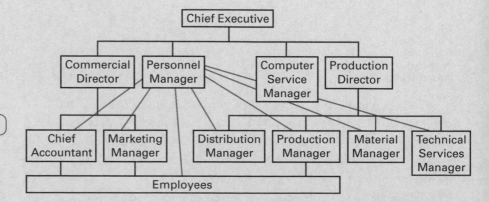

The organization chart shown on page 90 has divided its activities by *function*. Other organizations might use *product*, *process* or *geographical area* as the basis for division. The organization chart below uses the **matrix structure**.

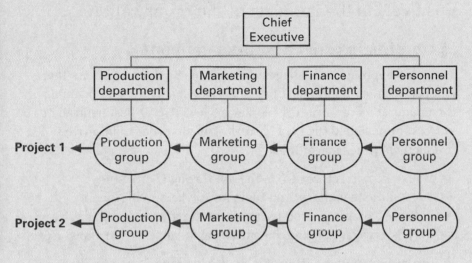

The major advantages of the matrix structure include

→ interdepartmental barriers are broken down and a team approach to work is encouraged
→ tighter control of the project is achieved through co-ordination by the project leader

Delegation ●●●

To function effectively a manager must **delegate** – by this we mean that certain parts of the job are passed to subordinates for action. This allows the manager to concentrate on the more important aspects of the job whilst also training the next generation of managers. There are three important aspects to delegation

→ *Responsibility*   The employee accepts the responsibility to ensure that the job is carried out correctly and on time. These responsibilities must be properly defined.
→ *Authority*   For delegation to work, the subordinates must be given the necessary authority to carry out their responsibilities. This may include the hiring of labour, the spending of money or other uses of resources.
→ *Accountability*   Subordinates are responsible to their superiors for the outcome of their job (but remember the superiors are in turn responsible to their own bosses for the performance of subordinates).

Exam question   answer: page 107

(a) Distinguish between consultation and delegation. (10 min)

(b) Consider the impact upon a firm of changing its approach to decision-making from being based on consultation to delegation. (20 min)

Don't forget

→ the departmental structure still exists as a resource bank for project teams
→ project teams cut across functional boundaries
→ client has a point of contact close to his immediate interests
→ however matrix structure may create conflicts of interest and result in a loss of efficiency in the use of resources

Checkpoint 3

List the circumstances where a manager might not delegate work to a subordinate.

Checkpoint 4

Distinguish between delegation and decentralization.

Watch out!

You should be aware that a business's organizational structure may change over time in response to changes in the external environment.

Examiner's secrets

Make sure you define these terms and distinguish between them. Think about time periods, e.g. short term and longer term.

Motivation in theory

Most managers have to delegate because the job that they have is too big for one person to do. In having to work through other people it is necessary that managers understand what motivates an employee to act positively in the interests of the organization.

Scientific approach to management

This is an approach to management by F. W. Taylor and others that emphasizes the importance of managers being involved in planning the organization of work. The worker is viewed as at best neutral, or at worst opposed, to the idea of work. Thus in order to improve productivity the manager must

→ devise the correct way to do the job through work study
→ develop the techniques and tools for workers to do the job
→ motivate workers to produce to a consistently high level, e.g. by using low basic wages and high incentive payments for exceeding targets

The results of these ideas of F. W. Taylor can be seen in the car production assembly lines of many motor manufacturers. The approach did improve productivity tremendously at factories where it was introduced. It also produced major labour problems. Such factories were fruitful grounds for trade unions seeking new members.

Human relations approach to management

This relied heavily on the work of Elton Mayo, who undertook work on the link between productivity and working conditions. He found that productivity rose even when working conditions deteriorated. Mayo conducted a whole series of experiments at the Hawthorne Plant of General Electric between 1927 and 1932. His conclusions, which were radically different to F. W. Taylor, were as follows

→ people are motivated by social needs
→ division of labour has destroyed much of the earlier meaning of work, which involved inter-personal relationships
→ work groups have a greater impact on employee motivation than financial incentives and organizational controls
→ to motivate the employee, managers must pay far greater attention to ensuring that the workers' social needs are met

Mayo's ideas were adopted in many firms. Unfortunately the expected improvements in motivation and productivity often failed to materialize.

Maslow and Herzberg

Maslow argued that workers have a **'hierarchy of needs'**. The first three needs, physiological, safety and social needs, are identified as *lower-order needs* and are satisfied from the *context* within which the job is undertaken. Self-esteem and self-actualization are identified as *higher order needs* and are met through the *content* of the job.

Maslow went further. He argued that at any one time one need is *dominant* and acts as a motivator. However, once that need is satisfied

---

Checkpoint 1

Briefly outline the contribution of Frank and Lillian Gilbreth to the scientific management revolution.

Example

Mayo found that the productivity of research teams rose in the Hawthorne plant because of increased personal attention and a perceived rise in status.

Checkpoint 2

Explain the term 'Hawthorne effect'.

Check the net

A wide range of motivational theorists are considered at www.westrek.hypermart.net

Checkpoint 3

Can you outline some criticisms of Maslow's ideas?

it will no longer motivate, but be replaced by the next higher level need which remains to be satisfied.

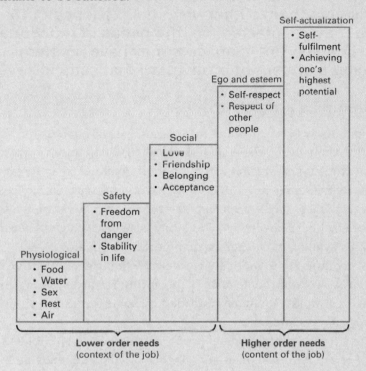

The implications of this theory for managers were that they had to try and satisfy their workers' needs within the organizational context. Some examples of how this might be achieved are shown below

→ *physiological* – pay, rest periods, holidays
→ *safety* – health and safety measures, employment security, pensions
→ *social* – formal and informal groups, social events, sports clubs
→ *self-esteem* – power, titles, status symbols, promotion
→ *self-actualization* – challenging work, developing new skills

Herzberg's 'two-factor theory' was based on a survey of what made managers feel good or bad about their job. He discovered that the factors which created dissatisfaction about the job related to the *context* within which the job was done. He termed these factors **'hygiene' factors**. However, ensuring that these factors were met did not result in positive satisfaction.

The factors contributing to positive job satisfaction related more to the *content* of the job. The presence of each of these factors (motivators) was capable of causing high levels of satisfaction, though their absence did not cause great dissatisfaction.

The implications for the practising manager were twofold. First, to ensure that the hygiene factors are met adequately to avoid dissatisfaction, but not to expect these to motivate employees. Second, to provide the motivators to create positive job satisfaction.

Exam questions   answers: page 108

1   To what extent does the Japanese approach to the management of employees seem related to Herzberg's theory of job satisfaction? (30 min)

2   Herzberg believes pay is important but does not motivate. Why? (15 min)

Don't forget

Motivators could therefore include achievement, recognition, responsibility, promotion, work itself, growth.

Watch out!

Be aware that higher order needs may be satisfied by activities outside of work.

Checkpoint 4

How have Victor Vroom and Edgar Schein contributed to our understanding of motivation?

Check the net

Use the search engine to look for Frederick Herzberg. There are many good sites which also often consider other theorists.

Checkpoint 5

Can you list the hygiene factors?

Watch out!

Herzberg also made a distinction between movement and motivation. *Movement* occurred when an employee did something, motivation occurred when he wanted to do it.

Examiner's secrets

Make sure you know, and can apply, Herzberg's analysis.

Motivation in practice

It is important for the practising manager to find out what the needs of his employees are and the ways of satisfying them. Otherwise the efficiency of the whole firm may be affected. Yet the needs of individuals vary considerably and managers may have problems in introducing a system of motivation that satisfies everyone.

Money as a motivator

It is not always clear how important money is as a *motivator*. We can distinguish between the *need* to have a job, where money may be a key factor, and *motivation* within a job. Here money may be far less important and may have little influence on how hard employees work. However where pay is seen as being too low it may become a source of dissatisfaction. Conversely, where pay is seen as a sign of success and a status symbol, it may act as an important motivator.

Many firms try to motivate workers by the use of **incentive schemes**. For direct workers, some form of piecework reward system is possible. Non-direct workers may be rewarded by some form of merit or performance-related pay.

An alternative approach is **profit sharing**. Like shareholders, workers are now paid an annual dividend, which depends on the level of profits. The benefits of profit sharing are

→ it does not discourage teamwork
→ it makes the employee look at profits in a positive light
→ employees may develop a strong sense of identity with the firm

Job design and motivation

Herzberg's work pointed to the importance of workers enjoying their jobs. Yet many jobs today are dull and uninteresting because they have been reduced to small or repetitive tasks. However, it is possible to restructure work so that it becomes less monotonous.

Job rotation
Staff are trained in a number of different jobs so they can be rotated. This does not really make the work any more interesting but it can give the workers greater variety. From the employer's point of view there is greater labour flexibility. Frequent changes, though, may be counterproductive as social relationships are disrupted.

Job enlargement
This involves widening the duties of the employee, thus making the job less repetitive. The aim isn't to make the employee work harder but to increase the variety of the job.

Job enrichment
This involves the worker in the *vertical extension* of the job. The additional tasks given to him/her carry greater responsibility than those he/she is doing at the moment. Thus with job enrichment the worker may be given responsibility for planning and prioritizing work.

Watch out!

You should be aware that motivational factors vary between people and even within one person over time.

Links

Herzberg again! See page 93.

Checkpoint 1

Many managers enjoy 'fringe benefits'. Explain this term.

Checkpoint 2

How does performance-related pay work?

Example

The John Lewis Partnership pays annual dividends to employees.

Watch out!

A major problem of some payment systems is that they discourage teamwork.

Checkpoint 3

Job rotation and enlargement are both examples of the *horizontal extension of the job*. Explain this term.

Checkpoint 4

Is *empowerment* a motivator?

Teamworking

This involves employees working together in a small team to complete a *whole task* rather than just one part of it. The most famous example was the Volvo car plant in Kalmar, Sweden where, under a production line manufacturing system, absenteeism and labour turnover were very high. By creating *workstations* at which a team of workers built a complete sub-assembly, absenteeism and labour turnover were reduced and the plant became the most profitable in Sweden.

For the *workers* the system meant that they had more control over their work, it gave them more interesting jobs, a sense of responsibility and greater social interaction. For the *employers* it meant a more motivated and productive workforce, as well as greater labour flexibility.

The jargon

Teamworking is sometimes referred to as establishing 'autonomous work groups'.

Symptoms and causes of poor motivation ●●●

It is important to distinguish between the symptom and cause of poor motivation. The *symptom* is the outward manifestation of the problem. The *cause* is the reason the problem exists. Thus if workers limit output, this is the symptom of a deeper problem. The cause may be a disagreement over incentive payments or that the workers are concerned about redundancies. Some of the more common symptoms and causes are listed below.

Symptoms	Causes
poor quality work	job insecurity
failure to meet deadlines	poor pay and working conditions
high absenteeism	monotonous work
high labour turnover	poor communications
disciplinary problems	not part of social group
sullen agreement to orders	changes to work groups

Checkpoint 5

How can *culture* affect the motivation to work?

Checkpoint 6

Many senior managers are provided with share options. Few other employees are. Assess the implications of this policy.

Examiner's secrets

When analyzing a motivational issue you should emphasize that whilst theories may help you understand the issues, motivation is really a very complex issue.

Exam question   answer: page 109

A large supermarket has adopted a number of different measures to motivate its employees. Critically evaluate the measures shown below in the light of any motivational theories with which you are familiar.

(a) Listening groups to discuss how the store is run and improve customer service. There is also a suggestion scheme with financial benefits given to individuals whose ideas are adopted. (15 min)

(b) The store gives a 'Team of the Month' award to the group that has the best record for sales, customer service, attendance and stockholding. During the following month they wear a special badge and have their photos displayed instore. They will also be entered for the Team of the Year competition. (15 min)

(c) The store also operates a contributory pension scheme, an annual share incentive scheme based on company profits as well as a share save scheme allowing employees to save to buy shares at a discounted rate. (15 min)

Examiner's secrets

'Critically evaluate' is asking *to what extent* do these measures accord with what would be expected having regard to the theory.

Leadership

Leadership is a key managerial role in any setting. It has been defined as the process by which individual and group activities are influenced towards organizational goals. A major issue is why some people are more successful than others in getting people to follow them.

Checkpoint 1

Leaders often gain subordinates' compliance because of some *power levers*. Explain the following power levers: reward, coercive, organizational (legitimate), personal, expert.

The jargon

These different approaches are sometimes described as *'styles'* of leadership.

Classifying leaders

The basic *approaches* to leadership include the following

→ *Autocratic leaders* These leaders make the decisions which others carry out. There is no employee involvement in decision-making. This style is most suitable for use in a crisis situation.
→ *Democratic leaders* These leaders involve the group in setting the objectives, devising the strategies and allocating the work. This style can produce a high level of commitment and 'ownership' of the work.
→ *Laissez-faire leaders* These leaders give little direction so that responsibility lies with the group.

It is also possible to categorize leaders on their *attitude* to getting the job done.

→ *Task-orientated leaders* Primarily concerned with the planning, organizing and output of work – i.e. 'getting the job done'.
→ *People-orientated leaders* They are more concerned about the responses and feelings of their subordinates.

Examiner's secrets

Trait theory may be criticized for ignoring
→ the task situation
→ the followers' needs

Trait theory

This starts from the assumption that there is a set of characteristics (*traits*) which every good leader has. However the findings from studies have been inconclusive with individuals regarded as strong leaders, exhibiting remarkably varied characteristics. Nevertheless researchers have generally agreed on some of the characteristics involved in 'good leadership'

→ intellectual skills   → interpersonal skills
→ task-based knowledge   → task motivation

However, no *single* characteristic has been identified as essential.

Action point

Find out about McGregor's Theory X, Theory Y, then think about why managers might use the autocratic or democratic styles of leadership.

Behavioural theory

This approach looks at leadership *behaviour*. The change of approach is significant – leadership behaviour can be learnt or modified. Thus individuals may, through training and experience, be capable of undertaking a leadership role.

Lewin's research in the 1930s concentrated on *group behaviour* under autocratic, democratic and laissez-faire styles of leadership. The results are summarized as follows

Style	Results
Autocratic	Group didn't plan at all. Considerable aggression amongst members. Output high when leader around, otherwise much lower. Quality levels low.
Democratic	Level of motivation high. Group worked well together. Work output and quality was high in all situations.
Laissez-faire	High levels of frustration amongst members. Group did not work well together. Output and quality levels were low.

One interesting fact is that when the leaders changed groups but maintained their management style, the behaviour of the group quickly changed to reflect that new style. Lewin and others have concluded that in many situations the *democratic* leadership style was the most effective.

Contingency approaches

These relate leadership to the situations in which it is being exercised. Thus a leadership style which is appropriate for one situation may not be appropriate in another. A good leader, then, is one who can identify the 'forces' in the situation and select the right style. Tannenbaum and Schmidt have set out a simple model to illustrate the options available. The right leadership style will depend on issues such as: **forces in the leader**, e.g. willingness to delegate, confidence in subordinates; **forces in the subordinates**, e.g. need for responsibility, ability to handle problems; **forces in the situation**, e.g. importance and complexity, time and money constraints.

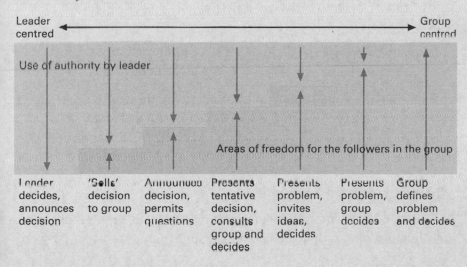

Leader decides, announces decision	'Sells' decision to group	Announces decision, permits questions	Presents tentative decision, consults group and decides	Presents problem, invites ideas, decides	Presents problem, group decides	Group defines problem and decides

Exam question   answer: page 109

The productivity of a workforce may be influenced by the leadership style of the manager.

Identify the kind of leadership style you would expect to find in the following situations and explain your reasoning (30 min)

(a) a research and development department

(b) an armed force group in war

(c) a youth club planning an outing

Don't forget

Leadership style may have an important impact upon morale and motivation.

Checkpoint 2

What do you understand by the term 'bureaucratic leadership'?

Watch out!

The *democratic* leadership style is the most popular today, but there are circumstances where it is inappropriate.

Don't forget

Every leader has 'power levers' to ensure compliance with his orders. They include the power to reward, the power to punish, personal power (charisma), superior knowledge and expertise, and higher position in the organization.

Examiner's secrets

Try to be aware of the characteristics of the various styles of leadership. Be prepared to apply this knowledge to particular situations.

Communication

Within an organization effective communication is important because it enables the firm to co-ordinate activities, give clear instructions to workers and establish satisfactory relationships with external parties.

Links

See the chart on page 90.

Don't forget

Managers will spend 80% of their time communicating with other people in order to do their job.

Checkpoint 1

Give examples of mechanisms that have been used for upward, downward and lateral communication.

Examiner's secrets

Advantages of the *informal* communication network include
→ it is fast
→ it is normally accurate
→ it can be used by senior managers for floating new ideas and obtaining the reaction of the workforce.

Checkpoint 2

What are the disadvantages of the 'grapevine'?

Checkpoint 3

Give examples of how each of these communication media could be used.

Checkpoint 4

Explain the term 'all channel communication network'.

Formal and informal communication ●●●

In any organization there exists an *organizational structure* which can be illustrated by an **organization chart**. This establishes both a command structure and a system through which the information needed to plan, organize, direct and control the activities of the organization is passed; i.e. it shows the *manager's communication network*.

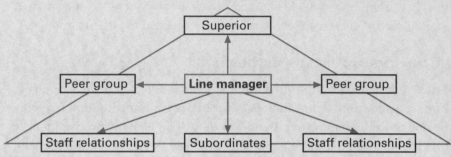

Downward communication is emphasized by the chart but there is also significant *upward* and *lateral* communication.

Upward communication provides senior management with information on items such as progress reports, quality circles, consultation committees and grievances.

Horizontal communication is important because it enables departments to

→ co-ordinate tasks → share information
→ solve problems → resolve conflicts

Alongside the *formal* communication network there also exists an *informal* one arising through the social relationships of employees. Where the formal communication channels of the organization are ineffective, the informal system will assume great importance.

Communication media ●●●

Whether an organization is communicating externally or internally there are a number of ways in which communication can take place. They are

→ written → oral
→ visual → electronic

Within each of these broad categories there are various forms the communication can take. Thus, *electronic communication* may arise through the use of local networks, facsimile or email.

In *selecting* the form of communication you should consider

→ cost → security
→ accuracy → speed
→ distance involved → efficiency
→ need for a written record

Barriers to good communication

Despite the importance of good communication within an organization often very little is done to ensure that communication is effective. In practice the barriers to good communication can be grouped into those resulting from the following problems.

Problems with words

Most people know and use only a few of the words available in the English language. Unfortunately, for many reasons we don't use the same words. Additionally, the same word may have alternative meanings. 'Jargon', because of its specialist nature, will not be understood except to those within that particular trade or profession.

Problems with perception

The way we interpret a communication is often affected by our personal feelings. For example, we often stereotype people. In an organization it could be 'them' and 'us'. In this case we are very much more likely to accept information from one of 'us' rather than from one of 'them'. Equally, our mood may affect the way we interpret a piece of information. In a negative frame of mind we would interpret information negatively. Finally, where we face too much information to absorb we often take in the information we want to hear and filter out that which is unwelcome.

Problems with distance

We are much less likely to communicate with people from whom we are separated *geographically*. An organization will always try to bring together in a single location those people whose work is interconnected.

Status within an organization may also be a barrier. Thus research has shown that people with a low status within an organization have difficulty communicating with those of higher status.

Examiner's secrets

In analyzing communication problems within a firm you should also consider leadership, motivational issues and organizational structure.

Checkpoint 5

How would you interpret the phrase 'the drill is boring'?

Don't forget

With face-to-face communication you also have to consider the impact of *non-verbal signals*.

Checkpoint 6

Give three examples of non-verbal communication.

Example

Open-plan offices are meant to encourage communication between different sections and departments.

Don't forget

The larger and more complex that a business becomes, the greater is the need for effective communication but the more difficult it is to achieve it.

Examiner's secrets

Make sure you read any quotations carefully. Examiners' reports frequently comment on candidates reading the information too quickly.

Exam question   answer: page 110

An extract from a consultant's report concluded:

'Despite a significant increase in size over the last decade, performance indicators from within the firm indicate that communications are good. The introduction of a "flatter" organization structure may however affect this. We are also concerned with the speed that new communications technology has been introduced.'

(a) List FOUR examples of new communication technology.

(b) Explain the link between size and communication within an organization.

(c) Explain TWO advantages of new communications technology.

(d) Explain TWO disadvantages of new communications technology. (30 min)

Collective bargaining

It is in the interests of both workers and management to avoid the problems caused by conflicts of interest. Collective bargaining is the process of negotiation between unions and employers about the major areas of conflict, i.e. working conditions and wages.

Trade unions and employers' associations

The principal purpose of **trade unions** is to protect the interests of the workers who are its members. Their objectives include

→ improvements in pay and working conditions
→ security of income and employment
→ protecting members against arbitrary management practices
→ worker involvement in decision-making

Trade unions also act at a *political* level and aim to

→ improve social security
→ ensure a fair share of income and wealth for employees
→ encourage industrial democracy

In 1979 trade union membership peaked at 13.5 million. Since that time membership has fallen to about 7 million because of

→ contraction of traditional areas of unionism (e.g. manufacturing)
→ inability to recruit in service sector
→ inability to recruit women
→ growth of part-time employment
→ growth of anti-union legislation

Employers' associations represent an attempt by employers to offset the power of the trade unions. They negotiate with trade unions on behalf of their members and also act as the industry's voice with the government and other national bodies. The Confederation of British Industry (CBI) represents many employers within the manufacturing industry.

Collective bargaining

This is the process by which the workers, through their trade union representatives, negotiate changes to their pay and working conditions with the employer or his/her representative. There are two important levels of collective bargaining.

→ *National or industry-wide level*   Many groups in the public sector have their pay determined this way.
→ *Local level*   National agreements have fallen out of favour as governments have tried to encourage agreements which reflect local rather than national conditions.

The state tries to avoid interfering in the collective bargaining and industrial relations process, believing that this is a private matter best left to the individual parties to sort out. However the state has intervened to provide

Watch out!

Some companies which are opposed to trade unions may still encourage the development of *staff associations* to represent the interests of their workers. Employers may consider these to be more accommodating.

Checkpoint 1

Give examples of the following types of union: craft, industrial, general, white collar.

Checkpoint 2

Outline the role of the TUC and the CBI.

Checkpoint 3

Give two examples of groups which have their pay determined
(a) nationally
(b) locally

Checkpoint 4

Distinguish between *procedural* and *substantive* agreements.

- legislation designed to protect the interests of the workers, e.g. anti-discrimination legislation
- legislation to curb the power of trade unions, e.g. calling a secret ballot before taking strike action
- institutions to arbitrate between conflicting interests. The most important of these is ACAS – the state-funded but independent Advisory, Conciliation and Arbitration Service.

Industrial action ●●●

Conflict occurs within the workplace primarily because workers and management may have different objectives.

Employee objectives	*Management objectives*
employment security	cost control/reduction
maximize earnings	profit maximization
good working conditions	the right to manage
industrial democracy	to satisfy shareholders
union representation	corporate growth

Industrial action may be taken by employees where trade unions and the employers cannot resolve a dispute. Methods of industrial action include work to rule, go-slow, overtime ban, strikes.

The advantage of the first three forms of action is that, whilst causing considerable disruption to the employer's operations, they are relatively cheap to the union and its members. Strikes are normally a sanction of last resort when all other forms of action have failed. The use of the strike as a form of industrial action was limited in the 1980s, so that unofficial or 'lightning' strikes are now illegal.

Strikes have many damaging effects upon employers including

- loss of output
- loss of customers
- harm to reputation
- loss of worker co-operation
- reduced sales revenue
- cash flow problems
- disruption of work
- demotivation

Union bargaining power can be defined in terms of a ratio

$$\frac{\text{employer costs of disagreeing to union demand}}{\text{employer costs of agreeing to union demand}}$$

The higher the ratio, the greater the union bargaining power. So where stocks are high and/or sales are low, the union will have little bargaining power.

Exam question   answer: page 111

'Strikes are a thing of the past.'

(a) What do you think are the grounds for this statement? (10 min)

(b) To what extent does a reduction in strikes represent an improvement in industrial relations within the UK? (20 min)

Check the net

For up-to-date information on trade union activities, consult
www.tuc.org.uk
www.tgwu.org.uk
www.unison.org.uk

Don't forget

Be aware that a breakdown in industrial relations may first become apparent through low morale, poor productivity and higher labour turnover.

Checkpoint 5

Industrial action doesn't only affect the firm. What are the implications for: the economy as a whole, customers, other firms?

Don't forget

Employers are also capable of imposing sanctions, for example refusal to negotiate, lock-outs and ultimately dismissal.

Watch out!

Firms might actually welcome a strike where stocks are high or sales low!

Examiner's secrets

A recent examiner's report stated some candidates had interpreted 'to what extent' as 'how could'. To achieve high marks you must answer the question set.

Industrial democracy

Industrial democracy is a general term used to express the idea that workers should be allowed to take part in the decision-making process of the firm. The aim is to create a platform through which matters of common interest to the employer and employees can be discussed. In doing so the motivation of workers may be improved and management may draw upon a source of knowledge and experience not normally available.

Examiner's secrets

You should be able to explain the value of industrial democracy through motivational theories.

Example

John Lewis Partnership and the Co-operative Retail Society are the best known British examples.

Watch out!

One major problem faced by co-operatives is raising finance for expansion.

Don't forget

As a worker director, a trade unionist may have to accept decisions that are against his members' interests.

Checkpoint 1

Outline the circumstances necessary for worker participation to succeed.

Watch out!

In many UK organizations collective bargaining is being expanded to cover issues normally dealt with by joint consultation.

Links

For more on the EU Social Chapter see pages 17 and 23.

Worker control

This refers to a situation where workers are the *owners* of the business and workers' committees are actively involved in deciding policy, and in appointing and controlling managers. In Western Europe there are numerous examples of worker control. Most successful examples are small because, once the **worker co-operatives** grows beyond about 20 members, some delegation to specialist managers is necessary. However, large scale co-operative enterprise is possible. The Mondragon co-operative enterprise in Northern Spain employs over 20,000 workers in a variety of co-operative ventures.

Worker directors

Here employees are allowed to elect representatives to the Board of Directors. These **worker directors** will take part in discussions representing the views of the workers.

In the UK, attempts to extend industrial democracy through the use of worker directors have not been particularly successful. Many managers believe that workers have little to contribute to policymaking decisions whilst trade unionists feel that acting as worker directors can undermine their position as worker representatives. Nevertheless, worker directors may improve employer/employee relationships through better communication with the workforce and closer worker involvement in decision-making.

In Germany the use of worker directors is required by law as part of their *two-tier board system*. In large companies the ratio of worker to shareholder directors may be as high as 50:50. However, the balance of voting power is still with the shareholders. Moreover there is no employee representation on the Management Board.

Joint consultation

This, as its name implies, is consultation between workers and management on matters of common interest that fall outside the area of collective bargaining. Within the UK **joint consultation** is widely practised in the public sector but not in the private sector.

In many countries joint consultation takes the form of a *works council*. This is a committee of employer and employee representatives. Under the **European Social Chapter** larger companies operating in two or more countries must now create a *European Works Council*. The aim of the legislation is to ensure that employees, as stakeholders in the business, receive information and are consulted on matters of interest to them. The aim of the legislation is to make it more difficult for a multinational operating in a number of countries to manipulate pay structures and working practices by the threat to move jobs from one country to another.

A European Works Council will consist of at least one elected member from each European Union country that the company operates in. There are also representatives of company management. The council would normally meet once a year to discuss matters such as

- → employment plans
- → future investments
- → business environment
- → new working practices
- → organizational structure
- → health and safety

Quality circles

A **quality circle** is a group of five to ten workers who would normally work for the same supervisor. The members are volunteers and meet regularly, in company time, to identify, discuss and formulate solutions to work-based problems. The solutions are then suggested to management.

The type of issue typically considered by the quality circle include

- → cost reductions
- → quality
- → safety issues
- → equipment usage

Quality circles are a means of achieving employee participation on the shop floor. The benefits are

- → circle members have a greater awareness of shop floor problems
- → circle members have greater confidence in tackling problems
- → improved productivity/quality via sharing of ideas
- → improved motivation amongst circle members

Teamworking

Production is organized into large units of work. Teams of people will work on these units of work (e.g. a washing machine), making decisions about output and who does which job. Having more control over their working lives is thought to improve motivation.

Checkpoint 2

Outline the benefits and problems arising from joint consultation.

Don't forget

Job enrichment and teamwork are also examples of employee involvement in decision-making (see pages 94–5).

Example

Quality circles reflect the Japanese concept of kaizen or continuous improvement.

Check the net

For information on this and other human resource issues try
www.ipol.co.uk
www.hrnetwork.co.uk

The jargon

Autonomous work groups are employees who are given the power to decide how best to complete a task, whether there should be a team leader, and who does which job.

Examiner's secrets

A recent examiner's report stated that many candidates lost marks through lack of exam question practice! Always get plenty of experience by going over past exam questions.

Exam questions   answers: page 111

1   F. W. Taylor said that in any job there was a planning element and a doing element. It was the manager's role to plan and make decisions while workers do the job.

    In the light of this statement how can moves toward employee involvement in decision-making be justified? (30 min)

2   Briefly discuss the criteria for the successful introduction of quality circles. (15 min)

Trends in employment

As the social and economic structure of the economy changes, so too do the supply and demand for labour. The trends we will consider here are the role of women in employment, the concept of the flexible workforce (including outsourcing) and the move to self-employment.

Women in the workforce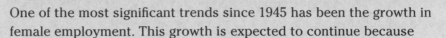

One of the most significant trends since 1945 has been the growth in female employment. This growth is expected to continue because

→ smaller families and labour-saving household items mean women have more spare time
→ it is now more socially acceptable to be a working wife and mother
→ growth of one-parent families where mother has to work
→ growth of career women using childcare rather than staying at home
→ gender discrimination now unlawful
→ growth in part-time work allows women to combine work and family responsibilities

Not only has the *supply* of women to the labour market increased, so too has the *demand* for female employment

→ there are many more women now with degrees and diplomas, which makes them more valuable in the labour market
→ growth in the service sector has provided many jobs that are more attractive to women

Despite the Equal Pay Act, women's gross average wages are, roughly, only about 75% of men's. Whilst some of this may be due to sex discrimination, women are more likely to take jobs that are less well paid and part-time or refuse to work overtime or unsocial hours.

Labour flexibility

Rapid changes in technology and consumer tastes have made the future far more uncertain for firms. The response of many firms has been to seek a more flexible workforce. This has taken several forms.

Flexitime – allows workers some degree of control over when they work. Extra hours will be put in at busy times of the year and fewer at other times.

Multiskilling – whereby workers are trained to undertake a variety of jobs. Workers are thus able to cover for absent colleagues.

A more fundamental way of introducing flexibility into the workforce has been to divide workers into 'core' and 'periphery'.

Core workers have characteristics such as

→ small in number   → well paid   → well educated
→ highly trained with permanent contract → career path employees

These are the employees who are vital to the firm. They are often difficult to recruit on the labour market. In return for the benefits they receive they may be required to move jobs or move location.

Periphery workers – Charles Handy divides the periphery into two separate parts, namely the flexible workforce and the contractual fringe.

The flexible workforce   This consists of full-time and part-time employees. The jobs these workers do are relatively routine, have few career paths and less job security. Labour turnover is quite high but the workers are easily replaced. The fact that labour turnover tends to be high provides the firm with the flexibility to adjust to changing economic conditions. Thus if the firm experiences a drop in sales, labour turnover will quickly reduce the size of the peripheral workforce.

Example

Retailing, catering and the health services tend to use such workers.

The contractual fringe   This has developed as a result of firms critically reviewing the extent of their business activities. Many firms have decided to concentrate on their core activities, that is those activities in which they have a particular specialism. Other activities which were previously done within the firm are now bought in. Such **outsourcing** of operations may include marketing research, recruitment and product development and gives the firm greater flexibility to meet changing market conditions. For example, outsourced activities can be bought in at short notice, as and when required.

Outsourcing is based on the belief that the economies of scale gained as the firm grows bigger are more than offset by the diseconomies of co-ordination, communication and control.

Examiner's secrets

The key to the success of *outsourcing* is in correctly identifying the core activities.

Links

For more on *economies of scale* see pages 22, 114.

Self-employment ●●●

The number of people in self-employment has virtually doubled since 1979 to reach 15% of today's workforce. Many workers made redundant over the past two decades have used their redundancy money to start a small business.

In the 1990s self-employment received an extra boost as a result of firms deciding to outsource their non-core activities. These activities were often sold to the existing workers and the firm then bought back the services they required.

The jargon

This is often called a *Management Buy-out (MBO)*.

Part-time employment ●●●

This is of interest to business as it allows for more flexible work patterns. It also allows the individual to balance personal needs with work. In October 2002 there were 7.1 million people working part time. Many of these were young people in higher education or 'working mothers'.

Links

For more on employment and unemployment see page 8.

Exam question   answer: page 112

(a) Explain the use of staff appraisal by many profit-making firms. (15 min)

(b) You have been appointed Personnel Manager of a medium-sized firm. It is apparent that the current staff appraisal system is resented by employees. They believe that their work is being criticized and their job security threatened.

   Write a short report to senior management commenting on the possible causes of the problem. You are also required to outline how you would ensure that in future employees regard the appraisal process more positively. (30 min)

Examiner's secrets

A *report* may contain the following
Title
Contents page
Objectives
Background
Methodology
Analysis
Evaluation
Executive summary
Appendices

Answers
People in organizations

Workforce planning

Checkpoints

1 A *job description* provides you with information such as
   - job title
   - to whom you are responsible
   - for whom you are responsible
   - your roles and duties

   With this information the applicant knows how they fit into the organization.

   A *person* or *job specification* goes beyond a job description by detailing the mental and physical abilities required of the jobholder. Thus a prison officer is expected to have qualities such as humanity, flexibility, enthusiasm and a sense of humour. A prospective applicant will be able to consider whether they have the attributes to do the job.

2 Training may be either 'on the job' or 'off the job'. Apart from induction training, training may also involve
   - basic skills needed to do the job
   - retraining – as part of a redeployment package or updating of skills
   - management trainees – intensive training for university graduates
   - management skills and operations – training in new management techniques

3 A firm can avoid compulsory redundancies by calling for volunteers. Voluntary redundancy is often encouraged through financial incentives such as redundancy payments or enhanced pension arrangements.

   Another opportunity is redeployment. This is often accompanied by a freeze on recruitment throughout the organization and retraining of those who are being redeployed.

   The other method is to rely upon natural wastage. In some industries labour turnover is high and this would therefore not be too expensive.

Exam questions

1 (a) • less costly
   - person learns in context
   - working with 'expert' in actual job
   (b) • number of accidents and their causes
   - rate of labour turnover
   - ability to promote from within
   - work quality
   - productivity
   (c) • improves profitability
   - improves staff motivation
   - improves skills
   - develops new skills
   - improves flexibility
   - reduces accidents

2 Points to make include
   - shop floor motivation
   - prevents 'them and us' situation developing
   - builds on expertise within the organization
   - ensures equal opportunities
   - need for academic intellectual ability
   - need for fresh ideas, 'new blood'

Workforce performance

Checkpoints

1 *Voluntary turnover* is a situation where an employee leaves the firm for reasons such as better pay, better prospects or job dissatisfaction. This is often used as a key indicator of discontent in the organization.

   Involuntary turnover occurs for unavoidable reasons such as death, ill-health, pregnancy or retirement.

   Management action occurs for reasons such as redundancy, misconduct or poor performance.

2 The causes of high absenteeism need to be investigated. Once the cause(s) have been identified some of the following actions may be appropriate
   - flexi-time
   - job enrichment
   - job enlargement
   - job rotation
   - improved working conditions
   - changed work processes
   - attendance bonuses

3 The more price elastic the demand for the product, the bigger the expansion of demand resulting from any price cut via improved productivity.

Exam question

The most appropriate form of communication would be an internal memo. You should ensure that it is properly drawn up.

(a) The facts should be summarized in a way that makes for easy assimilation. A table comparing labour turnover of this firm against other similar firms over two years would be appropriate.

(b) You should explain the following causes of labour turnover
   - poor recruitment policy
   - lack of motivation or effective leadership
   - lack of social contact
   - low pay

- poor working conditions
- more attractive opportunities elsewhere

(c) You should develop points around the following consequences of high turnover

Negative consequences
- cost of recruiting replacements
- cost of training new employees
- loss of productivity

Positive consequences (unlikely in this case but not excluded by the question)
- new workers bring new ideas with them
- can employ workers with required skills

Examiner's secrets

You should be aware that this is an important examination topic – particularly in case study examinations where it is linked to problems of change, change management, motivation, leadership and communication.

Organizational structure

Checkpoints

1 With regard to *managerial skills* the major differences are
- conceptual skills are used far more by senior managers
- technical skills are used far more by junior managers
- senior managers have a longer-time horizon than junior managers

With regard to *managerial functions*
- senior managers spend more time planning and organizing than their juniors
- junior managers spend more time directing and controlling

2 Mintzberg's managerial roles are

Interpersonal	*Informational*	*Decisional*
• figurehead	• monitor	• entrepreneur
• leader	• disseminator	• negotiator
• liaison	• spokesperson	• disturbance handler
		• resource allocator

3 A manager might not delegate work because
- he/she is not happy delegating
- the work is too important
- the work needs to be closely supervised
- the subordinate doesn't have the knowledge or skills necessary
- the subordinate is unwilling to accept responsibility

4 *Delegation* refers to the extent individual managers assign duties to subordinates.

Decentralization is the extent to which the organization as a whole pushes authority and responsibility down within that organization.

Exam question

(a) *Consultation* is the process of asking the views of those who will be affected by the decision.

Delegation is the process of passing authority for action to subordinates. Note that accountability remains with the superior.

Examiner's secrets

To obtain the highest marks you should explain where decision-making power resides.

(b) Short-term
- organizational change is always unsettling and may result in lower productivity and higher labour turnover
- increased costs arising from communication, consultation and training problems

Longer-term
- faster decision-making, closer to the problem
- effect depends on the quality, attitudes and training given to the staff with greater responsibilities
- does company culture tolerate mistakes?
- delegation can be highly motivating (link to theorists!)
- some staff may be demotivated if they do not receive delegated work

Your conclusion might mention that where change is introduced properly there will be short-term costs but gains in the longer term.

Examiner's secrets

Be aware that in any question about the impact of 'something' on a firm, industry or the economy there are likely to be short- and longer-term implications. Make sure you consider both time frames.

Motivation in theory

Checkpoints

1 The Gilbreths made significant contributions to what is now known as method study – though it is still often referred to by the old term of time and motion study.

First the work being studied was broken down into very small parts. Then it was decided how each of these tasks should be carried out by timing each action and the amount of effort required. Once the new method was introduced no employee was allowed to use any other method. With this approach the separation of the planning element from the doing element was complete.

For many workers method study was seen as 'making them work harder for the same money'. Management, however looked on it as making the worker work more effectively, not harder. Nevertheless time and motion employees and their work very quickly became a major cause of industrial unrest.

2 The *Hawthorne effect* is the improvement in efficiency brought about by better human relations rather than as a result of improved technology or working conditions.

3 Maslow's ideas were criticized as follows
(i) satisfaction of needs is not the only motivator; thus group allegiances may be a strong influence

(ii) some people have very low aspirations – particularly where their experience of life is limited

(iii) some people are motivated by higher-level needs even when lower needs aren't met (the hungry artist!)

(iv) higher-level needs may be obtained through social activities rather than work

4 Victor Vroom developed the value-expectancy theory. This stated that there were two factors that determined the degree of motivation, namely

- the value of the anticipated reward
- the likelihood of achieving it

Thus managers will find subordinates motivated where they prize the reward and believe that it is attainable. Conversely if the subordinate does not value the reward (e.g. promotion) or does not believe it is attainable they will not be motivated.

However it is unlikely that individuals always act so rationally. Edgar Schein puts forward the theory of complex man. He argues that people are motivated by a wide range of needs at any one time. In any individual these needs form a complex pattern. This pattern of needs, though, is constantly changing through experience. The managers' job is to optimize the motivational forces within their staff. In practice this means they need to be aware of

- individuals and their needs
- the demands and rewards of jobs together with the performance of staff
- the relevant styles of leadership and the prevailing organizational culture

5 *Hygiene factors* are those elements of working life that if missing have the potential to cause dissatisfaction. They include salary, working conditions, security and status as well as oversupervision.

Exam questions

1 Introduction: brief explanation of
- Japanese approach to employee management
- Herzberg's theory of job satisfaction

Main content

Hygiene factors

(a) single-status salaries, common conditions of service, uniforms and exercise

(b) lifetime employment

Motivator factors

(a) involvement, quality circles

(b) continuous improvement

Not mentioned by Herzberg:
teamwork/human relations

Examiner's secrets

The analysis marks are awarded for identifying ways in which Herzberg and Japanese management practices are related. The evaluation marks are awarded for assessing the extent to which the two are related.

2 Herzberg believes pay is a hygiene not a motivating factor. A hygiene factor is something that causes dissatisfaction if it is absent but does not motivate when present. The importance of this is that if a person feels he or she is underpaid this will cause dissatisfaction. Where a person is paid highly this is soon taken for granted and therefore does not motivate.

Examiner's secrets

Again, a familiarity with the principles and applications of Herzberg's analysis is important here.

Motivation in practice

Checkpoints

1 These are rewards other than income. They may take the form of a company car or an expense account. Banks and building societies offer low interest loans and mortgages. Transport companies often offer cheap travel. In all cases the aim is to encourage consumer loyalty.

2 Performance-related pay works through, establishing individual objectives, establishing rewards, and measuring performance against objectives. Many firms have found that PRP causes jealousy and employee unrest.

3 With *job rotation* additional or different work is provided. It is of the same order of difficulty and does not give the worker any more responsibility. Conversely *job enrichment* is referred to as a vertical extension of the job because the jobholder has more responsibility than before. An example of job enrichment is asking a production worker to check the quality of his own output.

4 *Empowerment* is rather like delegation. The significant difference is that the empowered worker has the authority to decide what the task should be as well as the authority to carry out that task. Empowerment motivates because it gives the worker extra responsibility.

5 The *culture* of a group may be such that it supports or undermines organizational objectives. Thus a group may not even try to achieve a specified output level in order to obtain a bonus as it would conflict with the group norms.

Equally the culture of an organization may encourage an employee to undertake extra tasks when they have spare time. In many organizations, though, the work culture is weak and does not encourage people to make good use of company time.

6 Depending upon the nature of the target set, senior managers are likely to be highly motivated by the offer of share options. Where other employees are not provided with similar or equivalent incentives they may become demotivated. A divide between the senior managers and the rest of the workforce, 'them and us' will develop. There will be no incentive for the 'us' group to strive to achieve organizational objectives – their value has not been recognized.

Exam question

(a) *Listening groups*

This is a formal group created by management to assess store operation. According to Mayo groups provide individuals with a sense of identity or belonging. Equally, in Maslow's theory this could provide for either safety or social needs. Again, according to Herzberg you could argue this was a hygiene factor (inter-personal relationships and security) which will cause dissatisfaction if not present.

It is also possible to argue that membership of the group satisfies some of Maslow's higher level needs or Herzberg's motivators in that the group are involved in important and challenging work which may gain the recognition of management and other groups through recommendations for changes being accepted and implemented.

Suggestion scheme/financial benefits

Money would normally be considered a lower level need, according to Maslow, satisfying physiological and safety needs. Equally, in the Herzberg two-factor theory a lack of money would normally be considered a dissatisfier. In this situation though, where money is given in recognition of ideas being implemented it could be argued (as above) that this satisfies higher level needs or acts as a motivator.

(b) *Team of the Month award*

Such an award gives the individual and the group self-respect as well as the respect of other people. In this sense it is a higher order need according to Maslow and a motivator in Herzberg's terminology. The work of Vroom, though, might suggest that this idea could be demotivating for some groups. For example, even though the anticipated reward is valued, if the group believes that they will not gain the award then they will not be motivated.

(c) *Contributory pension scheme/share incentive scheme/share save scheme*

All these relate to the context of the work rather than the content and thus are lower-order needs or dissatisfiers providing for physiological, safety or social needs.

Leadership

Checkpoints

1 *Reward power* This is the ability to offer pay increases, promotion or the granting of other privileges to those who follow orders.

Coercive power This is the perception that a leader has the power to punish those who do not follow instructions. Punishments might include dismissal, demotion, reprimand or the withdrawal of overtime or allocation of unattractive work.

Organizational or legitimate power The right to give orders stems from a person's position in the organizational hierarchy.

Personal power This is based upon the characteristics of the individual. Charisma and charm are important. So too are physical characteristics of height, size and strength.

Expert power This arises from having superior knowledge and expertise. This may relate to a functional area such as marketing or more general problem-solving skills.

2 Bureaucratic leadership emphasizes the importance of following rules and procedures. Many people will be frustrated by the inability to exercise any form of initiative. Unlike the autocratic leader though, the bureaucrat is unable to exercise leadership qualities in situations where the rules and procedures are inapplicable.

Exam question

(a) The employees in a research and development department are assumed to be highly qualified, self-motivated professionals. The nature of their work and their interest in it lie behind this assumption. In these circumstances the leadership style most appropriate would be free rein or laissez-faire. The nature of the task will be outlined by the leader who will then allow the subordinates to take control.

(b) This is a situation where someone must take control. There is no time to open up discussion and involve subordinates. This must be a situation for autocratic leadership where an order is made and obeyed by the subordinates.

(c) This is a situation which all members of the youth club understand and is therefore a decision they can all contribute to. Indeed to deny them the opportunity to contribute to the decision would be extremely unwise and very demotivating. In this situation a consensus decision based on democratic leadership must be sought.

Communication

Checkpoints

1 *Upward* communication methods used include Joint Consultation Committees, suggestion schemes, trade union channels, grievance procedures.

Downward communication methods include briefing groups, staff meetings, bulletins, notices and circulars.

Lateral communication methods include inter-departmental committees, special project groups.

2 The grapevine is the informal communication network. From the organization's point of view the major disadvantages are that it may undermine information provided by senior management. The information may also be factually incorrect.

3 *Written* – letters, reports, memos, company magazines, sales brochures, job advertisements, press releases
Oral – telephone, face-to-face meetings, staff meetings, committees, conferences, the grapevine, tannoy
Visual – OHP, corporate videos, business television, teleconferencing, posters, wallcharts
Electronic – fax, email, intranet

4 There are various forms of communication network including the chain, wheel, 'Y', circle and all channel. The all channel network is a situation where members of the net are encouraged to talk to one another direct and not through the leader. Research has shown that where complex problems are involved that a decentralized network such as this will provide the best results. Conversely, where the problem is relatively simple the best network will be one which is centralized such as the 'Y' or wheel.

5 Think in terms of the army, the dentist's chair or an oil rig!

6 Non-verbal communication or body language can communicate attitudes or feelings as strongly as words. Normally verbal and non-verbal communication reinforce one another. However, at times the two conflict and the recipient then has to decide which to believe. Forms of non-verbal communication include facial expressions, hand motions and body postures.

Exam question

(a) Telephone, teleconferencing, fax, modem links, Internet, intranet, mobile phones, pagers.

(b) As a firm grows in size you often find that the levels of hierarchy within the organization increase and this reduces the clarity and speed of communication. Communication becomes more formal and the use of written messages grows. This is to ensure that both parties know what has been said. Once again the speed of communication slows and the amount of written material as well as other forms of communication may result in communication overload.

(c) *Speed* Information can be transmitted in an instant from one side of the world to another.
Cost effective Electronic technology is cheaper than many traditional forms of communication.
Accuracy Less human involvement and therefore less likelihood of error.
Retrieval Information can be accessed easily and quickly at your desk.
Reliability Electronic equipment is more reliable because it does not get tired nor can it be distracted.

(d) *Cost* The cost of electronic technology can be considerable. There are also installation costs, running costs, and the costs of training staff.
Security Widespread use of computers has raised concerns about security and confidentiality.

Breakdown Considerable damage to the reputation and interests of an organization can be done where communications technology breaks down.
Quality Information may be corrupted.
Staff resistance Many staff dislike change finding it difficult and stressful to adapt to new working conditions.

Collective bargaining

Checkpoints

1 *Craft* – membership based on specific skills, e.g. National Union of Journalists.
Industrial – cover most of the workers in a particular industry regardless of occupation, e.g. National Union of Mineworkers.
General – recruit semi-skilled or unskilled workers in a wide range of industries, e.g. GMB union and Allied Trade Union.
White collar – technically not a separate category but have grown in importance over recent years; they recruit from managerial, administrative, supervisory and technical staff, e.g. National Union of Teachers.

2 The TUC seeks to represent the interests of the individual unions that are affiliated to it and to arbitrate in disputes between members. The TUC also seeks to establish links with organizations in other countries which have similar objectives.

The CBI represents the interests of its members who include employers' associations, trade associations, chambers of commerce as well as individual employers. Its stated objectives are to
• represent industry's views at a national level on a wide range of issues
• promote efficiency in British industry

3 Most groups working in the public sector have their pay determined nationally. This includes teachers and nurses. Most small firms will negotiate wages directly with their workers or unions locally.

4 *Procedural* agreements are the rules that govern the relationships between the employer and union.
Substantive agreements are the outcome of the parties' negotiations on pay and conditions of work, that is the new agreement.

5 *The economy* – loss of output, loss of taxable income, increased imports, bad industrial relations reputation
Customers – orders delayed, queries unanswered, look elsewhere (including abroad) for future supplies
Other firms – Those selling to this firm or relying on the firm's output will have their business disrupted. Competitors both at home and abroad will take advantage of the firm's problems.

Exam question

(a) The grounds for this statement are the published statistics which show the incidence of strikes is far less than in previous decades. The statement is rather sweeping though. Workers do still go on strike and the disputes are sometimes long and damaging. It is also very difficult to predict the future and it is possible to envisage circumstances in which the incidence of strikes increases. You could refer to changes in legislation, attitudes of workers and economic circumstances.

(b) Strikes are only one form of industrial action and it would be necessary to consider trends in these other forms of action as well before drawing any conclusions.

One point of view would be to accept the statement and draw attention to the changes of the last 20 years. Legislation has curbed the power of trade unions. Traditional industries with high union membership have declined and newer industries with fewer workers and no history of unionization have grown. Trade union membership has slumped dramatically. In many firms though there has also been a move toward better labour relations practices often through the introduction of Japanese management techniques. Involvement in decision-making, greater control of work and greater responsibility are powerful motivators for many people.

An alternative viewpoint would be to argue that fewer strikes do not indicate the improvement suggested. Workers don't go on strike now because they are scared that they will lose their jobs. There is less protection now for both workers and trade unions. If the law was different and it was easier to get another job workers might be more inclined to strike. Indeed, due to the lack of power employees have, employers have been able to introduce new work practices requiring the employee to work far harder than before.

Examiner's secrets

To obtain the evaluation marks you should draw some conclusions about how true the statement is.

Industrial democracy

Checkpoints

1 For worker participation to work there must be
   - adequate time to prepare and participate
   - adequate employee ability to contribute
   - relevance to employee interests
   - benefits greater than costs
   - no threat to either party
2 *Benefits*
   - acts as a safety valve for grievances
   - enables workers to have a say in matters of importance to them
   - draws on worker knowledge and experience
   - it encourages loyalty and a higher morale amongst the workforce

   - it improves communication
   - reduces 'them and us' mentality
   Problems
   - there are some issues where workers have little to contribute
   - it is costly and time-consuming
   - many employees are not interested
   - trade union power reduced if representatives are not union officials

Exam questions

1 F. W. Taylor's interest was in improving the level of efficiency within his factory. He has been described as 'the father of scientific management'. He believed that there was a right way to do a job and workers had to be taught that way. More importantly he believed workers were only motivated in the work situation by pay (preferably related to output) and threats of what would happen if they didn't comply with management rules. This is very like McGregor's Theory X assumptions.

Of course theories on motivation have developed somewhat since the 1900s. The work of Mayo, McGregor, Maslow and Herzberg suggest that employees often adopt a much more positive approach to the organization and its objectives. This is best summarized by McGregor's Theory Y.

Thus although moves toward employee involvement in decision-making cannot be justified by this statement, we can justify employee involvement as a result of our more up-to-date knowledge of motivation. The case for employee participation in decision-making rests not only on improved employee motivation but also on
   - the extension of democracy into the workplace
   - greater loyalty and commitment from workforce
   - improved industrial relations
   - improved information flow
   - the utilization of knowledge and experience of the employees

Examiner's secrets

This is really a question on motivation. To obtain high marks you must use your knowledge of the theorists to back up the points you make.

2 (i) Don't expect success quickly. Quality circles must be given time to settle down.
   (ii) They should be introduced quietly without publicity. Otherwise there is pressure on them to be seen to succeed quickly.
   (iii) All managers must support the introduction of quality circles.
   (iv) Adequate resources, time and money, to ensure effective operation.
   (v) Group leaders and members should receive training.
   (vi) Style of management within the organization must be supportive of employee initiative and freedom of action.

Examiner's secrets

Identify the key characteristics and objectives of quality circles, e.g. continuous improvements, etc. Relate these to the circumstances which would best suit their use.

Trends in employment

Checkpoints

1 Benefits include
  • cheaper operations
  • better use of resources
  • faster response to changes in market
  • greater use of specialists
  Problems include
  • organizational culture needs to change
  • demotivating effect on existing workforce
  • future operations may provide less secure and less skilled jobs for employees so morale and motivation will fall
2 Employees dislike flexible working because
  • redundancy
  • many jobs are less secure
  • may have to change career direction
  • need for constant training

Exam question

(a) Staff appraisal is undertaken because
  • it identifies employees who are failing and need help or need to be watched
  • it identifies employees who are promising
  • it enables superior and subordinate to understand each other's position
  • shows areas where they need to develop their skills
  • identifies areas of conflict and dissatisfaction and the ways of resolving them
(b) Reasons for resentment
  • misunderstandings as to the purpose of appraisal
  • poor implementation of system, e.g. appraisers not trained, poor procedures
  • those doing the appraising held in low esteem
  • no development aspect after appraisal
  Ideas to ensure appraisal experience is positive
  • explanation of purpose and procedures
  • include self-appraisal in the scheme
  • training of appraisers
  • non-threatening appraisal interviews
  • appraisal report agreed by both parties
  • training provided where necessary
  • confidentiality

Examiner's secrets

Clearly not all the elements of a typical report need be presented here. The focus should be on reasons for resentment and practical ways of overcoming these.

Operations management is about the efficient transformation of inputs into outputs that satisfy consumer needs. It includes not only the production of goods but also services such as banking, insurance and transport. The aim is to use labour, machines, raw materials, money and technology to *add value* at each stage of the production process.

Exam themes

→ The main features and applications of each production system.

→ The sources and types of economies of scale.

→ The importance and measurement of efficient capacity utilization.

→ The achievement of quality control and quality assurance.

→ Methods of stock control and waste management.

→ The role of research and development, with particular reference to new technologies.

Topic checklist

O AS ● A2	AQA	EDEXCEL	OCR	WJEC
Scale of production	O	O	O	O
Methods of production	O	O	O	O
Capacity utilization	O	O	O●	O
Production control	O	O	O●	O●
Research and development	●	●	●	O●
Critical path analysis	●	●	●	●●
Stock control	O	O	O●	O●
Quality control	O	O	O●	O●
Location of production	●		●	O
Role of technology	●	●	●	O●

Scale of production

The scale of production problem has two dimensions, a *strategic* one concerning the size of the entire business and a *tactical* one concerning the size of the production run for a particular product or service.

Factors affecting scale

In both cases the business wants to take advantage of *economies of scale*. On a *strategic level* the expansion of the entire business (enterprise) can lead to technical, managerial, marketing and financial savings. These savings should lead to lower unit costs, which improves the competitiveness of the business in the market place and may, subject to competitor reaction, lead to an increase in sales and market share. On a *tactical level* the operations manager has the problem of establishing the size of production runs for each type and variety of product.

Most businesses start small and expand over time. They may aim to *grow* for a number of reasons.

→ *Survival* – staying small might mean that costs are too high. Even if small firms are successful and profitable they may face a takeover bid from a larger organization.
→ *Lower costs* – larger output levels allow firms to enjoy economies of scale that will reduce unit production costs and improve efficiency and profitability.
→ *Gaining market share* – obtaining a larger share of the market might allow a firm some degree of monopoly power and better control over its prices.
→ *Reducing risk* – larger firms can reduce risk through diversification, both in terms of product and market.

Despite these obvious advantages there are still some constraints on growth. The *size of the market* is one of the most important limitations. This explains the survival of many small firms that offer a local service. Another limitation is the *availability of funds* for growth. Many expansion plans involve high risk, and traditional sources of finance (such as banks) are often unwilling to fund risky projects.

The operations manager must evaluate the benefits against the costs of growth and then decide on the best method of growth. This can either be through *internal growth* by expanding the sales of existing or new products or more rapid *external growth* through mergers or takeovers. In both cases the principal aim is to reduce unit costs by exploiting economies of scale.

Economies of scale

Economies of scale are the cost reductions gained through expanding the level of output. The main causes of such economies are

→ **Purchasing economies** – larger output provides more scope for bulk buying and obtaining better discounts and more favourable credit terms.

Links

For more on *economies of scale* see below and on page 22.

Checkpoint 1

Why should the operations manager work closely with the marketing department?

Check the net

Explore the site www.bized.ac.uk It has several worksheets and many web links on operations management topics.

Checkpoint 2

Can you think of some examples of small local services?

Examiner's secrets

Be ready to discuss the advantages and disadvantages of each type of growth.

- **Marketing economics** – a wider range of promotion and advertising is possible since these costs can now be spread over a larger output. Specialist advertising agencies can be used to design more effective, better targeted campaigns.
- **Financial economics** – financial institutions often regard larger firms as less of a risk and are therefore willing to offer loan capital at more favourable rates of interest.
- **Technical economics** – a larger-scale plant costs proportionately less to build than a smaller one. Larger firms can also afford to apply the idea of 'division of labour' more effectively with the employment of specialist staff.
- **Managerial economies** – the 'division of labour', when applied to management, allows the employment of specialists in the functional areas of marketing, finance, production, purchasing and human resources.
- **Risk-bearing economies** – diversification can lead to greater security by not being reliant on one product, market, consumer or supplier. A range of products can be marketed internationally so that recession in one area will not adversely affect the whole organization.

Diseconomies of scale

Diseconomies of scale occur when costs per unit rise as output is increased. Eventually the firm or plant will reach its *optimum size* and expansion beyond this will result in one or more of the following diseconomies

- *co-ordination problems* – delegating the decision-making and empowering staff might lead to departments following different objectives; meetings of senior staff to ensure co-ordination represents a considerable extra overhead cost
- *communication problems* – large firms have many layers of hierarchy that might result in oral messages being distorted as they pass through the various intermediaries. To overcome this, firms rely more on written communication through memos and reports. This incurs an added cost both in materials and staff.
- *motivation* – as an organization grows it can become much harder to ensure that everyone feels valued and is part of the 'team'. Workers can feel isolated and demotivated, especially when senior managers have less daily contact with all employees.

Exam questions
answers: page 134

1 Why would a company seek to exploit economies of scale whilst attempting to avoid diseconomies of scale? (20 min)

2 Explain why large firms can command bigger discounts from suppliers than small firms. (15 min)

3 Explain why some firms may prefer to remain small despite the existence of economies of scale. (15 min)

Checkpoint 3

Doubling the size of a storage tank results in an eightfold increase in capacity but only a fourfold increase in materials to build it. Can you suggest why?

Checkpoint 4

Multinational companies such as Ford, BT, Sony and Coca-Cola produce and sell in many markets. Can you name five other examples?

Action point

Think of a company you know something about. List some of the reasons for possible economies and diseconomies of scale.

Examiner's secrets

Many candidates use the terms 'costs' and 'unit costs' as though they mean the same thing. As a firm expands, 'costs' will rise, but if economies of scale are achieved, 'unit cost' (costs divided by output) will fall.

Examiner's secrets

A balanced answer to economies of scale questions might also refer to the barriers that often prevent firms from growing. Try to give examples where possible.

Methods of production

The type of production method chosen will depend on the uniqueness of the product or service being provided, the number required and the *life cycle* of the item.

Job production

Used for the production of unique items where there is very little chance of a reorder; for example the Channel Tunnel, a portrait, the Millennium Dome, a special building. Each product or service is a 'one-off' which requires its own costings and its own production plan.

The main features of **job production** are

→ high set-up costs
→ flexible multi-use equipment required
→ skilled and versatile labour required
→ high worker motivation
→ a high priced product

The advantage of this form of production is that it creates a unique product to the exact specifications of the customer, for which a premium price might be charged.

Batch production

This involves the output of a limited number or 'batch' of identical items, such as shoes of a particular size and style or the printing of an edition of a book. The units in each batch pass through each production stage together. This larger output provides some *economies of scale*, resulting in lower costs per unit than job production.

The main features of **batch production** are

→ less skilled labour required
→ use of more specialized but flexible machinery
→ possibility of repeat orders
→ some standardization of product
→ ability to supply a larger market

The main disadvantage is that batch production can lead to high stock levels as items wait to move between process stages.

Flow production (mass production)

With this system, an item of production moves continuously from one stage of the process to the next, e.g. bottling plants, car assembly lines and oil refineries. The stages are linked by conveyor belts or pipelines to minimize production time.

The main features of **flow production** are

→ high capital investment
→ greater proportion of unskilled and semi-skilled labour
→ specialized plant and equipment with little flexibility
→ highly automated production
→ huge economies of scale available, especially in the purchasing of raw materials

Speed learning

Mnemonics can help. For examples of job production remember CHOMP
*C*hannel tunnel
*H*air style
*O*il painting
*M*illennium Dome
*P*alace

Action point

Make a two-column revision table listing the advantages and disadvantages of job production. Think about cost, market size, quality, skill levels, motivation and consumer satisfaction.

Links

For more on *economies of scale* see pages 22 and 114.

Checkpoint 1

Under what circumstances might batch production be used?

The jargon

Such stock levels may be referred to as '*work in progress*'.

Checkpoint 2

Under what circumstances might *flow production* be used?

To be profitable, flow production must be run efficiently; this means high capacity utilization and high demand levels, in order to spread the *fixed costs* over many units of output.

Lean production

Although mass production has many advantages it can always be improved upon. The Japanese adopted a 'total approach' to eliminating waste, i.e. removing anything that did not *add value* to the final product.

Lean production aims to produce more by using less, and is to be achieved by

→ involving both management and workers in the decision-making and suggestion-making process
→ minimizing the use of key resources such as materials, manpower, floor space, capacity and time
→ introducing JIT materials handling in order to lower *stockholding costs* and to minimize the need for *buffer stocks*
→ encouraging worker participation in *quality circles* where improvements can be suggested and discussed (TQM)
→ introducing *preventative maintenance*
→ using multiple-purpose machines for flexible production
→ employing and training multi-skilled operatives
→ encouraging teamwork with the introduction of 'cell' production methods

This approach slimmed down 'mass' production into a flexible or 'lean' production system. The main advantages of this are

→ an increase in quality of product and after-sales service
→ shorter product development time
→ faster reaction to changes in consumer preferences
→ reduction in unit costs of production without sacrificing quality
→ a better trained and more motivated workforce

The jargon

JIT refers to a '*just in time*' philosophy; TQM to 'Total Quality Management'.

Links

You can find more on JIT and stock levels on pages 126–7.

The jargon

Cell production divides the production process into stages assigned to individual teams. A team is responsible for a complete unit of work. This provides the workers with a greater sense of achievement and increased motivation.

Example

Ford of America took 24 hours to change a stamping machine from producing one model to another. Toyota reduced it to three minutes.

Action point

List the key aspects of each of the four production methods. Can you give any examples of each method?

Exam questions   answers: pages 134–5

1   What are the advantages and disadvantages associated with moving from a batch to a flow production system? (30 min)

2   What do you understand by TQM? To what extent does the achievement of TQM depend on teamwork throughout the organization? (30 min)

3   Discuss the benefits and drawbacks of using a lean production system for the manufacture of cars. (20 min)

Examiner's secrets

The examiner will expect to see the appropriate use of key terms such as JIT, TQM, quality circles and lean production. Define these terms and give examples if you can.

Capacity utilization

Capacity is the maximum output that an organization can produce in a time period with a given quantity of assets. Most businesses aim to produce close to full capacity in order to achieve economies of scale. Any significant change in capacity utilization has important consequences, both for the firm's profitability and for its workforce.

Measurement

Capacity utilization is a measure of the effective use of a firm's assets and is calculated using the formula

$$\text{capacity utilization} = \frac{\text{actual output per period}}{\text{full capacity output per period}} \times 100$$

Capacity use is expressed as a percentage, with most firms aiming to achieve at least 90% utilization. For a service business it is more difficult to arrive at an effective measure. The lengths of queues or response times to customer requests are some of the common criteria currently used by service firms.

Impact on costs

Capacity utilization is a key factor in the **cost strategy** of a business. Fixed costs must be met irrespective of the level of output. A business with fixed costs of £1m and operating at a maximum capacity of 100 000 units will have *fixed costs per unit* of £10. If capacity falls to 50 000 then fixed costs per unit rise to £20, which will significantly affect profit margins and overall profitability. Capacity utilization therefore has an *inverse* relationship with fixed costs per unit. High capacity utilization helps to keep fixed costs per unit down by *spreading the overheads* over many units of output. From a financial viewpoint a firm needs to be as close as possible to 100% capacity.

Achieving full capacity

For a firm operating at *below* full capacity there are two ways in which it can improve its position.

→ *Increase demand for its products* – this could be achieved by extra promotional activities, cutting prices or penetrating a new market with its existing range of products. A more radical approach would be to create an entirely new product. These activities, however, can take a long time to have any significant effect and may be part of a long-term strategy for solving capacity problems.

→ *Reduce current capacity* – this can be achieved by selling off surplus machinery, moving to smaller premises or reducing the workforce. Each of these options has a significant impact on a firm's human resources. Reduction in capacity must be seen as a long-term decision, only to be undertaken if the cause of the reduced demand is considered to be a permanent feature. Similarly an increase in capacity, by further investment in fixed assets, should only be contemplated where the increased demand is perceived as permanent. Sub-contracting (outsourcing) the supply of extra output might be a short-term response until further market research is available.

Advantages of full capacity

The main advantages of operating *at or very close to* full capacity are

→ fixed costs per unit are at their lowest level possible
→ variable costs per unit may be reduced by scale economies
→ lower average costs should lead to higher profits or the opportunity to cut prices and become more competitive
→ full capacity working helps to motivate employees as they perceive that the company is successful
→ the firm's reputation with its suppliers, bankers and shareholders is enhanced

Disadvantages of full capacity

Although 100% capacity utilization might seem the perfect scenario it has its own associated problems such as

→ no time for essential maintenance of machinery; this might result in increased breakdowns with adverse effects on delivery schedules for customers, etc.
→ employees are required to work at full capacity; this might require extra overtime (expensive) and place greater pressure on staff not to take holidays or to be off sick (stress)
→ no time for employee training; this might reduce productivity and be demotivating
→ unable to meet new orders; this might mean potential new customers are lost to competitors
→ development of new products tends to become a secondary concern in the light of the success of current products; this might be a short-sighted approach to the future health of the business

A permanent change to the capacity of a business is a *strategic decision* and should be taken with a long-term view in mind.

Exam questions answers: page 136

1 How can a firm improve its capacity utilization without increasing its output? (10 min)

2 Why might a multinational firm be reluctant to reduce its global capacity by closing entire factories? (15 min)

3 What do you understand by the term 'production must flow from demand'? (10 min)

Checkpoint 2

Calculate the *profits* at the following capacity levels for a firm with fixed costs of £40 000 per month and a full capacity of 10 000 units per month. Variable costs are £5 per unit and the selling price is £10 per unit.
(a) Capacity = 50%
(b) Capacity = 80%
(c) Capacity = 100%

Links

Note how many human resource issues are involved in the question of capacity utilization, e.g. links to *motivation theory* are important (see pages 92–5).

Examiner's secrets

Excess capacity is not only a problem in itself but might be an indicator of a much more fundamental problem such as loss of market share or products in decline. Placing capacity in this context is evidence of evaluation.

Production control

Production is the process of organizing resources in order to satisfy the needs of customers. It is also the means for the business to make a profit by producing the good or service at a cost that is lower than the market price of the output. To guarantee this, management must keep an effective control on all its resources and monitor their use through the entire production process. Measuring resource efficiency can do this.

Efficiency and its measurement

Efficiency can be defined as how well resources such as labour, raw materials and capital are used to produce saleable items and services. This will have a direct impact on the average costs of production and consequently the profitability of the business. Costs and profits are, however, only *indicators* of efficiency. It is better to measure the efficiency of inputs such as labour and capital *directly* and to monitor the degree of waste in the production process.

When this is done accurately and effectively it allows managers to:

→ identify strengths and weaknesses in the production system
→ compare business units within a plant
→ compare their own business with industry averages
→ negotiate with the workforce about wage rates and job specifications and practices

Labour productivity

This measures the amount a worker produces in a given time period. In manufacturing this is easy to assess because there is a definite and measurable output at the end of the working period. With services, however, it is far more subjective.

Labour productivity can be measured using the equation

$$\text{labour productivity} = \frac{\text{total output}}{\text{number of employees}}$$

Although this looks straightforward it is much harder to apply in practice especially in multi-product businesses and where workers constantly move from one process to another. Despite these difficulties it is a useful measure as rising labour productivity results in falling labour costs per unit. This makes the business more competitive in the market place and also allows the firm to share some of the improvement with the workers in the form of improved remuneration.

Capital productivity

This is increasingly important as businesses invest in more capital-intensive production systems. **Capital productivity** can be measured using the equation

$$\text{capital productivity} = \frac{\text{total output}}{\text{capital employed}}$$

Don't forget

If it can't be measured it can't be controlled!

Check the net

Search under 'productivity' at the DTI website
www.dti.gov.uk

Action point

Think about how the work of a typist, a driver, a security guard and a trainer might be measured.

Checkpoint 1

What would be the labour productivity of eight employees producing 200 000 bricks in a day?

Examiner's secrets

Labour productivity can be *improved* by investing in better capital, investing in better training or by increased motivation of the workforce.

Current practice has led to the replacement of labour by more sophisticated machinery. Although this has led to a reduction in costs per unit it has also meant redeployment of workers and in many cases the replacement of labour. The use of better capital improves not only capital productivity but also labour productivity as output is increased while the number of employees remains the same or falls.

In all these calculations it is assumed that quality remains unchanged.

Waste control ●●●

The third element to control is the use of the basic raw materials and energy inputs such as power and fuel. Waste can occur through poor workmanship, incorrect design and reworking of faulty items.

Waste rate can be measured using the equation

$$\text{waste rate} = \frac{\text{number of items scrapped}}{\text{total output of items}} \times 100$$

Although this gives an indication of the problem it cannot measure the effect on the reputation of a business when faulty goods reach customers. The organizational goal for zero defects is an important measure for all employees to work towards.

Waste of resources can also occur with the overstocking of raw materials that become unusable and with the overstocking of finished products that cannot be sold.

Waste management also incorporates the control of items that can be considered to be environmentally undesirable. Factory smoke, noise levels and water emissions must be monitored in order to comply with local and national regulations. Failure to do so would lead to fines and an increase in the costs of production. More importantly it could damage a firm's reputation in the eyes of its customer.

Checkpoint 2

What is the capital productivity per machine of three bottling machines which fill 150 000 bottles per hour?

Example

Forty items scrapped out of a total output of 2 000 gives a waste rate of
$$\frac{40}{2\,000} \times 100 = 2\%$$

Links

See quality control (pages 128–9).

Don't forget

Increasing productivity and minimizing waste will reduce unit costs and make a firm more competitive.

Exam questions   answers: pages 136–7

1   Analyze the ways in which a business can improve labour productivity. (15 min)

2   Why is waste considered to be more than just a problem of poor resource use? (20 min)

3   Under what circumstances can improvements in capital productivity be
    (a) a benefit for the workforce?
    (b) a problem for the workforce? (20 min)

Examiner's secrets

Improvements in productivity may have many causes. Candidates who recognize the complexity of the issues involved will be demonstrating evaluation.

Research and development

A business must be dynamic in order to survive and grow in a constantly changing world. Goods and services that satisfy consumers now may not be demanded in the near future as new processes, materials and products emerge in the market. Research and development is one way in which firms can overcome this problem. 'Research' involves the attempts to *discover* new ideas whereas 'development' involves the *application* of the ideas to a product or process.

Invention and innovation

Invention involves the creation of a new product or process. Some are the work of individuals such as James Dyson and his cyclonic vacuum cleaner or Trevor Bayliss and his clockwork radio. Most, however, are the result of corporate investment in scientific research. This is particularly true of the pharmaceutical, electronic and computer industries. Research is also undertaken at universities and government research centres whose results are often available to industry.

The majority of inventions never reach the production stage as they are either too expensive, difficult to make or there is not enough capital to fund development. Invention on its own may be insufficient without innovation.

Innovation involves the bringing of a new product or a new process to the market or the workplace.

Product innovation is important to a firm because

→ it can gain extra market share
→ it reduces risk by increasing diversity
→ it can improve its reputation as an innovator
→ it can be sold at a premium price as it is first to market

Process innovation is important to a firm because

→ it can reduce production costs
→ it can reduce production time
→ it can allow the use of new materials
→ it can improve the quality of a product

Invention and innovation are particularly important where competition is strong and where product life cycles are short. A firm's product portfolio must be constantly updated as some items reach the decline stage of their life cycle.

Design

The *design* of a product is not only about its appearance but also about its functionality and the ease with which it can be manufactured. This is known as the **design mix**, and includes the following three factors

→ **aesthetics** – the shape, texture, taste or smell associated with the product
→ **function** – the durability, quality and performance of the product. Does it work?

Example

Recent successful inventions include:
Sony Walkman
Dyson vacuum cleaner
Video and digital cameras
Satellite television
The tetrapak

Action point

Add ten more items or processes to the list above. Think about new features in vehicles, new electronic products and developments in medicine.

Example

The glass manufacturer Pilkington plc developed a new *float glass process* that not only reduced production costs but also earned the company significant licensing revenue.

Action point

Outline the stages in a typical product life cycle.

→ **economic manufacture** – does the design allow it to be made efficiently and at a suitable cost?

All three aspects need to be considered, though with a different emphasis for individual products. For a cheap disposable item, economic manufacture is crucial and aesthetic appearance of little concern. The reverse would be the case for an exclusive piece of designer jewellery.

A **design process** is followed in order to eliminate problems as the product moves from being an idea to a reality.

→ *original idea* – probably in response to market research
→ *design brief* – outline description for the designers
→ *design specification* – materials, shape, cost, etc.
→ *investigate alternative solutions*
→ *models or prototypes created and tested*
→ *consumer testing*
→ *production*

Patents and copyright ●●●

Invention not only gives the firm a competitive edge over its rivals but can also lead to extra revenue from licence fees. An invention can be protected from unofficial use by the granting of a **patent**. This is a legal recognition of the firm's exclusive rights to the product or process for anything up to 20 years.

The *benefits* to a firm in receiving a patent include

→ legal protection from unofficial copies
→ exclusive access to the market for a period of time
→ the encouragement of investment in research
→ the opportunity to command a premium price and higher profits in order to recover research costs and to fund further investigative work
→ the opportunity to earn royalties from licensing the use of the invention to other businesses

The equivalent protection for intellectual property (the work of authors, composers and artists) is by **copyright**. Trademarks such as a logo or brand name can be protected by registration with the Patent Office. This is important as a great deal of advertising expenditure is devoted to establishing the product or company name in the minds of the consumers. Customers also benefit in that they are presented with greater variety, more choice, lower prices and better value for money.

Watch out!

The importance of the various factors in the *design mix* depends on the product in question.

Links

See the discussion of market research on page 64.

Examiner's secrets

Make sure that you stress the importance of patents and copyright in protecting inventions and innovation. Without long-term security a firm will not invest large amounts of capital in research and development.

Action point

What qualities do you associate with the following trademarks?
Rolls Royce
BMW
Chanel
ASDA
Nike
Harrods

Exam questions answers: pages 137–8

1   What are the problems associated with innovation? (15 min)

2   Explain how market research assists the various stages of the design process. (15 min)

3   How can expensive research and development be justified to shareholders? (15 min)

Examiner's secrets

R&D is crucial to the long-term performance of a business. Stress must be placed on the strategic significance of invention and innovation.

Critical path analysis

The main objective of critical path analysis (CPA) is to produce a network model of a complex project in order to help plan and control an organization's operations.

Operational planning

The use of **critical path analysis** allows a business to

→ break down a project into its component parts and determine a logical sequence of operations
→ schedule the tasks to find the minimum time in which a project could be completed
→ identify whether resources are being used efficiently
→ identify those tasks that are critical to the completion of the project within the minimum time period

CPA will often result in a detailed daily plan of the project. The model can help to minimize the use of resources and to investigate alternative courses of action (referred to as 'what if' or 'sensitivity analysis'). CPA is particularly useful for highly complex projects such as those found in civil engineering, house construction or national marketing campaigns.

Network diagrams

The method involves the drawing of a **network diagram** using

→ **nodes** (*circles*) – to show the start and end of activities; they also carry information about the earliest start time (EST) and the latest finish time (LFT)

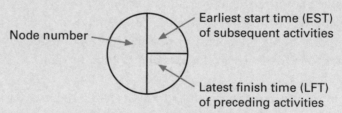

→ *arrows* – to show the flow of activities
→ *hatching* – drawn on the arrows of those activities that are critical to the completion of the project in the minimum time

Activity	Preceded by	Estimated duration (days)
A	–	4
B	–	7
C	–	8
D	A	5
E	C	4
F	B, E	4
G	C	11
H	F, G	4
I	D, H	12

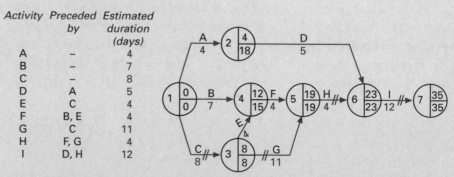

The network diagram is a visual representation of the activities of a project in their logical order. Taking into account the duration of each activity it is possible to determine the minimum project time by calculating the EST for each pathway. The **critical path** is found by

calculating the LFT for each pathway. In the diagram opposite CGHI is the critical path.

Operational control and the use of float

Once the network has been finalized it can be used as a **control mechanism** in that each period's progress can be mapped against the diagram. Non-critical activities have spare time or **float**. Where delays are being experienced resources can be diverted from non-critical activities to critical ones so that the project duration is not affected. This float can be calculated from the network. There are two types of float

→ **total float** (the amount of time an activity can be delayed without affecting the duration of the project) and
→ **free float** (the amount of time an activity can be delayed without affecting the EST of the next activity)

Float allows activities to be rescheduled to make efficient use of resources. Those activities with no total float are the critical activities.

Controlling the time taken for a project is important for a number of reasons

→ extra time often means extra resources and therefore extra costs and reduced profits
→ delays might incur contract penalties
→ completing projects on schedule improves the reputation of the organization and its goodwill with clients
→ completing tasks faster than other firms can provide a competitive advantage
→ reducing time taken provides a marketing opportunity that can command premium prices, such as 'while you wait' services

Advantages of CPA

The advantages of using the CPA are as follows

→ time between tasks is reduced to produce a smoothly run, co-ordinated project
→ construction of the network forces managers to plan forward and to consider all relevant tasks
→ by readjusting float the amount of resources can be minimized, thus improving efficiency
→ improved cash flow as stock can be ordered on a JIT basis
→ the network acts as a control technique to check the progress of the project, which is particularly important if there are penalty clauses for late completion, e.g. motorway construction

Exam questions
answers: page 138

1 Calculate the total float and free float for the activities in the network on page 124. (15 min)

2 Briefly explain the advantages of CPA as a control tool for management. (15 min)

The jargon

Calculation of *float*
Total float = LFT − duration − EST
Free float = EST at end − duration − EST at beginning

Examples

1-hour photo processing
Kwik-Fit car repairs
Same day dry cleaning

The jargon

JIT refers to '*just in time*' (see page 127).

Examiner's secrets

The examiner expects you to be able to interpret pre-drawn networks, particularly the application of float to a delay in an activity. Remember that the use of float can have knock-on effects causing other activities to become critical.

Test yourself

Make a list of four disadvantages of CPA. Using this list and the advantages from the text, write two paragraphs and a conclusion about the pros and cons of using CPA as a planning tool and control mechanism for large projects.

Stock control

Watch out!

The temptation would be to overstock so that all eventualities would be covered. In other words a policy of 'just in case'. Unfortunately this involves tying up financial resources in stock, expending funds on stock management and taking the risk of stock being damaged, becoming obsolete or unsaleable.

The jargon

Materials management is a recent phrase used to describe these aspects.

Links

Stock is also a *current asset* in a firm's balance sheet (page 150), a liquid resource that a firm would hope to convert back into cash during the year. Stock is also part of *working capital* (page 151).

Checkpoint 1

How would you expect
(a) order costs
(b) carrying costs
to vary with the size of order?

The jargon

Opportunity cost is the next best alternative use of the capital, e.g. the interest it could have earned in the bank.

Inventory or stock control is important because a business must ensure that it has sufficient raw materials and work in progress to supply the production line as well as provide finished goods for the customer. Firms have to balance the conflicting demands of holding sufficient stock for production and marketing purposes with the extra cost from maintaining higher stock levels.

Materials management

Managing materials is important as it ensures a flow of raw materials to the production or service activity as well as a flow of products to the consumer. It involves

- → sourcing and purchase of stocks
- → organization of delivery
- → handling, storage and monitoring of stock
- → issuing of stock to the relevant areas
- → reviewing stock held and making any necessary disposals of excess or redundant stock

The nature of stocks

Stock (inventory) is held for various reasons

- → *as raw materials and work-in-progress* – to be readily available so that the production sequence is not interrupted by any shortages
- → *as a stock of finished goods* – to act as a buffer between customer demand and supply from the production process, both of which can be erratic in volume and timing
- → *as a stock of tools and spares* – to help maintain essential plant and machinery in order to minimize costly downtime

The cost of stock

There are two main categories of costs: those associated with holding stock and those associated with running out of stock.

Inventory or **holding costs** include the following

- → *acquisition or order costs* – the cost of clerical and administrative work in raising an order, arranging transport inwards and clearance of stock on arrival
- → *handling or carrying costs* – this includes insurance, storage space, shelving, store personnel, security and loss through damage, deterioration and obsolescence
- → *financial costs* – the *opportunity cost* of having capital tied up in stock

Stock-out costs are difficult to quantify but are just as important

- → *stock-out of raw materials, work in progress or spares* – results in an increase in machine and operator downtime
- → *stock-out of finished goods* – results in loss of sales and missed delivery times, with possible penalties and damage to the firm's reputation and goodwill

Stock levels

One method of controlling stock is the use of **stock control charts**. These provide a quick visual image of the usage of stock as well as the current stock level. To construct a chart a firm needs to determine

→ *the amount of safety or buffer stocks* – to guard against unforeseen demand and late delivery
→ *the economic order quantity (EOQ)* – the order quantity that minimizes the sum of ordering costs and carrying costs
→ *the usage rate* – the stock items used per period of time
→ *the lead time* – average delay between order and stock arriving
→ *the reorder level* – (usage rate × lead time) + safety stock

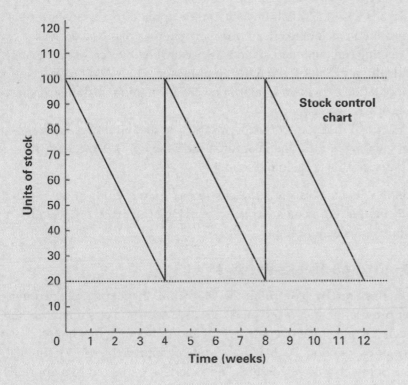

Stock control chart

Just in time (JIT) manufacturing

To minimize the problems of overstocking and understocking the Japanese developed a **JIT manufacturing system** where stock is carefully scheduled to arrive at the point of need at the right time. This requires meticulous planning and absolute delivery reliability.

Exam questions
answers: page 139

1 What are the objectives of stock management? (15 min)

2 What is meant by just in time manufacturing and how might a business benefit from it? (20 min)

3 From the stock control chart above determine the opening stock level, the EOQ, the usage rate, the lead time and the buffer stock level. (10 min)

Checkpoint 2

On a stock control chart which distance represents the Economic Order Quantity?

Examiner's secrets

A common exam question is to ask you to construct or interpret a stock control chart. Make sure you can calculate the EOQ.

Watch out!

Make sure your recommendations about stock levels take account of factors such as perishability, lead times and supplier reliability as well as the normal reference to cost.

Examiner's secrets

An understanding of the benefits and drawbacks of JIT manufacturing is often required. In most questions you must stress the need to balance the demands for adequate stock levels with the cost of stock holding.

Quality control

Quality is one of the ingredients in the purchasing decision of consumers, who demand ever-increasing levels of quality. Any firm that ignores the quality aspect of both inputs and outputs risks losing market share to those firms which make it a priority.

Quality defined

It is difficult to provide a single definition for **quality** as it means different things to different groups of people. Certainly the *perception* of the customer is a key element. Here are some minimum requirements for customer satisfaction

→ '*Fitness for purpose*' – the product can do what it is meant to do. This is a useful definition as it can be applied to a wide variety of products, including cheap products such as disposable pens.
→ Meeting the minimum standards prescribed by *Acts of Parliament* – 'Health and Safety', 'Weights and Measures' and 'Trade Description' legislation provide a legal framework for minimum standards across a wide range of goods.
→ Meeting *Trade Association standards* – some industries have self-regulating bodies that guarantee their members' work, e.g. the National House Building Council.

In the final analysis it is the customers' perceptions of quality that really matter. Firms must strive to convince the market that their product is value for money.

Quality control systems

In the past, **quality control** in the UK meant 'inspecting' the product after production had taken place. In other words it was a faultfinding exercise. Today quality control is all about 'building in' quality at each stage of production. Such a 'preventative' approach reduces the high costs of rejects and reworking. The Japanese perfected this approach which is known as **Total Quality Management (TQM)**.

The basic features of TQM are

→ the establishment of a culture of quality among all employees
→ the recognition of quality chains where each stage of production is treated as a separate customer to be valued and looked after
→ the use of quality circles (see page 129)
→ empowerment of the workforce
→ the emphasis on after-sales service as well as quality manufacture

TQM is not a management tool but a *philosophy*, requiring a complete mind shift on behalf of the entire company (managers and employees).

"Quality is defined by the customer."

W. Edward Deming (American quality guru)

Action point

List five more examples of inexpensive products that you *perceive* as being good quality.

Don't forget

Regulatory bodies such as Ofwat, Oftel and Ofgas help ensure quality standards are met in the newly privatized utility sectors.

Example

Skoda cars is finding it difficult to upgrade its reputation after years of unreliability despite being managed by VW, a recognized quality producer.

Links

For TQM to work effectively the employees must be motivated. Link this with the work of Maslow, Taylor and Herzberg (see pages 92–3).

Quality initiatives

In recent years there have been many initiatives introduced to assist firms to achieve 'quality assurance'. **Quality assurance** refers to all of the activities that ensure the satisfactory delivery of goods and services to the end customer. Key factors include

→ the quality of inputs such as raw materials and components
→ the quality of the design process so that the product meets customer requirements whilst still being economic to manufacture
→ the appropriate skill level of the workforce and its commitment to quality assurance
→ the quality control methods used in the production process
→ the quality of advice at the purchasing point and for after-sales service

The main initiatives have included

→ **TQM** – a philosophy of quality (see page 128)
→ **quality circles** – an informal discussion group drawn from all parts and levels of the business that meets regularly to discuss quality problems
→ **kaizen** – an approach that advocates 'continuous improvement' in small steps rather than a complete overhaul of the production system
→ **benchmarking** – identifying the best practice of the leading firms and using that as a yardstick with which to measure one's own performance
→ **ISO 9000** – an international quality certification procedure
→ **zero defects** – a philosophy that encourages all employees to strive for the ultimate goal of a 'perfect' product
→ **training** – where management has recognized that for quality to be assured a 'quality culture' must be implemented at each stage of the process; it is imperative therefore to train all employees to have the requisite skills, both for their direct tasks and for quality monitoring

Quality can be achieved in diverse ways but the ultimate goal is to satisfy the customer, which is of course a constantly moving objective.

Exam questions answers: pages 139–40

1 What are the five main factors associated with quality assurance? (10 min)

2 Why is quality not just the concern of the production department? (30 min)

3 What advantages does ISO 9000 provide for a firm? (10 min)

Example

IBM lost market share in the personal computer market because it failed to design flexible systems to meet smaller customer needs.

Check the net

Quality Digest magazine at www.qualitydigest.com

Examiner's secrets

The achievement of better quality is as much an HRM issue as it is about operations management techniques. Answers that recognize this will score well.

Checkpoint

Identify the costs and benefits involved in implementing these initiatives.

Don't forget

It is often said that 'zero defects is a journey rather than a target'.

Examiner's secrets

Examiners will be impressed with answers that recognize that quality is a way of working or a philosophy rather than a set of specifications.

Location of production

Production requires labour, capital, raw materials and power to be combined in a suitable location to produce a commodity that is then distributed to its market. The choice of **location** is one of the most important long-term decisions for managers, is likely to be one of the largest items of capital expenditure and once made is very costly to reverse. There are many location factors to take into account, each with its own associated costs and benefits.

The location decision

The **location decision** will be important to

→ new businesses wanting start-up premises
→ established businesses wanting to expand
→ businesses wanting to move into more modern facilities
→ businesses seeking to lower unit costs by reducing some of the input charges, such as rent, rates and fuel
→ multinational companies seeking to diversify their operations

For whatever reason location is being considered, the costs and benefits of each possible site must be carefully assessed. In traditional heavy industries the location chosen will often depend on whether the operation is 'bulk forming' or 'bulk reducing'. *Bulk forming* operations, such as furniture manufacturers, need to be close to their markets in order to cut transport costs. However for *bulk reducing* operations, such as the steel industry, the main need is to be close to the heavy raw materials used as inputs. Modern industries increasingly use lighter raw materials so that they, together with the service industries, tend to be more 'footloose'.

Input costs and availability

An important location factor to be considered is the cost and availability of the inputs into the production process.

→ *Raw materials* – especially important where the raw materials are bulky, heavy, fragile or perishable.
→ *Transport* – access to rail, road, sea and air links is important for both the inward movement of inputs and the outward movement of outputs (goods and services).
→ *Land* – not only is the cost important but also the topography and its load-bearing qualities. Potential for expansion and the ease of obtaining planning permission are also important factors to be considered.
→ *Labour* – the availability and cost of labour with appropriate skills is a key factor for most businesses.

Examiner's secrets

Different businesses will attach different weights to each of the location factors. For example, land costs may be more important for a hypermarket than for a doctor's surgery.

Check the net

Use the government index pages at www.open.gov.uk to access your local authority site, which should have a section on reasons for location in the area.

Example

Soft drinks firms are *bulk forming* and tend to be located close to motorway junctions for easy access to their markets.

The jargon

'*Footloose*' businesses are those with no strong commitment to any specific type of location.

Checkpoint 1

Compare and contrast the input needs of a *car assembly plant* with those of an *electricity generator*.

The jargon

Topography refers to the various physical features of the land-site in question.

Labour, particularly unskilled labour, is one of the least mobile factors, due to a host of reasons that range from family ties to housing costs. It is important to assess the availability of key personnel and the willingness of existing employees to move to a new location.

Closeness to market ●●●

Today the most powerful influence on location is often the *ease of access* to the market. As the service sector has expanded and transport links have improved, it has become more important to locate close to the customer base. This has been further strengthened by higher consumer expectations about after-sales service and prompt delivery times. The growth of business parks on the edge of towns and the drift of industries towards London and the South-East reflect the pull of the market.

Government incentives ●●●

Since the 1920s the government has attempted to influence the location of industry. For example, firms locating in areas with above average unemployment (known as *development areas*) are eligible for various financial incentives. As well as UK government incentives, the EU awards grants for new infrastructure projects such as business parks and new road systems.

International location ●●●

Multinational organizations take a *global* view of the location problem and seek to blend cost minimization with closeness to major markets. Increasingly their factories and plants are considered to be 'footloose'. They will locate in different countries in order to take advantage of grants and tax concessions and to avoid trade barriers. Some governments and trading blocs attempt to protect their own businesses by imposing tariffs, quotas and administrative barriers on imports. Multinationals establishing a plant *within the area* can escape these restrictions.

Exam questions   answers: pages 140–1

1 Give three problems associated with attempting to move an existing workforce to a new location. (10 min)

2 Compare and contrast the key factors in the location of a fast food outlet with that of a hypermarket. (20 min)

3 For what reasons and for what type of businesses is location close to motorway intersections important? (20 min)

> **Checkpoint 2**
>
> How has the move to telephone banking and telephone insurance services affected the demand for high street premises? Where are the call centres located and why?

> **Checkpoint 3**
>
> Find some examples of the types of incentives available. Such measures may help to reduce a firm's variable and fixed costs.

> **Checkpoint 4**
>
> Find out the meaning of 'screwdriver' plants. Why are they considered to be 'footloose'?

> **Example**
>
> Nissan located in the north-east of England in order to sell to the European market.

> **Examiner's secrets**
>
> A good location answer will always weigh up the costs and benefits of the various location factors. This demonstrates the higher order skill of evaluation. Examples will help to strengthen your answer.

Role of technology

Don't forget

Technology is the application of practical or mechanical sciences to industry or commerce.

Check the net

Institute of Operations Management at www.iomnet.org.uk

Action point

Write down five more examples of new products that have emerged during your own lifetime.

Links

See pages 116–17 for more on *flow* and *cell* production.

Watch out!

A decision to invest could leave a firm with an expensive technology that has been superseded whereas a decision not to embrace change could leave the firm trailing behind its competitors.

The advances in technology have affected all functional areas of business. Here the emphasis is on the impact technology has had on the operations function in terms of the *products made* and the *processes used.* Change is not new to the operations function but it is occurring much faster and more often than before.

Products materials and systems

The application of technology to business has produced a period of unprecedented change, not only in the products made and the materials used but also in the ways in which production has been designed and carried out. The advent of the microchip has revolutionized the approach to manufacturing in that the use of large numbers of skilled and semi-skilled operatives has largely been replaced by fully automated systems. The *operations function* has undergone radical change in the following areas.

→ *Products* – entirely new markets have been created with the development of products such as the television, the CD player, the video machine, the mobile phone, the microwave oven, the personal computer, the snowboard and the skateboard.

→ *Materials* – many of the new products were created because of the development of new materials. One of the major influences on product creation is the use of plastic. Its unique moulding capability and strength has made it the most common material used today. In the same way synthetic fibres have created a whole new range of fabrics. The invention of Teflon (polytetrafluoroethylene) led to the development of a wide range of non-stick cooking utensils.

→ *Systems and processes* – job and batch production systems have largely been replaced by fully automated *flow* and *cell production systems.* Computer-controlled machines and robots now do many of the repetitive tasks. Even the creative stage of designing has been revolutionized with the use of Computer Aided Design software. The difficulty facing the operations manager is one of choice: selecting the new technologies worth pursuing and the most appropriate time to adopt the changes.

Applications of new technology

Three major areas of the production process have undergone significant change with the application of technology. These are

→ **Computer aided design** (CAD) – a software system that allows designers and draughtsmen to design, store, retrieve and modify their work using multi-dimensional images. Designers and engineers can work on the same model simultaneously even when they are on different sites or even in different countries. CAD enables changes and modifications to be made easily. This allows a firm to customize mass-produced items to the greater satisfaction of its consumers.

→ **Computer aided manufacturing** (CAM) – this is integrated software that controls machinery. This reduces the lead time between the design process and the output of the finished product. Mistakes and errors can be corrected on line so that waste is minimized.

→ **Stock control** – the use of bar codes and laser scanners has allowed firms to keep better control of stocks and to monitor their individual use. This has led to the reduction of stock levels and the more effective use of resources. The use of computers has enabled concepts such as *just in time* manufacturing to be applied with significant effect on productivity and efficiency.

Benefits of new technology ●●●

Benefits to business from using new technology are as follows

→ *increased productivity* – fewer resources are needed to produce more products, reducing costs; routine and repetitive jobs on the production line are eliminated

→ *new opportunities* – new products for consumers are developed and new markets for firms are created

→ *reduction in waste* – machines can be programmed to use scarce resources more efficiently

→ *improvement in communications* – inventions such as the fax machine, mobile phones and email have allowed communication to be speeded up; it has also allowed employees to work from home

Disadvantages of new technology ●●●

The adoption of new technology can also cause problems, both for the firm and the workforce. The main difficulties are

→ *cost* – in financial terms there is the extra investment in new equipment and processes; in human terms there are training costs or the reduction of the workforce through redundancy

→ *uncertainty* – firms can never be certain as to the right time for investment to take place. When investment is adopted, the changes create uncertainty among the employees, both in terms of their skill level and job security; this might impact on productivity levels

→ *integration* – new technology must be integrated with existing processes, causing scheduling and synchronization problems

On balance, new technology has led to enormous increases in productivity and choice but it can have its downside both for individual firms and for the workforce.

Exam questions answers: pages 141–2

1 What do you understand by mass customization? (10 min)

2 What benefits might be derived from linking CAD to CAM? (15 min)

3 What is the business significance of reducing development lead time? (20 min)

Example

The Ford Puma car was designed in only 135 days.

Don't forget

CAD and CAM can be combined to form CIM, a Computer Integrated Manufacturing system.

Links

For more on JIT see page 127.

Examples

Mobile phones, telephone banking, Internet shopping, etc.

Test yourself

Questions on technological change require an integrated approach as new technology affects all of the functional areas. Can you identify two effects of introducing new technology on the marketing, finance, operations and HRM functions?

Don't forget

Large scale investment in new technology will affect the 'capital employed' figure in the balance sheet and some important ratios.

Examiner's secrets

Good answers will relate changes in technology to HRM issues such as resistance to change, redundancy and delayering.

Answers
Operations management

Scale of production

Checkpoints

1 The operations manager should work closely with marketing in order to fine-tune the output required for each product in each time period. This will reduce the amount of goods left in stock. Marketing will also gain a better understanding of the problems of operations and will, therefore, avoid making marketing claims or plans that are beyond the firm's production capability.

2 Small local services might include hairdresser, plumber, electrician, window cleaner, gardener.

3 A closed tank one metre square is made up of six panels of steel each 1 m² (materials = 6 m²) giving a volume of 1 m³ (1 m × 1 m × 1 m). Doubling the size of the tank to two metres square needs six panels of steel each 2 m² (materials = 6 × 4 m² = 24 m²) but has a volume of 8 m³. Materials has expanded four-fold but capacity has increased eight-fold. This is a real economy of scale.

4 Five other multinational companies might be Toyota, McDonalds, Microsoft, Nike, Kodak.

Exam questions

1 Start by defining the terms and giving one or two examples by way of illustration.
   Economies of scale lead to savings and lower unit costs of production. These lower costs allow a firm to enjoy either
   • a larger profit margin
   • or, by cutting prices, increased competitiveness and a greater share of the market
   Diseconomies add to unit costs and have the reverse effect.
   The thrust of the answer should explore the reasons for exploiting economies and avoiding diseconomies.

2 There are many small firms in the economy therefore a supplier knows that it can easily replace one firm with another. The number of large firms, however, is much smaller and their purchases are the equivalent of many small firms. Losing one large customer might be the equivalent of losing many small clients.
   Delivering large quantities to a single address is also much easier and much cheaper than organizing several small deliveries to different locations.
   Administratively a single invoice for a large quantity is the same cost as a single invoice for a small quantity.
   For these reasons a supplier is more willing to keep a large customer even if it means offering discounts. The savings in administration and transport easily compensate the loss in revenue from the discount. Large firms can obtain bigger discounts because of their market power.

3 Some firms prefer to remain small because
   • the owner wants to retain full control of the business
   • the owner is not prepared to accept the risk associated with expansion
   • the surrounding market is not big enough to support a larger operation; this is often the case with local services particularly in rural areas or highly specialized fields
   • capital is not available even when the owners are willing to expand
   • they want to avoid a confrontation with a larger company which might perceive a growing business as a new threat
   • the market that the small firm serves relies on personal service that would be lost if the business expands

Methods of production

Checkpoints

1 *Batch production* will be used where the order is of a reasonably large size for a standard product. Examples might be a school tie or a particular size of shoe. There should also be the chance of a repeat order so that the investment in design is worthwhile.

2 *Flow production* will be used where there is a constant mass demand for a standardized product. The product should lend itself to production-line manufacture.

Exam questions

1 Start the answer by giving accurate definitions of the two production methods. Each of the following points can be expanded with the use of relevant examples
   Advantages
   • increased output that can service a much wider market
   • purchasing economies
   • increased productivity
   • lower unit costs
   • lower labour requirement

- improved quality control
- reduced need for work in progress

Disadvantages
- raising finance for new machinery
- cost of training
- demotivation caused by breaking up social groups
- demotivation caused by deskilling
- cost of redundancies
- possibility of teething problems with new system
- need for constant high level demand
- breakdown results in total stoppage of production
- may not be able to offer as wide a variety of items

The final paragraph should come to a conclusion about the relative success of such a change. There is scope to link this operations question to other parts of the syllabus for example referring to the product life cycle of the good or the marketing issues surrounding the sale of the increased output.

2   TQM is the attempt to establish a culture of quality within a business that affects the attitudes and actions of all employees. It aims to make everyone in the organization understand, meet and exceed the expectations of its customers.

By 'customers' the organization means not only the end purchasers but also the 'internal' customers. Each individual and department serves another individual or group within the firm. TQM attempts to persuade each worker to regard the other workers as 'customers' who have specific needs and demand a certain quality service or product. The satisfaction of the needs of all these 'customers' must be the result of a team effort.

Quality can only be achieved consistently if people work together to discuss and implement new ways of achieving 'fitness for purpose'. TQM encourages the use of 'quality circles' as a means of identifying improvements while at the same time building team spirit. The views of the shop floor worker need to be given equal recognition with the views of line and senior management for the system to achieve continuous improvement. The overall objective is for the team to get it 'right first time and every time' and to aim for 'zero defects'. TQM is not a one-off target to achieve but a never-ending journey towards better and more efficient satisfaction of customer needs.

3   The opening paragraph must define what is meant by lean production. The body of the answer should concentrate on the following advantages and disadvantages but with reference to the car industry.

Advantages
- A reduction in unit costs that allows the manufacturer to enjoy wider profit margins or to reduce the price of new cars.
- Increased quality control that should reduce waste and reworking and produce increased customer satisfaction.
- A shorter product development time. This allows the car manufacturer to respond faster to changing consumer tastes such as the desire for safer vehicles or more fuel efficient ones.
- Involving the workforce in the changes can lead to increased motivation and a rise in productivity. This again can be passed on in the form of lower-priced cars.

Disadvantages
- The slimming down of stock and work-in-progress increases the risk of downtime on the production line.
- Significant change can result in worker resistance and poorer labour relations if not planned carefully in a co-operative manner.
- Lean production may become associated with rationalization and redundancy.
- It requires the full co-operation of suppliers who might not be willing to adopt such practices.

Capacity utilization

Checkpoints

1   The closure of the Halewood Ford Motor plant would have the following effects
- *Ford employees* – immediate redundancy and the prospect of long-term unemployment unless they were willing to move to another car manufacturing area such as the Midlands.
- *Surrounding businesses* – direct suppliers to Ford would suffer reduced demand and they in turn would

cut their workforce. General expenditure in the area would fall resulting in a loss of trade in the area that would further exacerbate the unemployment problem. Many small businesses would collapse.

- *Liverpool as a whole* – unemployment would rise and the local authority would have increased call on its services for deprived families. Businesses might leave the area to relocate elsewhere. Liverpool might experience an exodus of young people as they move out in search of employment.

2 The contribution per unit is only £10 – £5 = £5. The profit at any given level is given by the equation:

Profit = (sales x contribution) – fixed costs

(a) 50% capacity = 5 000 units
profit = (5 000 x £5) – £40 000
profit = –£15 000

(b) 80% capacity = 8 000 units
profit = (8 000 x £5) – £40 000
profit = 0

(c) 100% capacity = 10 000 units
profit = (10 000 x £5) – £40 000
profit = £10 000

The business makes a loss at 50% capacity, breaks even at 80% and earns a profit of £10 000 at full capacity.

Exam questions

1 A firm can increase its capacity utilization without increasing output by reducing its current production capacity. This can be done in a number of ways by
- selling off surplus machinery
- moving to smaller premises or renting out part of existing ones
- reducing the workforce

All of these actions will cut the total capacity and therefore improve utilization as long as current output is maintained.

Examiner's secrets

This method of improving utilization is often adopted in periods of recession or difficult trading circumstances. It is a means of ensuring survival.

2 A multinational firm would be reluctant to close entire factories for the following reasons
- the cost of redundancies
- the factory might have been established originally with the help of a government loan or grant, which might be repayable in part or in full in the event of closure
- it could damage the global reputation of the business
- in the event of an upturn in demand it might be too difficult for the remaining factories to increase supply quickly enough; this would give competitors the opportunity to gain extra market share
- investment opportunities in other countries might be damaged if the firm gets a reputation for short-termism

Examiner's secrets

In order to gain evaluation marks it would be necessary to comment on whether the firm thinks this downturn in demand is temporary or permanent. Closure of plants is a strategic decision and should, therefore, be part of the overall strategic plan.

3 The term 'production must flow from demand' refers to the policy of only scheduling production when firm orders have been received.

The advantages of this are that stocks are kept to a minimum and over-capacity is avoided. It also allows a more market-orientated approach by the firm.

The drawback of such a policy is that the firm cannot cope with sudden changes in demand. This might give a competitor the opportunity to gain some market share.

Examiner's secrets

This is a question of strategy and the firm must be sure that it can react fast enough to customer requests. In theory the policy is a sensible option but in practice it might not be so straightforward. Comments such as these will demonstrate evaluation.

Production control

Checkpoints

1 Labour productivity = 200 000/8
= 25 000 bricks per worker per day

2 Capital productivity = 150 000/3
= 50 000 bottles per hour

Exam questions

1 Labour productivity can be improved in several ways that need to be described in reasonable detail. The question, however, also asks for analysis. For each of the following methods you should mention some of the drawbacks as well as the benefits.
- Increase investment in more modern equipment. This should result in increased output per worker as well as improved quality. This will only be the case if the new machinery is reliable and the workforce is skilled enough in its operation. The cost of buying and installing the machinery must not exceed the planned improvements.
- Improve the skill level of the workforce by appropriate training. This not only improves ability levels but also has a motivating influence on the recipients of the training. This should be beneficial as long as the employees remain with the company after completing their training. It might be easier to recruit the right staff rather than to train existing employees.
- Improve worker motivation. This can be done in a number of ways from offering financial incentives to involving them in the decision-making process.

Reference to the findings and views of Herzberg would be useful.

- Change of management style. Closer co-operative styles tend to result in improved productivity as responsibility is devolved down the command chain and the views of the workplace are actively sought. Reference to the kaizen approach would also be suitable.

2 Many firms have too narrow a view of what constitutes waste. For many it is confined to the poor use of physical resources such as raw materials. In fact there are several types of waste that need to be actively monitored and eliminated. These include

- *capital and interest waste* – associated with the holding of too high stock levels; the opportunity cost is the return that could have been made if the capital tied up in stock was invested elsewhere
- *overproduction waste* – sales forecasts that are too ambitious lead to stockpiles of goods that can only be cleared through heavy price discounting and much reduced profit margins
- *quality waste* – goods that have to be reworked or are returned as faulty by customers are a form of waste as valuable time and resources must be used to correct the errors; it can also damage a firm's reputation

3 (a) Improvements to capital productivity are often achieved with the purchase of new machinery. This can be a benefit to the workforce in the following ways
- new machinery might be safer to operate
- new machinery or new working practices could demand further training and the raising of the employee's skill level
- better capital productivity can lead to better labour productivity with the opportunity for improved salaries
- newer work practices tend to be more environmentally friendly which could lead to better working conditions
(b) On the other hand improvements to capital productivity can be a problem to the workforce in the following ways

- new machinery might mean the need for a reduced workforce; this would entail either re-deployment or redundancy
- automated machinery might lead to the de-skilling of the operators' function
- skilled and semi-skilled jobs could be replaced with monotonous low-skilled routines that lead to dissatisfied and demotivated staff

Research and development

Exam questions

1 Innovation is the bringing of a new product to the market place or a new process to the workplace. The problems associated with innovation include
- the financial cost of turning a new invention into a marketable product
- the problem of someone copying the idea; this can be solved through copyright and patenting but it is expensive to protect an idea on a world-wide basis
- consumers need to be convinced that the 'new' product or improvement is really worthwhile. This often involves expensive and expansive advertising campaigns
- new processes in the workplace must first overcome the resistance to change of the employees. New practices are often associated with rationalization and redundancy

Despite these problems innovation is vital for long-term survival. This is especially the case in highly competitive markets. The innovation does not have to be radical in order to be successful. Small changes such as a plastic squeezable bottle or round tea bags have resulted in larger market shares for the innovating company.

2 At each stage of the design process it is important that customer viewpoints are gathered to ensure that the final product will meet consumer preferences. Different market research information is needed at the following design stages

- *Original idea stage* – an idea is generated often in response to qualitative research into customer preferences or problems.
- *Alternative solution stage* – the alternative solutions need to be investigated with a sample of the final end users. Likes and dislikes identified at this stage will eliminate expensive reworking later on.
- *Prototype stage* – it is imperative that exhaustive research is conducted prior to the design of the production layout as even small changes at a later stage can not only be expensive but also delay the launch of the product. Microsoft release advance copies of new software programs to a small group of interested users in order to identify faults or the need for improvements.
- *Consumer testing* – this is the final stage before the expense of a marketing campaign. Research here is attempting to shape or confirm the best method for launching the product. It is at this point that the name of the product is finalized.
- *Production and launch stage* – it is vital to test customer reaction to the product so that improvements and alterations can be planned for.

Examiner's secrets

Design is an iterative process where each small step forward is assisted by reaction from consumers. A market-orientated approach depends wholly on accurate and exhaustive market research. In some ways it is an insurance against failure.

3 Shareholders want two things from their investment in a company. The first is a stream of income that comes from dispersal of profits in the form of dividends. The second is a capital gain from a rising share price. With these two aims in mind expensive research and development can be justified to shareholders in the following ways
- Although R&D reduces current profits it leads to either cost savings in the future or new products that guarantee the long-term survival of the business.
- Current products have a finite life span as demonstrated by the product life cycle. A successful business must have a range of new products to replace existing ones, as they become dated or as consumer preferences decline.
- In a highly competitive market it is vital to match or better any advances by the main rivals. Ignoring innovation by competitors can result in a rapid loss of market share, which is often difficult to reclaim.
- R&D investment can be protected through patenting. A successful innovation can be licensed to other firms and prove to be a highly profitable business on its own. For example Pilkingtons plc earn significant sums from licensing its float glass process.

Examiner's secrets

In essence this question is about short-termism. Shareholders need to balance the desire for income now against the desire for long-term capital growth. The UK has been criticized for its short-term approach to investment in companies and it is no surprise, therefore, that firms in the UK invest much less in R&D than their major competitors.

Critical path analysis

Exam questions

1 To calculate the float periods you need to use the equations given in the margin of the spread to obtain the following results

Activity	Total float	Free float
A	14	0
B	8	5
C	0	0
D	14	14
E	3	0
F	3	3
G	0	0
H	0	0
I	0	0

Examiner's secrets

The activities that have no total float are the critical activities. The definition of these terms is a popular exam question.

2 The advantages of CPA as a control tool are
- it provides a checklist for each day's activities; it indicates when resources should be arriving and when jobs should be completed by
- in the event of a delay it allows management to reschedule tasks and to use any 'float' available
- it highlights which activities are critical to the completion of the project on schedule
- it allows 'what if' scenarios to be conducted so that management have a series of alternative plans available in the event of a major problem

Examiner's secrets

As with all of these operations research techniques, they are only as good as the data they are based upon. CPA is invaluable as long as the estimates are realistic. In exam questions the higher order marks will be awarded to those candidates who appreciate the use of the model in the context of the question. For example the use of CPA to organize a film shoot invites answers about rescheduling the arrival of actors, the use of alternative venues, etc.

Stock control

Checkpoints

1 (a) Order costs would be exactly the same no matter what size the order was.
   (b) Carrying costs would increase with the size of order as it would cost more to insure, transport, store and protect.

2 The vertical distance between the minimum and maximum stock levels.

Exam questions

1 The objectives of stock management are twofold
   - to minimize the cost of holding stock
   - to ensure there are sufficient stocks to satisfy the requirements of users

   The cost of running out of stock is just as important as the cost of holding stock. A stock policy needs to identify all stock costs such as delivery, administration, storage, labour, deterioration, insurance, security, obsolescence and the cost of tying up financial resources. To optimize the balance between stock levels and requirements, a stock policy must provide a means for ordering and holding stock at predetermined target levels. The stock policy should also be flexible so that stocks adapt to changes in demand or supply.

   In the end, the stock policy adopted often depends on the firm's attitude to risk which can range from a high risk 'just in time' approach to a low risk 'just in case' approach.

2 Just in time manufacturing is a production system that is designed to minimize stock holding costs by carefully planning the flow of resources through the production process. It requires a highly efficient ordering system and reliable delivery often directly to the production line. This type of system is highly sensitive to customer demand. In some cases production only begins when an order is placed. The system originated in Japan in the 1950s but is now universally applied, especially in firms using flow production such as car assembly, electronics and bottling plants.

   Benefits to a manufacturer from its introduction include the following
   - improved cashflow since money is no longer tied up in stocks
   - reduced waste from obsolete or damaged stock
   - reduced cost of handling stock (space, shelving, security, store personnel, etc.)
   - less space required for stock holding therefore more available for production
   - relationships with suppliers are improved
   - more scope for use of computerized information system to improve integration of departments
   - workforce are given more responsibility and encouraged to work in teams or 'cells'; this should improve motivation

3 Many exam questions about stock control require you either to draw a stock control chart or to interpret data from one. The data from the chart gives the following level
   - opening stock – 100 units
   - the EOQ – 80 units
   - usage – 20 units per week
   - lead time – 2 weeks
   - buffer stock – 20 units

Quality control

Checkpoint

Quality initiatives can have the following costs and benefits
Costs
- can prove expensive
- resistance to change from the workforce
- it takes a long time before results begin to show
- ineffective unless fully supported by management and workforce

Benefits
- build team work
- make everyone responsible for quality
- lead to job enrichment
- increased consumer satisfaction
- cost savings
- improved productivity
- better trained staff

Exam questions

1 Quality assurance is the attempt to ensure that quality standards are agreed and met at each stage through the organization in order to guarantee customer satisfaction.

   The five main factors associated with quality assurance are

- the quality of inputs such as raw materials and components
- the quality of the design process
- ensuring that the workforce has the appropriate skill level
- ensuring that quality control methods are used in the production process and delivery times are met
- the quality of advice at both the purchasing point and with after-sales service

2 As an essay this needs to be broken down into several parts.

The introduction should state what is meant by 'quality' and why it is important in an ever-increasingly competitive market.

The body of the question should stress the need for quality at each of the following stages

- *Design* – quality here means ensuring that the product or service meets the requirements of the consumer at the right price. Value analysis can be used to further enhance the quality of the product without necessarily increasing its cost.
- *Production* – quality control at each and every stage must be 'built in' to the production process. This requires the active and willing participation of all workers and not just reliance on 'inspection' at the end of the production line.
- *Sales* – quality advice is paramount. Discontented customers can seriously damage a firm's reputation.
- *After-sales service* – this has been a neglected part of quality assurance for many firms. The prompt settlement of customer queries and problems is a good way of building customer loyalty and ensuring repeat sales in the future.

Quality, therefore, is a concern of everyone in the organization no matter what stage he or she is involved in. Quality is not an extra. It is part and parcel of the product from its design to its delivery and satisfactory use by the customer.

3 ISO 9000 is an internationally recognized certification of quality management. As such it guarantees that a firm has a system of quality targets that it regularly monitors. It is not a guarantee of high quality.

The advantages which might be associated with having the certification are
- increased competitiveness
- increased customer satisfaction
- increased efficiency
- reduced waste
- improved communications both internal and external
- increased motivation among staff
- cost savings
- reduction in errors as the system documents the correct procedure which helps workers to repeat good practice

The combination of these can for many companies lead to increased profits as a result of lower costs and improved reputation.

Location of production

Checkpoints

1 A car assembly plant needs good access to transport links, a large area of reasonably cheap land but located close to a pool of skilled labour. The edge of a large conurbation is ideal.

A power station to generate electricity needs to be located well away from urban areas for safety reasons especially if it is nuclear. It also requires cheap land but the number of workers is much smaller so closeness to labour is not such a crucial factor.

2 Banks and insurance companies have closed many of their branches on the high street in order to reduce overhead costs. Call centres that are located on the edge of large urban areas, often on trading estates, have largely replaced the high street branches.

3 Incentives included
- relocation expenses for key personnel
- training costs
- capital grants to help cover the costs of land purchase and site preparation
- investment grants towards the purchase of new machinery
- free financial advice
- subsidised rents
- tax allowances

4 Screwdriver plants are those that only assemble predominantly imported components. They are not involved in the higher value-added manufacturing process. Footloose companies are those with no long-term commitment to any particular location. They often stay in one location until the incentives finish and then move to a new area.

Exam questions

1 The problems associated with moving existing employees to a new location are
  - The distance involved between the new site and the existing one. The larger the distance, the less willing are the employees to commute on a daily basis.
  - The relative cost of housing is a factor when the relocation entails moving house. Firms relocating to a high-priced housing area will experience strong resistance from the current workforce.
  - Employees with families are often reluctant to move because of family ties, children's education and their partner's employment. It would require a significant incentive to persuade a family to uproot itself for relocation in an 'unknown' environment.

  Overcoming these problems only adds to the cost of the move.

Examiner's secrets

Evaluation marks can be gained by weighing up the relative gains from keeping the existing workforce against the cost of recruiting or training suitable new staff. It might be the case that 'key' personnel are given financial incentives to overcome their inertia whilst the remaining staff is recruited locally.

2 Questions about location are too often answered in a descriptive manner with little regard for context. This question requires you to choose the most appropriate factors and to justify that choice.
  The main factors chosen should be

  Fast food outlet
  - closeness to market
  - cost of land
  - labour availability

  Hypermarket
  - cost of land
  - closeness to market
  - transport links

  The fast food outlet relies on passing trade and so its position relative to its customers is paramount. The hypermarket must be reasonably close to its customers but with a high car ownership most of these outlets are out of town to take advantage of cheaper land.

Examiner's secrets

The strict order of location preference is not as important as the arguments that you use to explain their choice. Top marks will be awarded for those answers that weigh up the relative strengths of the location factors for each type of business.

3 This question is asking for you to justify two or three types of business for which transport is an overriding concern. In general terms this will involve all those companies that trade in high volumes, bulky items or distribute on a national basis. Such companies might include
  - bulk forming industries such as soft drinks, e.g. Coca-Cola Schweppes at the intersection of the M1 and the M62
  - furniture manufacturers
  - haulage companies
  - supermarket distribution centres
  - import/export agencies
  - pharmaceutical distributors to the National Health Service
  - large retail outlets that rely on serving a large population, e.g. IKEA, Toys R Us, cinema complexes, etc.

Role of technology

Exam questions

1 Mass customization is the ability of a firm to apply flow production techniques while at the same time producing different types of product according to individual customer need. This is done by cleverly designing the components of the product so that they can be easily exchanged or substituted on a production line. This allows a firm to make to order but on a large scale. It is a mix of mass and job production but accomplished at high speed.

Examiner's secrets

This type of production can only work if the firm has an efficient just in time stock handling system. Each order 'pulls' specific components into the production line at the right time and in the right quantities. The use of computerized ordering is essential for this to be successful.

2 By linking computer aided design (CAD) with computer aided manufacture (CAM) it is possible to enjoy the following benefits
  - a reduction in the 'time to market' for new products therefore gaining a competitive advantage
  - a reduction in waste as problems are identified at an earlier stage
  - greater co-operation between the design department and the operations function which can lead to more user-friendly techniques and instructions
  - reduction in overall cost as changes made in one area are automatically made throughout the system, thus eliminating faulty production

Examiner's secrets

Integrating the design and operations functions should lead to significant time saving as well as greater co-operation between employees. The use of this type of technology produces a 'seamless' operation, thus avoiding the problems of co-ordination and departmental rivalry.

3 Reducing development lead time can deliver the following advantages
  - 'first to market' means that a firm can charge a premium price for its product (skimming) before competitors follow with 'me too' versions
  - enhanced reputation as an innovator can help build customer loyalty
  - able to enjoy longer product life cycles than its competitors
  - reduces the cost of R&D
  - faster and longer return on initial investment which will make shareholders more appreciative of spending on research

  - more chance of innovative products reaching the market before customer preferences change
    Reducing the lead time removes some of the uncertainty associated with new product investment.

Accounting is the process of recording a firm's financial transactions in a suitable format and of summarizing this in the form of accounting reports. Accounting can be divided into two types, financial accounting and management accounting. *Financial accounting* is concerned with the production of the principal accounting statements that provide stakeholders in the business with an accurate view of the firm's financial position. *Management accounting*, however, generates information for internal use to aid the analysis, planning and control of the firm's activities. Together the two forms of information provide insights into the success or failure of past decisions and operations, thereby helping management to assess the opportunities and difficulties of future plans. It is important that you regard accounting information as one piece of the decision-making jigsaw that is supplemented with information from the other functional areas.

Exam themes

→ The three principal financial statements: the balance sheet, the profit and loss account and the cash flow statement.

→ The use and interpretation of ratio analysis to investigate comparative performance.

→ The importance of sound cash flow management.

→ The matching of needs for finance with suitable sources of finance.

→ The construction and manipulation of the break-even model.

→ The budgeting process and the application of variance analysis.

→ The application of investment appraisal techniques to capital investment opportunities.

Topic checklist

○ AS ● A2

	AQA	EDEXCEL	OCR	WJEC
Use of accounts	●	○	○	○
Preparation of accounts	●	○	○●	○
Profit and loss account	●	○	○	○
Balance sheet	●	○	○	○
Cash flow management	○	○	○	○
Ratio analysis	●	○●	●	●
Costs and revenue	○	○	○	○
Break-even	○●	○	○	○
Sources of finance	○●	●	●	○
Budgeting	○	○●	○	○●
Investment appraisal	●	●	○●	●

Use of accounts

Accounting can be described as the collecting, recording and verifying of financial information. A broader and more helpful definition might see accounting as providing a database of information about the activities of an organization expressed in monetary terms. The role of the accountant is to accurately record transactions and to prepare reports on the finances of the business that will assist the decision-making process.

Don't forget

All businesses have a *legal obligation* to produce a set of accounts even if it is only for tax purposes. Private limited companies and plcs must file a set of accounts with the Registrar of Companies, which is then available for public scrutiny.

Links

See pages 148–53

Links

See pages 158–63

Examiner's secrets

Computers now do a lot of the record keeping. The accountant's role is now more of a consultant and manager rather than a bookkeeper.

Watch out!

Do not make a judgement of a company based on a *single year's accounts.* Always look at a spread of years in order to identify patterns and trends.

Financial and management accounting

Accounting is the process of recording a firm's financial transactions in a suitable format and of summarizing this in the form of accounting reports. Accounting can be divided into two types, financial accounting and management accounting.

→ **Financial accounting** is concerned with the production of the principal accounting statements that provide stakeholders in the business (management, employees, shareholders, creditors, consumers and government) with an accurate view of the firm's financial position. It uses *historical data* and is predominantly backward-looking in that it summarizes what has happened in the previous accounting period. The principal output would include profit and loss accounts, balance sheets and cash flow statements.

→ **Management accounts**, however, generate information for internal use to aid the analysis, planning and control of the firm's activities. They are principally *forward looking,* acting as 'information providers' to the management team. This information would be in the form of financial forecasts, budgets, contribution statements and break-even charts.

Together the two forms of information provide insights into the success or failure of past decisions and operations and enlighten management as to the opportunities and difficulties of future plans. It is important that you regard accounting information as one piece of the decision-making jigsaw that is supplemented with information from the other *functional areas* such as marketing, production and human resources.

Internal users

Most of the output of the accounting function is for internal use. The following groups are the main parties interested in the financial information.

→ *Management* – managers require financial information in order to review the success or failure of past decisions. In the light of these findings managers can then formulate future plans and strategy.

→ *Owners* – existing owners want to know how their investment has performed and what its prospects are for the future.

→ *Employees* – in the increasingly volatile labour market of the modern economy, employees are justly concerned with job security and the likelihood of future wage improvements. The financial performance of the business is an indicator of the long-term health of the company and of the employees' prospects within it.

External users

External groups, such as those below, have access only to the published accounts of the business. Their need is to build a picture of the firm's operations, efficiency and overall stability.

The main external users include the following

→ *potential owners* – to compare the organization's performance and prospects with those of other firms that offer investment opportunities
→ *suppliers* – to gauge the risk involved in extending credit to the firm
→ *government* – to assess the tax liability of a business and also to compile statistics about the performance of the economy as a test of government policies and as an indicator of potential problem areas
→ *banks* – to assess a firm's creditworthiness for the granting of a loan or its ability to repay a loan already granted
→ *competitors* – to measure their own performance against those of their nearest rivals and to indicate which firms are the most threatening in the market place. The accounts can also be used to estimate the cost of a takeover bid
→ *local community* – to assess the prospects for employment in the area both in the short term and in the long term
→ *pressure groups* – to provide them with information as regards the emphasis a firm places on the environment, such as money spent on waste management. The level of profits may indicate to consumer organizations whether the general public is being 'exploited'

Exam questions   answers: page 166

1   Why might a firm considering the takeover of another business be interested in seeing the management accounts as well as the financial accounts of that business? (15 min)

2   How has information technology affected the work of accountants in the supermarket trade? (15 min)

Don't forget

Trade unions representing employees might use the annual accounts as a bargaining point in wage negotiations.

Check the net

Investigate three different annual reports from major companies at the company reports section of the Internet site www.bized.ac.uk

Checkpoint

What term is sometimes used to describe *all those who have an interest in a particular organization*?

Examiner's secrets

Think about the different objectives of the two types of accounting. For each question relate your points to the particular area mentioned, i.e. a takeover and a supermarket respectively.

Preparation of accounts

The accounting process must produce statements that show a 'true and fair view' of the business's financial position and follow a series of accounting concepts and conventions. The final accounts of limited companies must also satisfy certain legal requirements.

Accounting concepts

There are four fundamental **concepts** that underlie the production of a set of accounts

→ **going concern** – assumes the business will continue to trade 'for the foreseeable future'
→ **accruals or matching principle** – relates revenues and costs to the period in which they occur
→ **prudence or conservatism** – avoids an over-optimistic view of the performance of the business; the accountant recognizes revenue only when it is realized in an acceptable form but provides for all expenses and losses as soon as they are known
→ **consistency** – maintains the same approach to asset valuation and the allocation of costs so that comparisons can be made over time

Accounting conventions

Many of the conventions have been adopted over time as tried and tested general rules. Here are five key **accounting conventions**

→ *objectivity* – accounts are based on measurable facts that can be verified
→ *separate entity* – the company is recognized as a legal person in its own right, entirely separate from its managers and owners
→ *money measurement* – all assets and liabilities are expressed in money terms.
→ *historical cost* – all valuations are based on the original cost rather than current worth. Where items fall in value through use, they are depreciated or written down in value. This gives the company an objective valuation of its assets
→ *double entry* – all transactions involve two sides: giving and receiving. This is acknowledged in the double-entry system of bookkeeping where the source of funds is balanced by the use made of them

These concepts and conventions underpin the work of the accountant and are critical for the production of accurate and meaningful accounts. Some are so fundamental that they have been incorporated into legislation. The overall aim of the concepts, conventions, legislation and professional standards is to ensure that accurate reporting adequately protects investors' funds.

Checkpoint

Explain why *independent auditors* are needed to confirm that accounts of public limited companies have been properly prepared.

Don't forget

The *accrual* or *matching principle* is important as the accounting statements are for specific periods of time (normally a year).

Watch out!

Intangible assets such as goodwill and brand names are included in the accounts only if they have been purchased, e.g. if the business has taken over another company.

Examiner's secrets

In examinations you can expect to be tested on these conventions, either by defining some of the terms or by recognizing the application of them.

Legal requirements

The *Companies Acts of 1985* and *1989* contain regulations which limited companies must follow in the preparation of their published financial information statements. The main points are

→ public limited companies and some larger private limited companies must have their accounts independently audited with confirmation by the auditors that they represent a 'true and fair view'
→ a set of accounts must be sent to shareholders and also made available for public scrutiny at Companies House

The annual report of a public limited company (plc) will include the following components

→ *Chairman's statement* – a general review of the past period of trading, comments on market conditions and an assessment of future prospects
→ *the directors' report* – a more detailed report on the company's activities and policies
→ *a profit and loss account, balance sheet* and *cash flow statement*
→ *notes to the accounts* – further explanation of the figures in the main financial statements
→ *auditor's report* – an inspection of the accounts on behalf of the shareholders to ensure truth and fairness

Professional requirements

Accountants must belong to one of the professional accounting bodies. The profession has an *Accounting Standards Board* (ASB) which lays down rules (*Financial Reporting Standards* – FRSs) that accountants should follow when dealing with various accounting problems such as stock valuation or depreciation. Older standards (pre-1990) are called *Statements of Standard Accounting Practice* (SSAPs), which are gradually being replaced by FRSs. Any serious breach of the Standards will result in the accountant being 'struck off' from the professional body's list and therefore be unable to practise as an accountant.

> **Action point**
>
> Compare the *Chairman's statement* from the 'Reports and Accounts' of three different companies. How do their views of the future differ and for what reasons?

> **Example**
>
> An example of a professional body is the Institute of Chartered Accountants in England and Wales (ICAEW) – www.icaew.co.uk

> **Check the net**
>
> Visit the website of the ASB at www.asb.org.uk

> **Check the net**
>
> Visit the website of the Financial Services Authority at www.fsa.gov.uk

> **Examiner's secrets**
>
> Make sure you can distinguish between *concepts* and *conventions* and can relate both to the needs of investors, firms and the public interest.
> 'Historic cost' and the 'matching principle' are often needed in answering exam questions.

Exam questions   answers: pages 166–7

1   Why are concepts and conventions needed in accounting? (15 min)

2   What difficulties are involved in assessing the current value of fixed assets? (15 min)

3   What is the difference between 'revenue and expenditure' and 'receipts and payments'? (10 min)

Profit and loss account

The profit and loss (P&L) account shows the revenues, expenses and the resulting profit (or loss) for a given time period, usually a year. The statement illustrates the performance of the business and how successful it has been in recent times. Careful examination can reveal how effectively the business is coping with the market and any changes in it. Examining the statements over several years will help identify the trend for sales, costs and profitability.

Measuring profit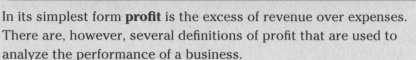

In its simplest form **profit** is the excess of revenue over expenses. There are, however, several definitions of profit that are used to analyze the performance of a business.

→ *Gross profit* – the amount of profit made on trading activities alone. It is calculated by subtracting the cost of goods sold from the turnover (sales). It does not include any indirect expenses (advertising, administration, etc.) or overheads (rent, rates, insurance, etc.)

→ *Net profit or operating profit* – the profit left after expenses and overheads have been deducted from the gross profit.

→ *Pre-tax profits* – net profit plus any non-operating income less interest.

→ *Profit after tax* – total profit minus tax due.

→ *Retained profit* – the amount of profit after tax and dividends that is kept within the business.

These measures are calculated at different stages within the three parts of the profit and loss account.

The trading account

The **trading account** shows whether the firm is making a gross profit from its core activities. It includes the revenue from sales (also referred to as turnover) minus the direct cost of production (the cost of goods sold). In order to conform to the 'matching principle' only the cost of those goods actually sold must be included. To achieve this the following formula is used

$$
\begin{aligned}
&\quad \text{opening stock}\\
&+\ \text{purchases}\\
&-\ \text{closing stock}\\
&=\ \text{cost of goods sold}
\end{aligned}
$$

This takes account of the stock brought forward from the previous year and available for sale, and the stock left unsold at the end of the year.

The format for the trading account is

	£m
Sales turnover	140
Less cost of goods sold	80
Gross profit	60

If cost of goods sold exceeds turnover a gross loss is made.

Watch out!

As the P&L account is a record of trading over a period of time, make sure that the heading reflects this, such as 'P&L account for the year ending December 2004'.

Checkpoint 1

Can you give an equation for *gross profit*?

Checkpoint 2

Can you give an equation for *net profit*?

The jargon

Non-operating income is money earned from activities not directly associated with a business's core function such as rent from property, dividends from shares in other companies, etc.

Examiner's secrets

The calculation of cost of goods sold is a common exam question. Many candidates forget to include either the opening stock or the closing stock in their answers.

The profit and loss account ●●●

The middle section has the same name as the whole statement: **the profit and loss account**. It shows whether the firm makes an operating profit, when all other expenses are deducted from the gross profit, such as administration, selling costs and depreciation. This is a useful indicator of the trading performance of the business. To this figure must be added any non-operating revenue, which then gives us the *profit before interest and tax* (*PBIT*). Interest payable is then deducted to give the *profit liable to tax*. Interest is dealt with as a separate item, as it illustrates the burden of how the company is financed rather than how it carries on its core business.

The format for the profit and loss account is

	£m
Gross profit	60
Less expenses	15
Operating profit	45
Add non-operating income	5
Profit before interest and tax (PBIT)	50
Less interest	2
Profit before tax	48

Example

In the 1980s *Sock Shop* expanded quickly by borrowing to finance the purchase of high street sites. Although the company traded at a profit it could not make enough to cover the interest payments when the government raised the rate to 15%. The business went into liquidation.

The appropriation account ●●●

The **appropriation account** explains how the profit after tax is dispersed. The after-tax profit could be used to pay dividends to shareholders or to keep as retained profits (reserves) for future use in the business. Shareholders generally expect dividends to rise in line with any improvement in the performance of the business. Management, however, may want to use profit to help expand, or to finance the future running of the business.

The format for the appropriation account is

	£m
Profit before tax	48
Tax	12
Profit after tax	36
Dividends	12
Retained profit	24

Examiner's secrets

A common mistake is to view dividends as an expense to be charged against revenue. It is not an expense but a distribution of profit.

Don't forget

Interpretation of the profit and loss account is likely to concentrate on 'profit quality' and 'profit utilization'.

Exam questions   answers: page 167

1 How is it possible to pay a dividend in a year when the business makes a loss? (8 min)

2 Is a rising level of operating profit always an indicator of a successful business? (10 min)

3 What other information is needed to put the profit performance in perspective? (8 min)

Examiner's secrets

Make sure you can relate the items in the profit and loss account to the firm's actions and concerns. Check whether any improved profit is the result of the actions of the firm or a result of changes in the market.

Balance sheet

The balance sheet is a financial snapshot of the business on a particular date. It illustrates an organization's resources in terms of what it owns (*assets*) and what it owes (*liabilities*). The balance sheet is important because it reflects the financial health of the business. It shows whether the business can meet its short- and long-term debts and by allowing comparisons to be made with earlier balance sheets, it also reveals any changes taking place in the business. It should be viewed as a 'window' through which an understanding of the business can begin.

Examiner's secrets

Do not worry about constructing balance sheets. In an exam you will only be required to read and interpret the data, particularly balance sheet strength.

The double entry system

Double entry bookkeeping is a system of accounting that recognizes that all transactions have a dual nature, a giving and a receiving. Each event is recorded in two accounts as a *debit* in one and a *credit* in another, e.g. £1 000 spent on materials will reduce cash by £1 000 but increase stock by £1 000, leaving the balance sheet in balance.

Don't forget

The accounting equation is 'assets = liabilities'.

Assets and liabilities

Assets are the items that the business 'owns'. They can be classified according to how long the business expects to use them.

Checkpoint 1

Define *tangible assets*.

→ *Fixed assets* – assets that are to be used for more than a year, for example machinery, vehicles and buildings.
→ *Current assets* – short-term assets whose value changes frequently during the year, for example stock, debtors and cash.

   Liabilities are the amounts that the business owes.

Checkpoint 2

Define *intangible assets*.

→ *Current liabilities* – those debts that have to be paid within 12 months and may consist typically of creditors, overdraft, declared dividends and tax due.
→ *Long-term liabilities* – money owed by the firm that has more than a year to maturity, such as bank loans and debentures.
→ *Shareholders' funds* – money or resources invested by the shareholders for the long-term use by the business, such as share capital and retained profit.

Use of funds

Don't forget

The balance sheet is a snapshot of the business taken on one particular day, normally the last day of the trading period. The *title* of the balance sheet should reflect this by being in the form of 'Balance sheet as at (date)'.

The *top half* of a vertical balance sheet displays the assets that a business owns less its current liabilities at the bottom. It is normally set out in a two-column format, so that individual items can be shown on the left leaving the main totals to be seen clearly on the right.

Balance sheet as at 31/12/2004

	£m	£m
Fixed assets		
Land + buildings	25	
Machinery + vehicles	2	27
Current assets		
Stock	8	
Debtors	4	
Cash	3	
	15	
Less: Current liabilities	(7)	
Net current assets (working capital)		8
Assets employed		35

Source of funds ●●●

For a limited company, assets employed are matched by share capital, reserves and possibly long-term loans.

	£m	£m
Financed by:		
Shareholders' funds		
Ordinary share capital	15	
Retained profit	9	24
Long-term liabilities		
Bank loan	5	
Mortgage	6	11
Capital employed		35

The balance between permanent capital provided by shareholders and borrowed funds ('gearing') is important. Too much borrowing places an interest burden on the business that legally must be met.

Working capital ●●●

Working capital is defined as current assets minus current liabilities. It is vitally important as many businesses fail not because they are unprofitable but because they lack sufficient liquid assets to pay their short-term debts. Small companies are often affected when they expand too quickly; cash is needed immediately to pay for extra materials and labour but problems arise when the increased sales are on credit. This situation forces the business to increase overdrafts or loans. This raises the firm's costs and places it at risk from a rise in interest rates.

Exam questions answers: pages 167–8

1 Does a balance sheet alone show a company's true worth? (15 min)

2 What form can capital reserves take? (10 min)

3 How can working capital problems be solved? (20 min)

Cash flow management

Cash is the most liquid of assets. It is the oil that allows the business machine to function smoothly. Without sufficient cash a firm could not pay its labour force, settle its bills as they fall due or take advantage of special offers. It is crucial that a business can estimate accurately the cash flows and identify problems before they happen.

The importance of cash

Purchases of resources (labour, raw materials, transport, etc.) are transformed into finished goods and eventually sold to customers. Some of the sales generate cash immediately but some are on credit and so the business will suffer a delay until the debtors eventually settle their bills. This can cause a problem because the firm, meanwhile, still needs to buy further resources. For this reason **cash management** or **cash budgeting** is crucial to the effective running of all organizations. Each time the cycle is repeated a firm should increase its cash holdings by the amount of the mark-up on the goods. A fall in sales or a lengthening in the time debtors take to pay will cause the cash cycle to slow down and decline, thus threatening the existence of the firm.

Cash flow forecasts

It is important to ensure that a firm has sufficient cash not only for its present level of operations but also for the future. The role of the **cash flow forecast** is to help management determine the future cash position and to plan remedial action for any problem periods. A cash flow forecast is an estimation of future receipts and expenses. The **cash flow statement** is set out as a simple table showing the opening cash position, the cash inflows and the cash outflows over the period, and the closing cash position.

Cash flow £m

	J	F	M	A	M	J
Opening cash	52	43	48			
Cash inflow	13	14	17	19	22	21
Cash outflow	(22)	(9)	(12)	(15)	(18)	(17)
Closing cash	43	48				

To be of any worthwhile use to the businessperson it must be as realistic as possible. Sales must be based on market research and not be over-estimated. Expenses can be based on quotations or historic costs adjusted for inflation. Wherever possible the convention of prudence must be applied.

Effective control of cash and the level of working capital will allow a firm not only to survive and expand but also to reduce business costs and add to profits.

Sources of cash flow problems

The cash flow can be affected by any of the following

- → *Overborrowing*   As businesses grow they require more cash and may resort to borrowing which increases the firm's interest payments.
- → *Stockpiling*   The holding of stocks of raw materials, work in progress and finished goods is an expensive exercise. Where a firm keeps unnecessarily high levels of stock it has valuable funds tied up in an unproductive area.
- → *Overtrading*   This occurs where a business is attempting to expand its operations without sufficient working capital. It is often seen among new firms which experience rapidly growing orders and an increasing level of debtors. The firm has to finance further production through an overdraft or extra loans.
- → *Poor credit control*   Not paying enough attention to the prompt payment of debtors leads firms to costly borrowing and the possibility of bad debts.
- → *Market changes*   Consumer demand is prone to change as new products come on to the market or tastes and fashion alter. This can seriously affect sales and reduce cash inflows.

Cash flow solutions

Without enough cash the business will have insufficient funds to pay wages, suppliers and running costs for the current level of output. This may cause the business to either request an overdraft or for the owners to inject more capital. If these options are not available then the firm must remedy the situation by a combination of

- → *cutting expenditure* – this can be achieved by reducing current output levels, reducing labour levels, ordering in smaller quantities (thus missing out on discounts), etc.
- → *delaying cash payments* – negotiating longer credit periods with suppliers, postponing the purchase of new assets, leasing or renting equipment rather than buying it, etc.
- → *increasing cash inflows* – boosting cash by the sale of stock at reduced prices (thus lowering profitability), selling off some fixed assets, selling debtors to a factor, etc.

These are in themselves only short-term measures. The business may need to address cash flow problems with a long-term solution, such as a fresh injection of capital or reducing operations to a level commensurate with the finance available.

Exam questions   answers: pages 168

1   What are the main advantages of constructing a cash flow forecast? (15 min)

2   What are the limitations of a cash flow forecast? (15 min)

3   Complete the cash flow forecast on page 152 and determine the closing cash balance for June. (10 min)

Checkpoint

How would the following affect cash flow?
(a) increase in inflation
(b) strike action
(c) unexpected breakdowns

Test yourself

Recall the elements involved in the working capital cycle. Draw a circular diagram to show the cash inflows and cash outflows experienced during the cycle.

Examiner's secrets

Do not confuse profit with cash. Many profitable firms are cash-starved because sales have been made on credit.

Ratio analysis

Ratio analysis involves the examination of accounting data to gain understanding of the financial performance of a company. It is useful to all stakeholders as it provides insights into the performance, financial liquidity and shareholder returns of the business over time.

Analyzing financial statements

Ratios used on their own are largely meaningless. The statement that 'profits have grown by 10%' might appear satisfactory but not if prices have risen by 15%, competitors have secured 20% increases in profits and the firm has used 20% more capital to generate the extra sales! It is essential to have a means of *comparison* either with previous years or with other firms of a similar size.

Profitability ratios

Profitability ratios measure the relationship between profit in its various forms and sales, assets and capital employed.

➜ *Gross profit margin* – this ratio examines the relationship between profit (before overheads are taken into account) and sales.
➜ *Net profit margin* – this ratio examines the relationship between profit (after all expenses are taken into account) and sales.
➜ *ROCE (return on capital employed)* – this is the most important ratio as it measures the efficiency with which the business generates profits from the capital invested in it.

These ratios provide a picture of the profitability and efficiency of the business. The desired result is to either generate more profits with less capital investment or to make the existing capital work harder by generating more sales. Increased profitability can be achieved by making more profit on each item or selling more items. This principle is very simple in theory but much harder to put into practice.

Activity ratios

Activity ratios measure how well a firm manages it resources.

➜ *Stock turnover* – this measures how long it takes for a firm to sell and replace its stock. Each time the stock is sold it generates more profit so the aim is to turn the stock over as quickly as possible. The ratio can be expressed as a number of days or as a number of times per year.
➜ *Debtor turnover* – this measures how quickly debtors are paying their bills, i.e. the average collection period.
➜ *Asset turnover* – this measures the sales generated from each pound of assets invested in the business. The aim is to create as much sales as possible as each sale should add to the profit figure. Some businesses, however, will by their nature have a slow turnover and must therefore have a high profit margin, e.g. a high-class jeweller. Other firms rely on a high turnover with a low profit margin such as supermarkets.

The jargon

$$\text{Gross profit margin} = \frac{\text{gross profit}}{\text{sales}} \times 100\%$$

$$\text{Net profit margin} = \frac{\text{net profit}}{\text{sales}} \times 100\%$$

$$\text{ROCE} = \frac{\text{operating profit}}{\text{capital employed}} \times 100\%$$

Don't forget

Investors and shareholders want to see a continually rising ROCE which in itself puts pressure on management to perform.

The jargon

$$\text{Stock turnover} = \frac{\text{stock}}{\text{sales}} \times 365 \text{ days}$$

$$\text{Debtor turnover} = \frac{\text{debtors}}{\text{sales}} \times 365 \text{ days}$$

$$\text{Asset turnover} = \frac{\text{sales}}{\text{net assets}}$$

Liquidity ratios

Liquidity ratios provide a measure of risk, as they are concerned with the short-term financial health of the business. Too little working capital and the business will not be able to meet its debts. However too much working capital represents an inefficient use of resources.

→ *Current ratio* – measures how well short-term assets cover current liabilities. For most businesses a ratio between 1.5 and 2 is ideal.
→ *Acid test ratio* – a more stringent test of liquidity as it only takes account of current assets that can easily be turned into liquid funds (cash and debtors). Most firms seek a value of at least 1.

Gearing ratio

The **gearing ratio** focuses on the long-term financial health of the business by showing how reliant it is on borrowings. Highly geared companies have a large interest burden that might prove difficult to sustain in an economic downturn.

Shareholder ratios

Shareholder ratios reflect the returns on investments.

→ *Earnings per share* (EPS) – a good indicator of management's use of the investors' capital as it measures the profit performance over time.
→ *The price/earnings ratio* (P/E ratio) – an indicator of investor confidence as it shows the relationship between earnings and the current market price of the share.
→ *Dividend yield* – this is the annual dividend expressed as a percentage of the current market price and shows the return that a new investor could expect. It is easy to compare this ratio to other forms of investment, such as savings accounts.

Shareholders want to see two trends, an increasing return on investment in the form of improved dividends and an increase in the capital value of the investment in the form of a rising share price.

Limitations of ratio analysis

Ratio analysis must be used with care as the ratios are based on historical data, whereas the economy is dynamic and ever-changing. Inter-firm comparisons are difficult because of different sizes, year-ends, company objectives and accounting practices. Non-quantitative information must also be considered, such as the quality of a firm's management and the skill base of its workforce.

Exam questions

answers: page 169

1 How might a finance house use accountancy ratios when considering a loan application from a firm? (20 min)

2 Must ratios have additional information to be useful? (30 min)

3 What does the debtor collection period tell you about a firm's financial control? (10 min)

The jargon

$$\text{Current ratio} = \frac{\text{current assets}}{\text{current liabilities}}$$

$$\text{Acid test} = \frac{\text{current assets} - \text{stock}}{\text{current liabilities}}$$

The jargon

$$\text{Gearing ratio} = \frac{\text{long-term loans}}{\text{capital employed}} \times 100\%$$

Checkpoint 1

What do you understand by the term 'highly geared'?

The jargon

$$\text{EPS} = \frac{\text{net profit after tax}}{\text{number of ordinary shares}}$$

$$\text{P/E ratio} = \frac{\text{market price (pence)}}{\text{EPS (pence)}}$$

Checkpoint 2

What type of value for the P/E ratio might indicate confidence in a business?

The jargon

$$\text{Dividend yield} = \frac{\text{dividends per share}}{\text{market price per share}} \times 100\%$$

Watch out!

Information expressed in figures is not always accurate. Stock values and depreciation are themselves subjective assessments.

Examiner's secrets

Interpret the ratio figures in relation to previous years, of other companies or industry averages. Try to identify trends, for example falling profits or rising debtor levels.

Costs and revenue

Cost and revenue information is crucial for decisions about price, output and new product development. It is important to understand the different types of costs and how they behave over time, in both the short run and the long run.

Cost classification and cost allocation

In order to make meaningful decisions a manager must have cost data for each product, department and function of the business. The problem with this is how to accurately *define* the costs and how to *allocate* the costs of the business to the various products and departments. Some costs are easy to allocate, such as raw materials, but many costs are shared among several products or departments, for example rent and security. Allocation becomes increasingly subjective especially where fixed costs are concerned. The management accountant attempts to overcome this problem firstly by classifying costs into *fixed* and *variable costs* or *direct* and *indirect costs*. These are then allocated as accurately as possible to the cost centres that generate them. In this way centres are made aware of their responsibility to control costs.

Fixed, variable and semi-variable costs

→ **Fixed costs** – those expenses that do not alter in the short run in relation to changes in output, e.g. rent, insurance and depreciation. These costs are linked to time rather than level of business activity.

→ **Variable costs** – those expenses that do alter in the short run to changes in output, e.g. raw materials, packaging and components. They are payments for the use of inputs.

→ **Semi-variable costs** – those expenses that vary with output but not in direct proportion, e.g. maintenance costs. They often comprise a fixed element and a variable element.

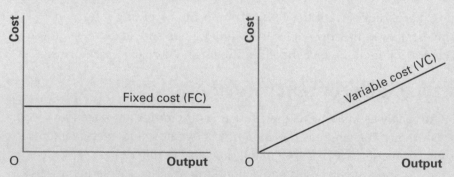

Direct and indirect costs

An alternative means of classifying costs is by means of allocation.

→ **Direct costs** – those costs that can be directly identified with a product or cost centre. They are mainly variable costs but can include some fixed costs, e.g. the rent of a building solely used for one product. They are also referred to as *prime costs*.

→ **Indirect costs** – are those costs that cannot be allocated accurately to a cost centre or product, e.g. administration costs, management salaries or maintenance costs. Another term for them is *overheads*.

Total cost

Total cost is the addition of all fixed and variable costs (plus any semi-variable costs). Where fixed costs form a significant part of total costs it is important for a business to maximize sales so that the fixed cost element is spread across as many units of output as possible.

The total cost is used by the business to see how much finance is required for each level of output.

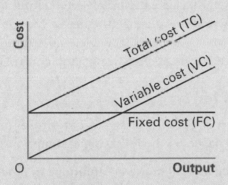

Average cost and marginal cost

Average cost is the cost per unit of production and is found by dividing total cost by total output. Average cost can be used to establish the basic price level by adding on a suitable *mark-up*.

Marginal cost is the extra cost incurred in producing one more unit of output. It is needed to calculate a product's *contribution*, which is used in some short-run decisions such as special orders (see page 159).

Revenue

Total revenue is the amount of money a business receives from selling its products. It is calculated by multiplying the number of units sold by the unit price. In order to make a profit a business must ensure that its total revenue is greater than its total costs. In order to *increase profits* a business must increase total revenue, reduce total costs or both.

Total revenue can be increased by
→ increasing the number of products sold at the current price (better advertising, promotions, etc.)
→ reducing the price in the hope that the number sold will increase by a greater proportion (see price elasticity of demand, page 71)

Total cost can be reduced by
→ reducing the overheads or fixed costs (selling surplus machinery, renting out or selling unused premises, cutting management costs)
→ reducing the variable costs per unit (obtaining cheaper raw materials, improving productivity, etc.)

Exam questions   answers: pages 169–70

1   What do you understand by the term 'cost centre'? Give examples. (15 min)

2   For what reasons might a business seek to maximize sales revenue? (15 min)

3   Reducing the workforce may not cut costs. Discuss. (15 min)

The jargon

Total cost (TC) = fixed cost (FC) + variable cost (VC)

Don't forget

Cost and revenue information help the business to calculate the break-even level of production. See page 158 for more on break-even.

The jargon

$$\text{Average cost} = \frac{\text{total cost}}{\text{total output}}$$

Contribution = price − marginal cost

Total revenue = price × quantity sold

Checkpoint 2

How would you define *total profit*?

Examiner's secrets

Accurate definitions and appropriate examples are needed to score high marks on cost-related questions.

Break-even

The most important goal in business is to survive and that means breaking even, i.e. making sufficient revenue to cover total costs.

Importance of break-even

Break-even provides the firm with its first target, i.e. covering all its costs. Any output beyond break-even will then generate a profit. Rising costs and/or falling prices will cause the break-even output to *increase*. Falling costs and/or rising prices will cause the break-even output to *decrease*. This approach also helps to focus management's attention on the importance of limiting fixed costs and ensuring good control of variable costs.

Break-even charts

A **break-even chart** is a graphical means of representing cost and revenue data. It is based on the following assumptions

→ all output is sold and there are no additions to stock
→ prices and costs per unit remain unchanged
→ there are no economies of scale associated with higher output
→ economic conditions are static, i.e. no changes in market demand, competitor reactions, government regulations, taxes or technology

A new business with fixed costs of £3m, variable cost of £8 per unit and a selling price for its product of £20 would have the following chart

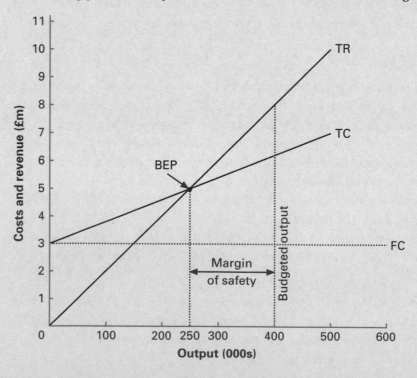

Break-even point and margin of safety

The **break-even point** and **margin of safety** can be determined by graphical means or by calculation.

→ *By graph*   The break-even output level is where the sales and total cost lines cross. From the chart it can be seen that the business

---

The jargon

Break-even point is that level of output that earns sufficient revenue to cover all costs. An alternative name for break-even is *cost-volume-profit analysis*.

Don't forget

Management must ensure that break-even is achieved on a long-term and continuing basis if the business is to survive.

Watch out!

The total revenue line always starts at the origin. The total cost line starts on the 'y' axis at the level of fixed costs.

Action point

Draw a break-even chart with fixed costs of £2m, variable costs of £5 per unit and a selling price of £15. Check that the break-even occurs at an output of 200 000 units.

The jargon

Projected sales (output) is sometimes called *budgeted output*.
   Margin of safety is the amount by which demand can fall below projected output before a firm starts to make a loss. It is sometimes shown as a percentage of the projected sales (here 37.5%).

must produce and sell 250 000 items to break even. The project's sales are 400 000 which would give the firm a margin of safety of 150 000 items (projected or budgeted output minus break-even output).

→ *By calculation* using the equation

$$\text{Break-even (B/E)} = \frac{\text{Fixed costs}}{\text{Contribution per unit (c/u)}}$$

where c/u is given by 'price minus variable costs per unit'

$$\text{B/E} = \frac{\text{£3m}}{\text{£20} - \text{£8}} = \frac{\text{£3m}}{\text{£12}}$$

$$\text{B/E} = 250\ 000 \text{ items}$$

Advantages ●●●

The *advantages* of this model are that

→ the model is easy to understand and use
→ the break-even point (or output) is easily determined
→ the profit/loss of other levels of sales can easily be found
→ the impact of price changes can be seen by altering the *slope* of the TR line
→ the impact of changes in the fixed costs can be seen by altering the *starting point* (intercept) of the TC line
→ the impact of changes in variable costs can be seen by altering the *slope* of the TC line
→ sensitivity analysis can be performed for any change of circumstances

Limitations ●●●

The *disadvantages* of this model are that

→ it is too simplistic in assuming that price/costs are constant
→ the conclusions drawn are only as good as the accuracy of the data they are based on
→ it is assumed all output is sold and no additions to stock are made
→ there are no economies of scale associated with higher levels of output
→ economic conditions are assumed to be static, i.e. no changes in market demand, competitor reaction, government regulations, taxes or technology

---

Exam questions answers: page 170

1 Outline two reasons why a firm might want to use break-even. (10 min)

2 'Break-even analysis is not very useful because it is a static model!' How far do you agree with this statement? (30 min)

3 Using the chart above or by calculation determine what happens to the break-even point and margin of safety when
   (a) variable costs rise to £10 per unit
   (b) as well as (a) price falls to £16 per unit. (20 min)

The jargon

Contribution per unit = price – variable cost per unit
Since total cost is a straight line, *variable cost per unit* is the same as *marginal cost*.

Checkpoint

What will happen to the chart if
(a) price falls
(b) fixed costs rise
(c) variable costs rise?

The jargon

Sensitivity analysis means conducting 'what if' scenarios to see what would happen to B/E and profit if various factors changed.

Don't forget

The model is only valid in the short term and when conditions are reasonably stable.

Examiner's secrets

Break-even is a fairly powerful tool that is easily understood. Ensure that you stress that it is only useful in the *short term* when some of the assumptions hold true, such as prices and costs being constant as output changes. Be able to find the break-even point, margin of safety and projected profit.

Sources of finance

Every business needs finance and there is a growing number of financial institutions willing to supply it. The skill required is to match the needs for finance with the most appropriate sources in terms of time, cost and risk.

The need for finance

There are two main areas where finance may be required.

→ *Funding of extra working capital*   This is particularly important when sales are expanding and more raw materials, work-in-progress and stock is needed. This type of finance tends to be short-term, often on a rolling basis, where more credit is taken out as earlier debts are repaid.

→ *Financing of fixed assets*   This requires a medium- and long-term commitment of the lender.

Once the need has been identified the next stage is to determine the total capital required, how long it is required for and how much can be generated *internally*. Any extra must be sought from *external* sources.

Internal sources

The majority of business finance is generated internally by the organization from its own profits. The advantage of this source is that there is no interest to pay or repayments to be made.

In extreme cases assets can be sold to raise funds, but only when more conventional means have failed.

Internal sources, however, are often not enough on their own and so funds must be generated from outside the business.

External sources (short-term)

Short-term sources of external finance are normally required to fund extra working capital. The three main methods available are

→ *Bank overdrafts* – banks allow the borrowers to overdraw funds in excess of their bank balance up to an agreed total limit. For businesses, overdraft facilities are often provided on an indefinite basis, thus providing a continuous line of credit.

→ *Trade credit* – a supplier grants a period of credit of between 30 and 90 days before payment is required for goods delivered. It is in effect an interest-free loan for the period of credit. Trade credit is the largest single source of short-term finance.

→ *Debt factoring* – outstanding debtors are 'sold' to a factoring company, which advances up to 80% of the debts outstanding. The remainder is paid, less commission, when the total debts have been collected. This improves immediately the cash flow of the business and removes the burden of credit control, which is taken over by the factoring company.

External sources (long-term) ●●●

Long-term sources of external finance are normally required to fund fixed assets. Finance for between one and five years is mostly used for the purchase of capital such as plant, machinery and vehicles. Finance for five or more years is used principally for the purchase of capital assets that have a long life, such as land and buildings.

The principal types and sources of long-term finance are

→ *Loans* – a formalized agreement between the borrower and the lender, normally a bank. The capital borrowed must be repaid over a stated period together with interest in regular instalments.

→ *Hire purchase* – the purchase of a capital asset by paying a deposit and regular instalments over a period of time. Finance houses, which retain ownership of the equipment until the last payment has been made, provide the funding.

→ *Leasing* – the firm (the *lessee*) pays an agreed rental for the leasing of equipment from the leasing company (the *lessor*). This eliminates the need for the firm to commit large sums of money to the out-right purchase of an asset. At the end of the lease the equipment is returned to the leasing company.

→ *Share issues* – this is the most important form of funds for limited companies. The principal advantages of share issues are that the company receives a 'permanent' injection of capital and can raise further funds in the future.

→ *Mortgages* – a long-term loan for the purchase of property provided by banks and building societies.

→ *Debentures* – a type of fixed period loan secured against the firm's assets and paying a fixed rate of return.

→ *Venture capital* – risk capital mainly provided by merchant banks in return for interest and part ownership of the business.

Choice of finance ●●●

Informed choice will match the duration of the need to the duration of the source of finance. For items required in the short term, such as an expansion of stocks at Christmas, a combination of extra trade credit and a larger overdraft may suffice. For items lasting longer than one year it is best to use a more permanent form of finance. This is where medium- and long-term sources should be used. The financial manager must consider criteria such as availability, flexibility, duration and risk, as well as the cost of borrowing, in making a final choice of supplier.

> **Checkpoint 1**
>
> Compare the advantages and disadvantages of loans as compared with share issues as a source of finance.

> **Action point**
>
> Compare the cost and terms of hire purchase agreements offered by high street retailers in your area.

> **Checkpoint 2**
>
> How might the risk to the business vary with the type of finance used?

> **Links**
>
> The type of finance chosen may change the *financial ratios* of a business (see page 155).

> **Watch out!**
>
> The cost of any extra borrowing should be offset by the extra profit from increased sales.

Exam questions   answers: page 171

1   Why might it be difficult for a new firm to obtain external finance? (10 min)

2   What are the advantages and disadvantages of raising funds from the sale of shares? (15 min)

3   Compare factoring and an overdraft as suitable sources for financing an increasing amount of debtors. (20 min)

> **Examiner's secrets**
>
> Cost is not always the overriding element in finance decisions. Appropriate finance means matching the type of finance to its use. The element of risk may also play a part.

Budgeting

One of the main problems that a business has to face is planning for the future and controlling events or reacting to them as the future unfolds. A budget aims to help overcome this problem. It is a plan of action, quantified in monetary terms, for the forthcoming period. The main purposes of a budget are to plan the activities of the next accounting period, to help control the business as it progresses through the period and to analyze any variations from the plan. Remedial action can then be taken before any problems become too serious.

Planning the budget

Planning the budget should involve the whole business. Management often initiates the process by recommending some *short-term goals* (such as a sales target) in line with the firm's *long-term goals* (such as a growth in market share target). These targets are then communicated to the various departments (production, marketing, sales, distribution, etc.) for their assessment as to the feasibility of the targets and the resources needed to achieve them. The separate department budgets are then co-ordinated into a final or *master budget*. The final budget should, therefore, act as a motivator as it is a combination of 'top down' target setting by senior management and 'bottom up' resource planning by departments. An 'agreed' budget should be demanding but at the same time attainable and realistic.

Control

Control is exercised through 'management by exception', i.e. by investigating items that differ significantly from the projected budget. A typical annual budget will be divided into *monthly review periods* at the end of which the planned and actual costs and revenues are compared. Differences are referred to as **variances**. Some will be 'favourable', such as lower than expected costs or higher than expected revenues. Others will be 'adverse', such as higher costs or lower sales and revenue. Variances regarded as 'significant' will be investigated further.

Variance analysis

Variances can be significant because of their size (costs over-running by thousands of pounds) or because of their importance (a continued fall in sales of a main product). Variances may help to alert management that activities are deviating from the proposed plan and to suggest that remedial action is required. This is not unusual in an economic environment that is constantly changing due to increased competition and rapid technological change. Variance analysis is both an *early warning system* to highlight problem areas and a *monitoring system* to reassure the business that its plans are accurate.

In examinations it is common for questions to highlight differences in material costs, labour costs, sales volume and sales price.

The answers involve an analysis of the true cause as being one of either 'volume' (too few sold or too much material used) or 'price' (a lower than expected selling price or higher manufacturing costs). Variance analysis is a problem-finding technique not a problem-solving technique. Management must investigate the *causes* behind the variance and take appropriate action, such as an improved advertising campaign for flagging sales.

Advantages

The main benefits of budgetary control are

→ the use of resources is regulated, drawing attention to waste and inefficiency
→ problem areas are highlighted in time for corrective action to be taken
→ department managers are made aware of their financial responsibilities and the importance of good cost control
→ communication is improved through the need for co-ordination of departments
→ budgets provide targets that can be motivational for managers and workers

Disadvantages

The drawbacks of budgetary control are

→ unrealistic budgets are demotivating in that staff will not attempt to achieve targets that are not feasible
→ budgets 'imposed' by management can create resentment among the workforce as they have not taken any part in their preparation
→ budgets can be inflexible in times of rapid market change; they are only as good as the assumptions they are based on.

Meeting the budget target might become the manager's main goal instead of concentrating on the market. For example, advertising might be reduced to meet the month's target just when a close competitor is launching a new product. In this case slavish adherence to the budget could result in permanent damage to sales.

Exam questions   answers: pages 171–2

1   What might cause a sales variance? (10 min)

2   Why should budget holders be consulted in the preparation of their budgets? (10 min)

3   Pollard Industries budgets to sell 30 000 units at an average price of £30. Actual sales revenue from 35 000 units is £98 000. What are the total sales variance, the volume variance and the price variance? (15 min)

Examiner's secrets

Adopt a two-stage approach to variance analysis. First identify the *size* of the variance, then identify the *cause* of the variance (volume, price or both).

Take note

'The budget is a tool not a master.'

Don't forget

Budgets can be used as a motivator. Employees can gain satisfaction from being given responsibility for a budget and achieving the firm's goals within the agreed financial limits.

Examiner's secrets

Be able to suggest likely reasons for variances (e.g. material price variance caused by seasonal shortages).

Investment appraisal

Capital investment decisions are part of the strategic decision-making of a firm. They are important decisions in that they can determine the future success or failure of a business. They are difficult to reverse without accepting a significant loss and contain a greater element of uncertainty as they deal with long-term changes in the market.

The capital investment decision

The decision-making process should contain the following elements

→ the identification of possible projects
→ the estimation of all cash flows
→ assessment of profitability using a range of techniques
→ consideration of qualitative factors
→ selection, implementation and monitoring of a project

Cash flows

The first step is to establish the **expected cash flows** associated with the capital investment. The start of the investment is labelled as Year 0 (meaning now). Years 1, 2, 3, etc. show the net cash flows that it is estimated will take place by the end of each year. The table illustrates a project with an initial investment of £10m and net cash flows over a five-year period. At first glance the project looks viable as it produces a surplus of £4m.

Payback

The **payback** technique estimates the length of time it will take to recover the initial capital outlay of an investment project. A simple *cumulative cash flow column* is required (see table).

Payback occurs half-way through the fourth year, i.e. after $3\frac{1}{2}$ years assuming that the cash is received evenly throughout the year.

The technique is useful when a firm is 'cash starved' or when the market is 'volatile' and there is a need to recover the investment capital as quickly as possible. Payback is therefore a measure of risk. Using this technique alone the project with the shortest payback would be the one favoured. Unfortunately the method does not measure the overall profitability of the project as it ignores the cash flows after payback.

Average rate of return (ARR)

$$ARR = \frac{\text{average annual profit}}{\text{initial capital outlay}} \times 100$$

where average annual profit is the total profit earned over the lifetime of the project divided by the number of years involved.

ARR provides a percentage figure that can be compared with the percentage rates of return of other projects or the cost of borrowing the initial capital. Unfortunately this does not take into account the *timing* of the net cash (or profit) flows. A project receiving most of its

Year	Net cash flow	Cumulative net cash flow
	£m	£m
0	(10)	(10)
1	2	(8)
2	2	(6)
3	3	(3)
4	6	3
5	1	4
Total net cash flow	4	

Example

In the above table:

$$\text{average annual profit} = \frac{\text{total profit}}{\text{no. of years}}$$

$$= \frac{£4m}{5} = £0.8\text{m p.a.}$$

$$ARR = \frac{£0.8m}{£10m} \times 100 = 8\% \text{ p.a.}$$

profit flow in the early years may have exactly the same ARR as one receiving its profit in the later years. The two projects obviously have different risks which are not shown by the ARR method.

Net present value (NPV)   ●●●

This technique recognizes that cash sums received in the future are worth less than the same sums received today. It takes account of the time value of money by 'discounting' the future sums by a suitable percentage (the discount rate). This is known as the *discounted cash flow (DCF)* method. The discount rate chosen may be the current interest rate or more likely the firm's preferred investment return. The method is relatively simple. Each year's net cash (profit) flow is reduced by multiplying it by the appropriate *discount factor* (these will be given in the question). The initial investment outlay and the discounted annual net cash flows are added together to give a **net present value** for the project. If the NPV is positive, the project is worthy of consideration, but a negative NPV should be rejected, as future profits are insufficient to cover the initial investment outlay.

Internal rate of return (IRR)   ●●●

The IRR is the discount rate which, when applied to a series of net cash flows, reduces the NPV to zero. The IRR of different projects can easily be compared against one another and against the firm's cost of capital. It is found by discounting the net cash flows at different rates until the NPV diminishes to zero.

Comparison of methods   ●●●

The NPV and IRR methods of estimating the profitability of capital projects are considered to be superior to ARR and payback. ARR ignores the timing of returns while payback ignores cash flows after payback. Despite these problems some firms may still choose to use more than one method. Whichever method is used, they all depend on the accuracy of the cash flow forecasts that are themselves subject to a wide margin of error. There are also *qualitative factors* to take into account such as

→ the relevance of the project to the firm's overall objectives
→ the impact on the workforce
→ the reaction of shareholders

Year	Net cash flow £m	Discount factor at 10%	Present value £m
0	(10)	1	(10)
1	2	0.91	1.82
2	2	0.83	1.66
3	3	0.75	2.25
4	6	0.68	4.08
5	1	0.62	0.62
	4	NPV	0.43

Example

In the table the project has a positive net present value of £0.43m, so it should be considered.

Checkpoint

What impacts would you expect a rise in business optimism to have on an investment decision?

Watch out!

Cash starved firms will place emphasis on payback as will firms which are averse to risk taking.

The jargon

Present value is the value of a future stream of income from a proposed investment converted into its current worth.

Exam questions   answers: page 172

1   Suggest and explain four factors that might be taken into account when making an investment decision. (15 min)

2   Under what circumstances would payback or ARR be the preferred investment method? (15 min)

3   Why should forecast cash flow figures be treated with caution? (10 min)

Examiner's secrets

Be prepared to argue the merits and weaknesses of each method. This will display the skill of evaluation.

165

Answers
Accounting and finance

Use of accounts

Checkpoint

Stakeholders.

Exam questions

1 The management accounts include budgets, cash flow statements and contribution statements. These would be useful to a bidding company in the following ways
   - Budgets – from these the company could see how accurately the target firm estimates cost and revenue. Overestimation of costs would indicate scope for significant cost cutting with the resultant increase in profits.
   - Cash flow forecasts – these would indicate the expected future sales and income patterns. This would provide information on the firm's expectations in the market with the current range of products.
   - Contribution forecasts – these indicate the relative strengths and weaknesses of the current product portfolio. From this it would be possible to identify products that are 'cash cows' and those that are 'dogs'.

2 Accountants in the supermarket trade have seen a technological revolution in the way that information has been gathered and analyzed. The main changes and benefits have included
   - The use of bar codes on goods – this has helped with stocktaking, stock ordering and the recording of sales at the cashout. This has largely eliminated human error as well as speeding up the process.
   - Bar code readers – these are linked directly to head office, which can monitor sales in real time. This allows management to order replacements more accurately as well as seeing the effect of instore and local advertising.
   - Consumer profiling – the use of store cards allows management to analyze each customer's purchasing habits. This knowledge can be used to more accurately target promotions to those customers more likely to respond to offers on certain items. Ultimately this makes better use of the marketing budget as well as boosting sales.

   As far as the accountant is concerned the data is available faster and in much greater detail, which allows the supermarket to use its finances more effectively.

Preparation of accounts

Checkpoint

Independent auditors are needed so that an unbiased opinion is provided about whether the final accounts published really give a 'true and fair view' of the business. Without this outside assurance many people would not risk investing in companies.

Exam questions

1 Concepts and conventions are needed in accounting in order to
   - ensure objectivity – accounts must be based on verifiable facts and not on guesswork
   - guarantee consistency – the same approach must be used over time otherwise valid comparisons would not be possible
   - ensure that revenue earned in a period is accurately matched by the costs incurred in its generation
   - provide a common approach to the valuation of assets and the recognition of debts
   - provide a common language that accountants can use to communicate and interpret financial information

   All of these are needed for the accountant to produce an accurate business statement of the 'true and fair view' of a firm's financial position.

2 Fixed assets are items that have a long-term use and can be used repeatedly such as buildings, machinery and vehicles. The current value of a fixed asset will be influenced by
   - the wear and tear on the asset
   - the expected useful life of the asset
   - the demand for the final product that the asset is helping to make
   - the rate of technological change
   - the emergence of alternatives

   Most of these factors and influences can only be estimated. Any method used to 'depreciate' assets is, therefore, at best an approximation.

3 Revenue and expenditure refer to the earning of income or the incurring of a cost in a financial period. Revenue is earned when a sale is made whether that sale is on credit or is paid for by cash. In the same way expenditure is recognized when there is a legal charge against the business. For example, telephone charges are incurred at the time of the call but the bill for payment might not be presented for several months.

Receipts and payments, on the other hand, refer to the actual transfer of cash in and out of a business that may occur after the transaction or in advance of it. For example invoices are often paid in arrears whereas deposits are paid in advance.

Profit and loss account

Checkpoints

1 Gross profit = turnover – cost of goods sold

2 Net profit = gross profit – (expenses + overheads)

Exam questions

1 Limited companies are obliged to pay dividends to shareholders but the size and regularity of payments is at the discretion of the board of directors. In a year when a loss is made the board might suspend payment of dividends. This might also be the case in a profitable year when profits are earned but the board decides to reinvest the profits in an expansion of the business. It is in the firm's interest, however, to retain the loyalty of shareholders by paying dividends on a regular basis even in years of loss. In these circumstances the dividends will be paid from reserves or from borrowing.

2 A rising level of profits is not always an indicator of a successful business. The following factors should be considered

- Is the profit the result of a sudden increase in prices that might produce a short-term gain but damage long-term market share?
- Is the profit the result of short cuts being taken with health and safety or environmental issues?
- Is the profit the result of exploiting the workforce with the result that labour relations have been permanently damaged?
- Is it the result of using lower quality materials that might lead to future customer complaints and dissatisfaction?

Short-term gains often lead to long-term suffering.

3 Even in cases where the profit performance is genuine it must be put into perspective by considering the following factors

- The rate of growth of the market – profits could be growing not because the firm is performing significantly better but because consumer demand is expanding faster than competitors can enter the market. Conversely increasing profits in a declining market indicates improved competitiveness.
- The company's corporate objectives – is the profit being earned in the sector that the business wants to develop in the future?
- The prospect of future profit growth – is the profit earned now likely to attract fierce competition, price-cutting and the erosion of profit margins?

Answers to these questions are needed before the profit growth can be deemed to be quality profit.

Balance sheet

Checkpoints

1 *Tangible assets* – those assets that can be seen and touched, such as machinery and stock.

2 *Intangible assets* – those assets that do not have a physical existence, such as goodwill, patents and copyright.

3 If the company cannot meet the interest payment to its creditors then it will be insolvent.

Exam questions

1 The balance sheet does not show the true worth of a business as it is a snapshot of the firm on one particular day. For a meaningful analysis to be made it must be compared with previous balance sheets in order to determine the trends in trading and profit.

The balance sheet does not show items such as the quality and dedication of the workforce. The ownership of intangible assets such as trademarks, patents and goodwill are also not included.

An appreciation of the market and the threat from competitors would also be needed to give a true picture of the future potential of the firm.

2 One example of a capital reserve arises when the business's fixed assets such as buildings are revalued to reflect their increased market value due to inflation. This recognizes that the true worth of an asset is more than it was at purchase. As this tends to be a gradual increase, a revaluation is only carried out every five or ten years unless there is a sudden increase in value.

3 Working capital is the difference between current assets and current liabilities. Boosting current assets or reducing current liabilities in the following way can solve insufficient working capital
- an injection of new cash by the owners
- taking out a loan
- increasing sales and retain the profit
- converting an overdraft into a longer-term loan
- selling shares
- sell some fixed assets

Cash flow management

Checkpoints

1 Inflation, strike action and breakdowns would affect cash flow in the following way
(a) inflation – costs would rise resulting in increased outflow of cash; inflow might increase depending on the degree of competition and how price sensitive the products are
(b) Strike action – inflow of cash from sales would be seriously affected as soon as existing stocks were used up.

(c) Breakdowns – this need not affect cash flow as long as sufficient stocks of finished goods exist to meet demand while repairs are carried out. Where the firm operates a just in time system with minimum stocks, the cash flow could be seriously affected in a short period of time.

Exam questions

1 A cash flow forecast sets out the anticipated inflows and outflows of cash of a business over a time period – usually a year. The forecast shows the effect of each month's cash flows upon the firm's cash balance. It will highlight periods when there is insufficient cash in the business which will allow management to arrange finance or to readjust the cash flows by delaying expenditure or boosting inflows.

In a similar way, periods of surplus cash can be identified and plans made to make good use of the funds. A bank will insist on seeing a cash flow forecast when any loan is requested so that they can see the ability of the business to repay the interest and capital.

2 The limitations of cash flow forecasts are
- the figures are only estimates
- it assumes that debtors will pay on time
- it assumes a certain inflation level and a certain interest rate level
- it assumes a particular rate of sales that can easily be affected by changes in the economy or by changes in consumer preferences
- it assumes that periods of cash shortage will be covered by the bank through an overdraft facility
So many of these variables can change that the forecast must be viewed as an approximation or guideline.

3 *Cash flow £m*

	J	F	M	A	M	J
Opening cash	52	43	48	53	57	61
Cash inflow	13	14	17	19	22	21
Cash outflow	(22)	(9)	(12)	(15)	(18)	(17)
Closing cash	43	48	53	57	61	65

The closing cash figure for June is £65m.

Ratio analysis

Checkpoints

1 A business is often regarded as highly geared if 50% of its capital is provided by loans.
2 A P/E ratio of 15 is the average on the London Stock Exchange. Anything above this is usually regarded as favourable for the future of the business.

Exam questions

1 The examiner is looking for the application of the gearing concept to the taking on of more debt. Use should be made of the gearing ratio of long-term liabilities to capital employed and the interest rate cover to explain the impact of servicing extra debt. The finance house wants to be assured that the business has sufficient profit and cash flow to keep up payments of both interest and capital.

2 You should be aware that this question is not solely about ratios and how they are calculated. This is a common examination fault. The essay is principally about the limitations of ratios and asks specifically for examples of information other than ratios. You must stress that ratios must be analyzed in context, over a period of time and alongside other information in order to score highly. Other information might include
   * size of company
   * type of market
   * extent of competition
   * industrial relations
   * economic outlook
   * future plans of the business
   * accuracy of the figures
   * the company's objectives
   Each point should be discussed with reference to ratios, e.g. the impact of greater competition on profitability ratios.

3 The lack of liquidity is one of the main problems for firms, particularly small concerns and new businesses. The debtor collection period is crucial, therefore, to keeping a tight control on the amount of credit extended to customers. A long period might indicate poor control of debtor collection and a reliance possibly on an increasing overdraft facility. A short period might indicate an efficient control over debtors with quick follow up as invoices become due.

Costs and revenue

Checkpoints

1 The business must cover its running or variable costs for it to keep trading in the short run.
2 Total profit = total revenue − total cost.

Exam questions

1 A cost centre is a department or section of a business to which specific costs can be accurately allocated. The centre could be a department, a project, a person, a process or a machine.
   For example, a firm might have individual cost centres for its marketing operations, its photocopying service and for its sales representatives.

2 The main reason for maximizing sales revenue is to increase profit. As revenue is made up of sales multiplied by price there are two main options available
   * Adopt a high price, low sales volume policy. This is typical with firms that have a product that does not face keen competition such as some pharmaceutical products and new technology equipment.
   * Adopt a low price, high sales volume strategy. This is typical in markets where goods are fairly similar and consumers do not have strong brand preference.
   Another reason for maximizing sales revenue might be to build market share. In this case profits are secondary to the drive for new customers. Firms attempting to enter a new market or to force some competitors out of the market adopt this policy.

3 In the short term, the reduction of the workforce is often seen as the quickest way of cutting costs. Its impact on expenditure is immediate. The long-term effect, however, might not be to decrease costs. The reasons for this are that
  * productivity might fall if experienced staff are lost
  * when the firm wants to expand it will incur recruitment costs
  * new staff will need to be inducted and possibly trained
  * remaining staff might suffer lower morale and not work as enthusiastically
  * the company's image might be damaged which might deter good workers from applying

Break-even

Checkpoint

(a) The TR line will pivot downwards, break-even output will rise and margin of safety fall. Budgeted profit will also fall.
(b) The TC line shifts vertically upwards (and parallel). Break-even output will rise and margin of safety fall. Budgeted profit will also fall.
(c) The TC line will pivot upwards with the same intercept on the vertical axis. Break-even output will rise and margin of safety fall. Budgeted profit will also fall.

Exam questions

1 A firm might want to use break-even for the following reasons
  * to help determine a selling price that will cover all costs and give an acceptable level of profit
  * To conduct sensitivity analysis in order to explore the likely impact of changes to costs and prices

2 The opening to this essay should explain that break-even is a static model because it assumes no change in costs and prices over the range of output. This is simplistic, as there should be some economies of scale.

This apart, the rest of the essay should argue that the model is still useful because
  * it relates scale of output to profitability
  * it provides insights into the impact of changes in costs
  * it shows the effect of price changes on the break-even point and the margin of safety
  * it can be used to set output or sales targets
    The counter argument would highlight that the model
  * assumes that all output is sold which is simplistic given the changing tastes and buying habits of consumers
  * ignores the dynamics of the market place such as the actions of competitors or changes in technology
    Evaluation marks can be earned by presenting a balanced conclusion. An acceptable comment might stress the usefulness of the model in the short term but note that it is simplistic in the long term.

3 Use the equation

$$\text{Break-even} = \frac{\text{fixed costs}}{\text{contribution}}$$

where contribution = price − variable cost

(a)
$$\text{B/E} = \frac{\text{£3m}}{\text{£20} - \text{£10}}$$
B/E = 300 000 units
margin of safety is now only 100 000 units.

(b)
$$\text{B/E} = \frac{\text{£3m}}{\text{£16} - \text{£10}}$$
B/E = 500 000 units
The firm would see its break-even point double from 250 000 to 500 000, that is 100 000 above the projected sales. There is no margin of safety as the firm is now in a loss-making situation.

Sources of finance

Checkpoints

1 Share issues may not require any extra borrowing (therefore a lower gearing ratio). If the firm earns low

profits then it is at less risk of insolvency since shareholders are owners who take risks rather than creditors of the company. Dividend payments may be lower than current rates of interest, so that share capital may be cheaper.

2 See parts of answer to Checkpoint on page 170.

Exam questions

1 A new firm might find it difficult to raise external finance because
  - it may not have any collateral to offer as security
  - it has no track record of debt repayment
  - new firms are considered high risk ventures as many will fail in the first three years
  - it takes time to build profitability therefore the lender risks delayed repayment
  - inexperienced owners, particularly in the area of financial management, might control new businesses

Examiner's secrets

New businesses are high-risk ventures. Lenders need to be assured that their investments are safe otherwise loans are rejected or charged at premium rates.

2 The main advantages and disadvantages are:

Advantages	Disadvantages
• large amounts of capital can be raised	• cost of share issue and sale
• capital is free of the burden of interest payments	• ownership and control is diluted
• capital is permanent	• shareholders will expect growing annual dividends
• capital does not have to be repaid	

Examiner's secrets

To obtain high marks you should weigh up the merits and drawbacks of gaining more capital in this way but in the context of the firm in question.

3 An overdraft is an expensive means of finance. It should be used only where the need for finance is short-term. In this case it would not be suitable if the increase in debtors is deemed to be permanent.

The use of factors is really to improve the cash flow of a business and to reduce the firm's administration costs. The fee charged by factors (usually 5% of the invoice figure) can seriously reduce the profit margin particularly with low margin products.

Although factoring would be a better option there is no real substitute for the injection of more permanent capital into the business to fund the rising working capital need. This can be achieved through a loan, selling shares or by a further injection by the owners.

Examiner's secrets

Make sure that you accurately define the terms and then confine the discussion to the task in the question. Too many candidates reproduce standard answers that do not refer to the specifics in the question. In this case the problem is debtor finance on a long-term basis.

Budgeting

Exam questions

1 A sales variance might be caused by
  - a difference in the actual volume of sales compared to the predicted sales volume
  - a difference in the price actually charged
  - a combination of both

Variance analysis can isolate the two effects but the causes will need to be investigated. A drop in sales volume could range from a slow down in economic activity to increased advertising by close competitors.

Examiner's secrets

Variance analysis asks questions rather than provides answers. It gives early warning signs that management must act upon before a situation becomes serious.

2 Budget holders should be consulted in the preparation of their budgets because
  - involvement in the budget process will develop some ownership of the end budget
  - imposed budgets are often viewed as unfair even when they are not
  - targets set by the budget holders will act as a motivator
  - first-level operators are closest to the actual job and therefore are in the best position when cost control is needed

Examiner's secrets

Budgets are as much to do with motivating a workforce as they are to do with controlling finances. Stress the impact on the human dimension in any question involving budget setting and cost control.

3

	Units	Price	Revenue (£000s)
Budget	30 000	30.00	900
Actual	35 000	28.00	980
Sales variance			80

The first step is to calculate the price actually charged from the information given in the question by dividing total revenue by sales volume (£980 000 ÷ 35 000 = £28.00).

The sales variance was favourable by £80 000.

Volume variance = difference in volume × standard price

$$5\,000 \times £30 = £150\,000$$

Price variance = actual volume × difference in price

$$35\,000 \times (£2) = (£70\,000)$$

The *total variance* can be broken down into a favourable volume variance of £150 000 and an adverse price variance of £70 000 giving an overall favourable variance of £80 000.

Investment appraisal

Checkpoint

A rise in business optimism will raise the expected future returns on the project and therefore make investment more attractive to the firm at any given rate of interest.

Exam questions

1 The following factors need to be taken into account when considering an investment decision
   - The firm's belief in the future. This is needed in order to create a picture of the future market and will include forecasts about demand, costs, inflation, taxation, etc.
   - The investor's attitude to risk and project uncertainty. This is important when the project involves large amounts of capital.
   - The alternative projects available.

   - The finance available. Are there sufficient funds available internally or must the firm take on more long-term debt? What will be the effect on gearing?

2 Payback would be a preferred method when a quick return is needed. This is usually to maintain cash flow or to keep risk to a minimum. Firms that are cash starved prefer payback as an indicator.

   ARR is preferred when forecasts are reasonably accurate and the firm is not cash starved. In these circumstances high return projects are welcome even when the cash inflow is spread across the project.

3 Forecast cash flow figures must be treated with extreme caution because
   - the collection of data might be inaccurate
   - the estimates might be over-optimistic
   - improvements in technology might render the project process obsolete
   - demand for the product could change significantly thus affecting revenue figures
   - government legislation might impose unforeseen costs
   - raw material supply might become more difficult to obtain or expensive

All the examinations covered by this book include a paper with structured questions and extended writing based on either pre-issued or unseen case material. Most also include a project option. All have a synoptic element as the final end of A2 course assessment. The aim here is to provide guidelines on how to deal with each of these assessment areas.

Much of your success will depend upon your efforts in the examination room. In a very short period of time you will have to show the examiner your mastery of the subject. There is, however, no short cut to mastering this, or any other, subject. Success will be achieved by revision, not just in the few weeks prior to the examination but consistent revision throughout your course.

As part of your preparation for the examination you should practise answering past examination questions. It is important, therefore, that you have a supply of these for each topic area. The questions at the end of each spread have been carefully selected to illustrate the various kinds of questions that might appear in a topic area. You should attempt all of these within the suggested time allocation. This will help you to revise the topic and improve your exam technique. Each of these questions has an outline answer provided at the end of the chapter with examiner hints.

Exam boards

In order to organize your notes and revision you will need a copy of your exam board's syllabus specification. You can obtain a copy by writing to the board or by downloading the syllabus from the board's website.

AQA (*Assessment and Qualifications Alliance*)
Publications Department, Stag Hill House, Guildford, Surrey, GU2 5XJ www.aqa.org.uk

EDEXCEL
Stewart House, 32 Russell Square, London, WC1B 5DN www.edexcel.org.uk

OCR (*Oxford, Cambridge and Royal Society of Arts*)
1 Regent Street, Cambridge, CB2 1GG www.ocr.org.uk

WJEC (*Welsh Joint Education Committee*)
245 Western Avenue, Cardiff, CF5 2YX www.wjec.co.uk

CCEA (*Northern Ireland Council for Curriculum, Examinations and Assessment*)
Clarendon Dock, 29 Clarendon Road, Belfast, BT1 3BG www.ccea.org.uk

Topic checklist

○ AS ● A2	AQA	EDEXCEL	OCR	WJEC
Planning revision	○●	○●	○●	○●
Command words and levels of response	○●	○●	○●	○●
Short answer and extended writing	○●	○●	○●	○●
Case studies – pre-issued and unseen	○●	○●	○●	○●
Synoptic writing	●	●	●	●
Projects – starting	●	●	●	●
Projects – finishing	●	●	●	●

Planning revision

Don't forget

Be serious about constructing a timetable and about following it!

Examiner's secrets

It is useful to display some reminders that will help to refocus your attention during revision sessions. For example:
Don't just sit there. Do something!
or
Be active not passive!
or
Coffee break starts when tasks have been finished. Not before!

Check the net

A series of revision notes is available at www.bized.ac.uk

A dictionary definition of a plan is '*a detailed scheme or method for obtaining an objective*'. This highlights three important points about your revision

→ it must be detailed
→ it must be methodical
→ it must have an objective or target

It is obvious, therefore, that a first step is to create a timetable that details the topics to be covered, the times and dates of revision and the tasks to be achieved. A few hours spent on this will provide enormous benefits not only in terms of improved exam performance but also in relieving the stress and anxiety that are associated with exam preparation.

Planning your revision

Your plan should be based on the four Cs. You should be

→ *careful* – ensure that all topics are covered
→ *conscientious* – ensure that you follow the plan
→ *conservative* – restrict the time allowance to manageable periods with plenty of planned breaks
→ *cerebral* (intelligent) – ensure that the tasks that you attempt make your brain *use* the information to answer the question set and not simply to regurgitate your notes

Step by step approach

→ Start revising in good time. Last minute revision may work for some people but, on the whole, it is too risky.
→ Try to allocate a set time each week when you are going to revise this subject and make sure you have enough 'slots to cover all the subjects you are revising for.
→ Be clear about what you have to learn. Make a list of topics covered in your course. Check that you have covered all the topics by obtaining a syllabus.
→ Be prepared to adapt your timetable as you go along. Some topics will take more or less time than you imagined. Build in rest periods for relaxation and treats. These will help to keep you going. If you are working hard, you deserve them, so take them without feeling guilty.
→ Everyone has a limited concentration span, so each revision session should be broken down into periods of approximately 30 to 40 minutes, after which a short break of 5 to 10 minutes should be taken.
→ Each spread (two pages) in this book could provide a useful revision session on a particular topic.

Revise actively. This means doing more than just reading over something. You may fool yourself into thinking you have learnt a topic simply because you understand it and recognize the ideas when you read them over. This is not the same as being able to reproduce those ideas in an exam. At the very least you should summarize your notes and then summarize them again. Your knowledge of a broad subject area should be capable of being reduced to a list of headings on several index cards.

Other ways of revising include

→ mind maps
→ reading aloud
→ taping notes and replaying them at odd intervals
→ getting someone to test your knowledge
→ discussing topics with a friend or the family
→ creating mnemonics

You should vary your methods of revising so as to maintain concentration.

→ Practise reproducing information by yourself without the aid of notes. Initially this may take the form of reproducing your summarized notes. Soon, though, you should be attempting to answer examination questions. Try to ensure you have a practice run of the exam before the real thing. You will find plenty of timed examination questions in this book.
→ Expect to work hard. Sadly, few of us are geniuses capable of soaking up information with little effort. You will need to put in the hours. But remember that it is the quality of your revision, not the quantity of time spent on it, that matters most.

Using exam questions in revision

After you have revised a topic area it is vital that you carefully consider examination questions of the type you will find in your exam. You must, of course, try the questions you will find at the end of each topic in this book. These are intended to highlight the important issues of the topic.

Trying past questions helps make your revision active and has a number of advantages

→ it will check whether you have really understood the topic you have been trying to revise
→ any gaps in your knowledge and understanding of a topic area will be revealed. It is better to find this out before the exam so that you can go back and revise more thoroughly. You can even make extra notes on a sub-topic where necessary
→ you will begin to identify the sorts of questions you can do well, and perhaps even the sorts of questions you might want to avoid
→ you will become more familiar with the type of language used in questions

Checking yourself against the outline answers will help you to see what the examiner was looking for. Nearer to the exam you should practise answering a whole paper in the length of time allowed for the exam.

Examiner's secrets

The use of *index cards* is a good way of condensing notes to a manageable size. Produce an index card for each topic or sub-topic containing important headings, diagrams, mnemonics and examples.

Don't forget

Once time has been allocated for reading the question paper there is usually about 1 minute left for each mark available, e.g. spend no more than 15 minutes on a 15 mark question.

Examiner's secrets

The 'command' word used in a question dictates the type of answer required and should be strictly followed.

Command words and levels of response

Many candidates lose marks because they fail to do precisely what the examiner requires them to do. It is imperative, therefore, to have a sound grasp of the differences between the various *command words*. Having established what is required, you need to write to the correct depth. For many essay-type questions this will be marked using *a level of response* marking scheme. You need to know the difference between knowledge and understanding, analysis and evaluation.

Command words

It is crucial to understand the examiner's instructions. For example the term '*outline*' is asking for only a superficial treatment of a topic whereas '*explain*' is demanding some reasons for an action or situation.

→ *Analyze* – to demonstrate an understanding of a topic area by breaking it down into its component parts and examining their relationship.

→ *Assess* – to make an informed judgement about how good or effective something is, based on an awareness of strengths and limitations of the argument presented.

→ *Compare/contrast and compare* – to consider similarities and differences between the stipulated topic areas.

→ *Consider* – to demonstrate knowledge and understanding of a topic.

→ *Criticize* – to appraise or evaluate the strengths and weaknesses of the topic.

→ *Define* – to explain precisely and accurately what a term means.

→ *Describe* – to present evidence of knowledge in the topic area without any explanation of the information.

→ *Discuss* – to consider or examine a topic by reference to different or contrasting points of view.

→ *Distinguish between* – to demonstrate an understanding of the differences between two topic areas.

→ *Evaluate/critically evaluate* – to make an informed judgement regarding the value or significance of a stipulated topic area, based on systematic analysis and examination.

→ *Examine/critically examine* – to present a detailed consideration of the stipulated topic area. This may also require the candidates to show an understanding of the strengths and limitations of the information presented.

→ *Explain* – to give an explanation of why something has occurred. It implies that more than a description is required.

→ *Illustrate* – to clarify by means of an example or visual material.

→ *Justify* – to consider the grounds for a decision, for example by offering supportive consideration of the logic behind that decision.

→ *Outline/state* – to offer a summary description of the stipulated topic area in brief form.

Levels of response

Many exam boards now use a '*levels of response*' marking scheme for essay-type answers. In order to obtain a higher level you must demonstrate the harder skills such as analysis and evaluation. It is not good enough to produce a simple list of facts, as the example below demonstrates for a 12-mark question:

Level 4 (10–12 marks) Evaluates the problem in context and is able to justify or prioritize courses of action.
Level 3 (7–9 marks) Analyzes the problem in context.
Level 2 (4–6 marks) Applies knowledge and critical understanding to the problem.
Level 1 (1–3 marks) A simple list of facts with little development. Demonstrates knowledge and understanding.

To obtain the highest marks you should practise analyzing and evaluating problems, suggesting alternative solutions. Pointing out the benefits and drawbacks of recommended courses of action is part of the evaluation process that is required for level 4.

Let us look at some of the higher academic qualities on which you will be tested.

Analysis (breaking down)

→ Identification of cause, effect and interrelationships.
→ The appropriate use of theory or business cases/practice to investigate the question set.
→ Breaking down the material to show underlying causes of problems.
→ Use of appropriate techniques to analyze data.

Synthesis (bringing together)

→ Building the points/themes within the answer into a connected whole.
→ Logical sequencing of an argument.
→ Clarity through summarizing an argument.

Evaluation (judgement)

→ Judgement shown in weighing up the relative importance of different points or sides of an argument in order to reach a conclusion.
→ Informed comment on the reliability of evidence.
→ Distinguishing between fact and opinion.
→ Judgement of the wider issues and implications.
→ Conclusion drawn from the evidence presented.
→ Selectivity – ensuring material is relevant to the question.

Analysis and evaluation are the route to top grades in all exams.

Examiner's secrets

Illustrate your statement with an example drawn from the case study. This will ensure you are writing in context!

Examiner's secrets

Only answers *in context* can achieve above level 1! To reach level 4 you must provide a judgement, or considered conclusion, or weighing up of the evidence, or a justified course of action.

Don't forget

Evaluation is a high order skill that leads to high order marks!

Short answer and extended writing

All exam boards will require you to do *short answer* or *restricted response* questions. These are often comparatively simple but many candidates lose marks by not following the command correctly or by not recognizing the range of treatment indicated by the mark allocation. You will also be required to demonstrate the skills of extended or discursive writing. Essay-style questions allow examiners to discriminate between students by posing problems that require them to display *higher-level skills*.

Restricted response questions

These are designed to test recall and comprehension across the whole of the syllabus. Although most candidates feel that this is an easy part of the examination, many do not have the necessary breadth of knowledge to achieve high marks!

When you answer these questions you should look carefully at the *mark allocation* and the *command word*. Often no more than one or two concise statements are required.

Thus if you come across a question such as

'State two ways in which an office manager may motivate his workers' (2 marks)

you could respond by writing

higher levels of pay
involvement in decision-making

Here it is fairly obvious that you receive one mark for each brief statement you make.

Words such as *State*, *Give*, *Name*, *Outline*, *List* and *What* indicate a simple answer with little development or explanation required. Some answers require slightly fuller treatment. Again, the mark allocation and the 'command' words are normally helpful.

For example, if the question is

'Define income elasticity of demand' (3 marks)

you are being asked to go further than a statement without explanation.

Words such as *Explain*, *How*, *Why*, *Describe*, *Define* and *Compare* commonly indicate some form of development or explanation in the answer.

Short answer questions often form the first part of a larger question. The question is structured so that marks on the first part are fairly easy to obtain but later parts become more difficult. Through this 'incline of difficulty' the examiner is able to distinguish between candidates of differing ability.

Extended writing – planning your answer

Once you have decided what questions you are going to tackle you can start to *plan* your answer. You should plan to allocate an appropriate amount of time according to the mark allocation (and also ensure that you answer the required number of questions).

Some candidates, having selected a topic that they understand, immediately begin writing. This should be avoided. At A-level the questions asked are very specific and are unlikely to be answered directly from the notes you have memorized. The examiner is looking for thoughtful, well-planned answers. You need to think about how you are going to respond to the question set.

A lot of candidates will write a brief plan at the top of their answer, adding to it as they go along. Other candidates will draw a spider diagram. Whatever method you use, planning is an effective way of marshalling your thoughts. A plan will help to ensure that you

→ cover all the points you have thought of
→ don't repeat the same point

The introduction

The *introduction* sets the scene for the rest of the essay. It should be short and to the point. You should define any technical terms that are used in the question. Where a question can be answered in a number of different ways you should explain the approach that you are taking.

The core

In the *core* of your essay you will be developing your major points. It is important that these points are developed properly or you will lose many marks. Many examiners' reports criticize students for merely listing a large number of points rather than developing the most important ones. Remember, providing a list of points with little or no development can never provide that depth of analysis or evaluation that A-level Business Studies demands.

You should also consider the order in which you make your points. Leave the less important points until later (just in case you run out of time). Thus, in a question on why a business might prefer to adopt company rather than partnership status, if you believe that limited liability is a key consideration it should be mentioned first.

The conclusion

Many students do not leave much time for the *conclusion*, believing that it is of little importance. This is very wrong. In practice, it is the conclusion that is the key to gaining high marks. For example, where the command words are 'assess' or 'analyze the extent to which', it is in the conclusion that you summarize and make some kind of judgement on the relative importance of the various points you have made.

Examiner's secrets

Remember – it is always easier to move from 0/20 to 5/20 than to move from 15/20 to 20/20. This is because the marks for knowledge and comprehension are gained far more easily than the marks for synthesis and evaluation.

Watch out!

Many candidates lose marks because they answer the question they wanted to come up rather than the one that did!

Examiner's secrets

Examiners regularly comment that candidates earned low marks because they failed to interpret the key or command words in an essay title. Make sure you understand what command words require you to do (see page 176).

Don't forget

You can also use the *introduction* to indicate the stages that will appear in the core of the essay.

Links

See page 177, 'Levels of response'.

Examiner's secrets

Demonstrate your depth of knowledge. Use business terms and concepts. Use up-to-date examples or examples from the case study to illustrate your points. When referring to a theory, identify the author or source of that theory.

Watch out!

Including even one or two appropriate sentences in the conclusion may help to move you up to level 4 in the mark scheme.

Case studies – pre-issued and unseen

A *case study* is a simulation of a 'real life' situation. Questions based on the case study seek to test your understanding of the syllabus. The examiner expects your answer to be related to the case material, but business ideas, concepts and theories should always substantiate your ideas and arguments.

Pre-issued and unseen case studies – the difference

Unseen case studies tend to be about 1 000 to 1 200 words. Pre-issued case studies are substantially longer, more detailed and may contain tables, graphs and charts. AS case studies commonly relate to operational issues whereas at A2 level the cases focus on decision-making, problem solving and strategy.

You will be expected to have a deeper understanding of the issues arising from a pre-issued case study. However, both types of case study can be approached using a similar analytical method.

Case analysis

Getting started

You should first read through the case quickly. Don't stop and ponder. The aim of this first reading is to familiarize yourself with the general situation before undertaking a more detailed analysis.

Assessing the situation

You are now at the stage where you need to become more familiar with the information in the case study. This may be done in a number of ways.

The most popular way is *highlighting* those aspects of the case study which are considered important.

Another method that students often use is to *index information*. This is done by selecting key ideas, for example marketing or production, and indicating by the initial M or P in the margin of the case study any point relating to marketing or production.

This method of grouping information under headings such as marketing, accounting, production or human resources can be used as a more detailed framework for studying the case. Thus if you were studying a case where the emphasis was on marketing, you would be looking for information on products, price, promotion, place.

Not all the information in the case study will be of the same quality or have the same degree of precision. Some information will be very concise. Distinguish between opinion and fact. Decide which information should be treated with caution.

Identifying the problems

You will, by now, be very familiar with the case material and will already have identified some problems. Now

1 List all the problems you have identified. Many will be stated explicitly in the text. Others, though, will only be identified by the careful analysis you have just undertaken.
2 Ask yourself whether any of the problems are connected. For example, high absenteeism and high labour turnover may (but not necessarily) be connected. Equally you may find that one problem causes another. Thus low profitability may be caused by poor stock control.
3 Ask yourself – are the problems stated the real problem or the sign of a more deep-rooted problem? Thus high labour turnover may merely be the outward manifestation of low morale.

Generating alternative solutions

Having identified the problem and its cause, we now need to generate *alternative solutions* to that problem. In doing so we need to be clear exactly what we are trying to achieve. You should state your objectives, i.e. 'what you are trying to achieve' and 'what outcomes you expect'. These objectives should be kept in mind at all times.

For each problem you have identified you need to generate a number of solutions. The more alternatives you have to consider, the better the final decision is likely to be.

The subject matter of business studies provides you with a whole range of principles, analytical tools, strategies and tactics that have been used and found successful in real-life situations. Make sure that your answer utilizes business theory.

Evaluating the alternatives

The key question to answer is 'how well does each alternative solve the problem?' In practice you will find that all solutions have good and bad points. None will solve the problem perfectly. You should list the 'pros' and 'cons' for each alternative solution before making a decision.

In making a decision between alternatives you will have to assess the impact of each solution on the whole organization. It is important to realize that the solution that is best for one department may incur high costs in the rest of the organization. It may be necessary, therefore, to select a solution which is less than perfect for that department in order to minimize costs elsewhere.

Evaluation requires you to compare alternatives and justify your choice.

Examiner's secrets

Look for the connections. Thus increased unit cost may result from poor machine maintenance.

Watch out!

In many case studies questions will have different values. Make sure you allocate your time accordingly!

Don't forget

If you are working in groups analyzing a pre-issued case, try brainstorming the situation.

Don't forget

You may find the framework introduced under 'assessing the situation' helpful here.

Examiner's secrets

For many case study questions there is no right answer. The examiner is looking for your ability to analyze, evaluate and draw conclusions from the case study material.

Synoptic writing

A key part of studying business at A2 level is to develop an integrated approach. Instead of concentrating on individual functional areas of a business you must adopt an integrated approach, recognizing that decisions and actions taken in one part of the organization will have direct consequences on other areas. For example, increased production will lead to overstocking unless additional marketing creates further demand.

All specifications include a minimum of 20% synoptic assessment to be taken at the end of the course. Synoptic writing is defined as the explicit integration of knowledge, understanding, analysis and evaluation. It requires you to make connections between different topics and to demonstrate the interactive nature of the business world.

The requirements

Most synoptic units will require you to

→ examine the external influences on business activities which affect decision-making and the ability of firms to meet their objectives
→ recognize the inherent conflict between the different stakeholders in a business
→ suggest and evaluate possible resolutions of stakeholder conflict
→ recognize the inter-relationship between a firm's objectives and the operation of an uncertain, dynamic business environment
→ devise and evaluate strategies that aim to anticipate, respond to and manage a changing environment

All of these skills must be demonstrated within the context of the question.

Examples of synoptic studies

The exam question might focus on one particular area.

→ *Marketing* – analyze and evaluate the effectiveness of different marketing strategies, tactics and techniques for a business that is trying to adapt to a changing market.
→ *Operations management* – analyze and evaluate the use of different management tools to improve the decision-making process to achieve higher efficiency and quality.
→ *Accounts and finance* – use and evaluate a range of performance measures in a critical manner to assist the achievement of an organization's strategic objectives.
→ *Human resources* – analyze and evaluate the relationship between organizational structure, leadership style and motivation and their impact on the successful management of human resources.
→ *External influences* – analyze the impact of market change on a business, e.g. increased competition from abroad.

- *Communication* – recognize the central importance of good communications for the successful achievement of business objectives.
- *Industrial relations* – the impact of poor industrial relations on productivity, efficiency, morale, motivation, absenteeism and labour turnover.
- *Ethics* – the role and influence of external pressure groups on corporate policy and practices, e.g. the use of genetically modified plants in food production.
- *Government policies* – increasing legislative demands on firms and the implications for location of industry, e.g. call centres re-locating to south-east Asia to take advantage of lower labour costs and less expensive working conditions.
- *Objectives and strategy* – refocusing the business towards a new opportunity, e.g. the emerging markets of Eastern Europe or the growth in low-cost airlines.

Answering synoptic questions

- Take note of any restrictions in the question and do not stray outside them.
- Plan your answer carefully – logic rather than length is required.
- Be analytical – look at several alternatives or viewpoints.
- Look to compare and contrast the advantages and disadvantages in each alternative strategy with reference to the objectives required.
- Be evaluative – in your conclusion weigh up the alternatives and make some form of considered judgement.
- Use examples and detail from the context to reinforce your arguments and to ensure you are writing in context.
- Synthesis – be aware that high marks are awarded for the logical sequencing of an argument and clarity in summarizing an argument.

Good and bad answers!

A bad answer will

- show gaps in basic knowledge of business theory
- write in very general terms basing answers on general knowledge
- fail to relate answers to the case study
- fail to read the synoptic material carefully
- make assertions without justification

A good answer will

- use relevant business theory to underpin arguments, e.g. Porter, Ansoff
- write specifically about the scenario
- identify the key personnel and key issues
- identify the advantages and disadvantages of different strategies
- justify the chosen solution

Projects – starting

We can define a *project* as some kind of investigation undertaken by an individual student. It will relate to an issue, topic or management problem on which the student is required to collect data, undertake analysis, draw conclusions and make recommendations. It will be presented in a report format.

Most of the examination boards include a project as part of their assessment criteria. The phraseology may differ, it may be called a project, dissertation or assignment, but it combines those elements outlined above.

Choosing a topic

Look at past projects

Projects provide you with a chance to select a topic that you personally are interested in. This should mean that motivation is less of a problem than in other parts of your course. Selecting an appropriate topic is very important. A lack of thought at this stage may affect the successful outcome of the project.

Past project material may be available within your school or college. You should ask your tutor whether it is possible for you to look at a representative selection of these projects. You should also ask your tutor to discuss the projects with you. What did he think were good and bad points in each? What difficulties did they face?

Successful project titles

How can AB Hotel solve its staffing problem?

Should CD Co computerize its accounting system?

How can EF Ltd improve its stock control?

Is it feasible to open a Thai restaurant in Batley?

Should GH Ltd relocate its production facilities to Eastern Europe?

How should a local boutique decide its pricing policy?

Is it profitable to renovate an old building into student accommodation?

How should a company introduce a *no smoking* policy?

Most examination boards insist that you submit your proposed title to them for approval, some ask for rather more detail, but even if they don't you would be well advised to do more than just 'think' of a title. You should discuss with your tutor

→ the aims of the project
→ potential sources of information
→ methods of investigation
→ criteria for assessing project results

Some examination boards insist that the project considers a work-based problem. Others may suggest that it covers more than one functional area of the organization. If in doubt, check with your tutor.

Take note

All sources of information must be duly acknowledged. Failure to do so will be penalized as plagiarism.

Examiner's secrets

Choosing a title in the form of a question will ensure that your project is analytical and has an investigative focus.

Check the net

Alternatively go to the exam board's website. See page 173.

Is the project tackled from a business studies angle?

The aim of the project is to show that you can *apply* business studies concepts and techniques to a given situation. Thus it follows that projects may fail because

→ They deal with a topic in an incorrect manner. For example, whilst 'the ethics of advertising' may be considered too vague, 'evaluating the effectiveness of XYZ Co's advertising campaign' would be acceptable.

→ The project is merely descriptive and fails to use the appropriate concepts or techniques. Thus in a project 'Should ABC Co invest in new machinery?', the concept of opportunity cost should be introduced, as should the various techniques of investment appraisal.

→ Is there a clear question (hypothesis) to answer or investigate? In submitting their project titles, candidates are encouraged to ask a question. Experience has shown that titles such as 'Personnel policy in ABC Co' or 'The advertising strategy of PQ Charity' will result in a project which is too descriptive to gain high marks. In many cases the general area of research is perfectly acceptable, but by asking a specific question the research is more clearly focused, analysis is undertaken and conclusions drawn.

Is it feasible?

Due to the constraints of time, money and student ability, students are often recommended to limit their area of research. Thus a study of a large organization is legitimate, but if it is too large and complex the end project is likely to be very descriptive. It is far better to tackle one problem within a particular department of that organization.

An attempt should also be made at the outset of the project to see whether the information needed is readily available. Where the information has a value to the organization itself or to its competitors, it is unlikely to be available for student use. Equally, where the conclusion of a project is likely to be critical of an organization's actions, co-operation is unlikely. If in doubt, ask the organization whether information will be available. Be specific – indicate precisely what you will need.

Can high marks be gained from undertaking this project?

You should be aware of the *assessment criteria* against which your project will be judged. Generally speaking, a large proportion of the marks will be given for higher level skills, e.g. analysis, evaluation, conclusions and recommendations. Once more we emphasize, avoid purely descriptive projects, as you will deny yourself many potential marks. It is far better to undertake some investigation into a practical problem within an organization.

It is important that you use both secondary (desk) research and primary (field) research. In such circumstances candidates are expected to use a variety of methods, draw together the findings and undertake some form of critical evaluation.

Example

What are the implications of the Euro for the UK? A likely examiner response would be that it would be better to avoid a purely economics topic. Instead, consider the impact on a specific firm or industry.

Example

Better titles would be
How could ABC Ltd's human relations strategy be improved?
or
Is advertising an effective form of promotion for PQ Charity?

Example

'Does consumer protection work?' Likely examiner's comment would be that this is far too complex a project for a student.

Example

'A study of equal opportunities policy in XYZ Ltd.'
Likely examiner's comment would be that key information would not be readily available. The student would then be forced to rely on bland public relations statements. The title is not in the form of a question and is likely to be descriptive.

Examiner's secrets

Make sure you use business concepts and techniques. To gain high marks you would have to refer to various sources of information, such as data, government sources, quality newspapers, magazine articles and reputable sites on the Internet. These are *secondary sources*; *primary sources* might be devising and using your own questionnaire.

Projects – finishing

In the previous section (pages 184–5) we were concerned with the need to identify a *project title* that could reasonably be undertaken by an A-level student. We now turn our attention to the *presentation* of those findings.

Presenting your project

All examination boards use a project or extended essay as part of their scheme of assessment. Some examination boards require a *presentation* in the form of a report. Although some require you to adopt a suitable format, in the vast majority of cases this would involve a report format.

Despite *reports* being a common form of written communication in both business and government, there is no one agreed format. Try to obtain examples of past projects from your tutor and study the report structure. You may find that there is considerable variation. You should select a report structure that you feel happy with and one that suits the kind of project that you are undertaking. One logical format which has been used by students for many years is given below.

→ Project title
→ Table of contents
→ Introduction
→ Findings
→ Conclusions and recommendations
→ Appendices

Project title and table of contents

These first two items provide basic information for the reader. It informs them of the area of study and how the report on that study is to be structured. The *contents page* is particularly important as it enables the reader to find their way quickly round the report. A well thought out structure, as illustrated by the contents page, will immediately make a good impression on the reader.

Introduction

The *introduction* sets the scene for what comes in the main body of the report. This is done in a number of ways.

→ Firstly you should describe the nature of the project to be tackled, amplifying the main aims and defining the points of the project.
→ Secondly you should provide such background information as is necessary for the reader to understand what is written in the main body of the report.
→ Finally you should explain your plan of action, including the techniques and methods of enquiry you intend to adopt (it is also useful to explain why you may have rejected other lines of enquiry). This can be done as a separate section entitled 'Project Objectives'.

Obviously, the length of the introduction will vary between reports but, as a general rule, it should not be more than two or three pages long. Examiners often comment that poorer candidates tend to produce overlong and very descriptive introductions. For example, you might question whether the history of Company X since 1900 is particularly relevant.

Findings

The *findings* section is the body of the report. Here you will present the results from using those techniques and methods of enquiry outlined in the introduction to generate your findings. This is normally the longest part of the report. The details should be arranged logically, and where different points are being made or different techniques used, this section should be divided into subsections. Careful editing is necessary to ensure that the points you make are not obscured by too much information. If necessary use appendices for the additional information.

Conclusions and recommendations

In this section you will

→ briefly restate your findings
→ draw conclusions from those findings
→ make recommendations based on your conclusions

There are several points worth noting here

→ First, no new material should be presented in this section – you are merely summarizing your findings.
→ Second, your *conclusions* should relate to the facts. You must avoid unsubstantiated conclusions and should not let personal prejudices cloud your judgement.
→ Third, this section gives you the chance to evaluate critically what you have done. For example, the sample size may not be large enough to be sure of your conclusions or your cash flow predictions may be suspect. It is better to let the examiner know that you are *aware* of these shortcomings than let him believe you are ignorant of these problems.

The *recommendations* are the final part of your project. As they are supposed to be acted upon, they are essentially practical points. It is not sufficient to say 'something must be done', it is up to you to explain what that 'something' should be. You should also avoid suggesting that 'further investigations' are necessary. This could imply that your investigations are flawed. Finally you must consider the impacts of your recommendations. Thus if the introduction of new technology is likely to displace staff, you need to indicate (at least in general terms) how this problem may be overcome.

Appendices

There are times when the inclusion of relevant information renders an argument more difficult to follow. In these circumstances you should relegate this information to an *appendix*. Each appendix should be referred to at the appropriate place in the report.

Don't forget

Keep a record of all your sources of information. You will need to record this information in the report.

Watch out!

Check that the main ideas emerge clearly from your report.

Examiner's secrets

Have you written an effective conclusion? It should
→ be brief and concise
→ restate the main points of the findings
→ refer and relate to the aims and objectives detailed in the introduction

Examiner's secrets

If you are using abbreviations or specialist terms, you should create a *glossary* at the end of your report.

Glossary

The following list contains some of the terms you should be familiar with. The list is not exhaustive – keep your own glossary of other concepts you encounter.

audit

An independent check on an organization's accounts.

average cost

The total cost divided by the number of units produced. Also referred to as unit cost.

average rate of return

The average annual profit of an investment expressed as a percentage of the sum invested.

balance sheet

A statement of an organization's assets and liabilities at a particular point in time. The liabilities (capital employed) must be equal to the assets of the business (the assets employed).

batch production

The production of a limited number of similar products. At each stage of production the whole batch will be processed before passing on to the next stage.

benchmarking

The setting of standards based on the best practice observed in the industry.

break-even

The output level where total revenue is just sufficient to cover total cost.

budget

A financial plan that details the expected revenue and costs in a future trading period.

bureaucratic leadership

The leader emphasizes the importance of following rules and procedures. Where rules and procedures are inapplicable, the bureaucrat is unable to exercise leadership.

business culture

An unwritten code that affects attitudes, decision-making and management style within an organization.

business cycle

The regular pattern of upturns and downturns in economic activity.

CAD

Computer aided design – the use by designers of multidimensional images to assist product design.

CAM

Computer aided manufacture – the use of computers to manage and control the production system.

capacity utilization

The extent to which the maximum capacity of a business is being used. It is calculated by expressing the actual output as a percentage of the maximum output.

cartel

An illegal agreement by firms to control output and prices.

cell production

The division of production into small, self-contained units.

competition

The rivalry between firms trying to win our custom.

competitive advantage

Organizations achieve a competitive edge over their rivals through the possession of some assets or attributes. For example, low cost plants, reputation for quality, innovative products, brand names.

core activities

The firm's activities seen as central to its corporate strategy.

corporate plan

The formulation of an organization-wide strategy to meet that organization's objectives. Functional objectives must contribute to the attainment of the overall strategy.

creditor

A person or organization to whom you owe money.

critical path analysis

The process of breaking down a project into its component parts, placing them in sequence along with the appropriate duration. The shortest possible route through the project is the critical path.

debenture

A fixed interest, long-term loan secured against the assets of the business.

debtor

A person or organization that owes you money.

Delphi technique

A form of subjective long-range forecasting produced by a panel of experts reaching a consensus view.

demand

The desire to own a good or service.

de-skilling

The process of breaking down a job into smaller parts, thus making it easier to perform. It enables the firm to use less skilled and therefore cheaper labour.

distribution channel

The process by which goods move from maker to the consumer.

division of labour

The breaking down of work into smaller parts. By specializing in a specific job the worker becomes more familiar with the task and therefore more productive.

economies of scale

The advantages available to larger scale fims that cause the average costs to be reduced, e.g. larger discounts for buying raw materials in bulk.

elasticity of demand

A measure of the degree of responsiveness of demand for a product to a given change in some economic variable – especially its own price.

empowerment

Providing subordinates with the authority to decide the tasks to be done and how to do them. It is wider than delegation.

entrepreneur

Individual creating a business and accepting the associated risks.

EPS (earnings per share)

A ratio that shows the after-tax profit that is available for distribution to shareholders.

externalities

Costs or benefits borne by society as a result of a firm's activities (e.g. pollution).

factoring

A service that allows an organization to receive up to 80% of its invoiced sales immediately in cash and the balance less commission when the invoices fall due.

fixed costs

Those costs that do not alter in the shot term in relation to changes in ouput.

flexible working

Practices introduced by management to achieve a more efficient use of human resources.

flow production

The manufacture of an item in a continually moving process where one stage is linked to another in a constantly moving stream.

footloose business

A firm that has no commitment to a particular location and can operate in a variety of areas.

franchise

A business based upon the name and operating method of an existing successful business.

free trade

The export and import of goods and services without any form of hindrance (e.g. tariffs or quotas).

grapevine

The network of informal communication within an organization.

historical cost

The original purchase price paid for an asset.

internal rate of return

The discount rate that makes the net present value of a series of cash flows equal to zero.

investment appraisal

A variety of techniques that allow different investment opportunities to be ranked in order of desirability.

joint consultation

Meetings between management and workers to discuss issues other than those related to collective bargaining.

JIT (just in time)

A system that attempts to minimize the amount of stocks required at all stages of production so as to reduce the costs of stockholding.

job production

The production of one-off unique items to the specific requirements of a customer with very little chance of a repeat order.

kaizen

A Japanese term for continuous improvement.

lean production

The elimination of all 'waste' from the mass production system.

limited liability

The restriction of a shareholder's responsibility for the debts of a business to the amount invested.

margin of safety

The amount that sales can fall before an organization reaches its break-even level of output.

market leader

The firm that holds the largest market share. This position is often achieved by establishing some competitive advantage over its rivals.

market orientation

The strategic thinking that puts the consumer at the centre of all that the organization does.

marketing mix

The variables, product, price, promotion, place, through which the firm carries out its marketing activities.

matching concept

The allocation of costs and revenue to the period in which they were incurred or earned.

matrix organization

A project-based organization structure cutting across departmental boundaries.

multinational

A firm having manufacturing bases throughout the world.

net present value

The current value of a series of future cash flows associated with an investment.

niche market

A narrow and well-defined segment of the market. Many smaller specialist firms survive by targeting such a segment.

non-verbal communication

Communication through body language.

oligopoly

A market structure where a few large firms supply the bulk of industry output. A key feature is that the actions of one firm will affect all other suppliers in the market.

outsourcing

The hiving-off of non-core activities and subsequent purchase from outside the organization.

overdraft

A facility provided by banks that allows an organization to withdraw funds from their account up to an agreed limit.

payback

An investment appraisal technique that calculates the minimum period for a project to repay the cost of its initial investment.

P/E (price/earnings) ratio

A ratio that shows how highly the stock market values an organization's shares. Calculated using the equation P/E = market share price ÷ EPS.

primary research

The collection of first-hand information that is directly related to the firm's particular product, market and customers.

profit

The residue after costs have been deducted from revenue. Within a market it is a spur to efficient use of resources.

profit sharing

The distribution of a portion of the firm's profits to its employees. It is thought to improve employee loyalty and productivity.

public interest

A test often used in competition policy to determine whether the actions of a firm are good or bad when considering efficiency or consumer interests.

quality circles

Informal discussion groups that meet regularly to identify quality problems and alternative solutions.

ROCE

Return on capital employed – a measure of the profit generated from the capital invested in a business.

satisficing

A compromise strategy that takes account of the objectives of several stakeholders rather than just profit maximizing for the shareholders.

secondary research

The collection of data from second-hand resources such as reference books, government publications or market intelligence reports.

segmentation

Breaking down a market into smaller parts with recognizable characteristics.

single market

The removal of barriers to the movement of goods, labour and capital to create a single market within the EU.

sponsorship

A means of promoting a product, service or organization through the provision of finance to help an event take place.

stakeholders

Any person or group of people who have an interest in a firm's performance.

supply

A firm's willingness to produce those goods demanded by consumers.

total quality management (TQM)

A business culture that concentrates on persuading all employees to adopt working practices that place the accent on quality.

turnover

Another term for sales revenue.

variance

The amount an actual figure differs from a budgeted figure.

wholesaler

A business which buys goods in bulk which it then sells on to retailers in smaller quantities.

work to rule

Refusal by employees to undertake work outside the terms of their job description.

workers' co-operative

An organization that is owned and controlled by those who work in it.

working capital

The finance needed for the day-to-day running of a business, defined as current assets minus current liabilities.

Index